AMONG THE LAKES AND FELLS

AMONG THE LAKES AND FELLS

Published by The Reader's Digest Association Limited

LONDON • NEW YORK • SYDNEY • MONTREAL

ABOUT THIS BOOK

'LET NATURE BE YOUR TEACHER' wrote William Wordsworth, undoubtedly the most celebrated of all Lakeland residents, past and present. For Wordsworth, nature, whose handiwork in the Lake District is more dramatic than in perhaps any other corner of England, was indeed the ultimate teacher—and muse, providing inspiration for his verse and nourishing his soul with ceaseless wonder.

So it is for countless others in our day. People can't help falling in love with the Lake District. Hunter Davies, a lifelong resident, penned the heart of this book, 'A Walk Around the Lakes', and his account betrays his own continuing affair with the region. Travel writer John Kahn sets the scene with his introduction. Within a few days of arriving he, too, was spellbound: 'My scholarly agenda and efficient schedule hadn't reckoned with nature's beguilements...My earnest resolutions wavered, and then gave up the struggle'. From page 150, a 'Highlights' section, with its useful map, will enable you, the reader, to sample the region's delights— and maybe fall in love with it as well.

AMONG THE LAKES AND FELLS was edited and designed by The Reader's Digest Association Limited, 11 Westferry Circus, Canary Wharf, London E14 4HE

A Walk Around the Lakes Original full-length version by Hunter Davies, published by Weidenfeld and Nicolson, 1979, paperback edition published 1980, revised 1989, revised 1993
© Hunter Davies, 1979, 1989, 1993
British condensed version © The Reader's Digest Association Limited, 1999
The author asserts the moral right to be identified as the author of this work.

CONTRIBUTORS

Series Editor Steve Savage

Volume Editor Charlotte Rundall

Assistant Editor/Researcher Miriam Sharland

Associate Editors David Blomfield, Hugo de Klee

Copy Editors Kate Green, Morag Lyall, Barbara Roby

Editorial/Picture Research Assistant Kate Michell

Art Editor Karen Stewart

Designer Carl Meek

Picture Researcher Helen Ashford

Additional material by Jeremy Hunt, John Kahn, Tim Locke, John Satchell, Frank Westwood

Cartography Anthony Sidwell (page 9), Malcolm Porter (pages 152–3)

Index Brian Amos

FRONT COVER *Wooden rowing boats nudge the shore of Buttermere, one of the more remote lakes.*
BACK COVER (TOP) *The Senior Guides Fell Race is one of the most gruelling events of the Grasmere Sports.*
BACK COVER (BOTTOM) *An unusually heavy snowfall transforms the pretty village of Troutbeck.*
TITLE PAGE *The sunlit vista of Wast Water beckons walkers over a wooden stile towards the lake.*

THIS PAGE *Dora's Field, planted with daffodils by Wordsworth for his daughter, lies below Rydal Church.*
PAGES 6–7 *Ashness Bridge provides a picturesque crossing point over Barrow Beck by Derwent Water.*
PAGES 24–5 *Bracken-covered fells surround Blelham Tarn and Ambleside on the shores of Windermere.*
PAGES 144–5 *Bowness, on Windermere, is a lively holiday centre specialising in boat trips and hire.*

CONTENTS

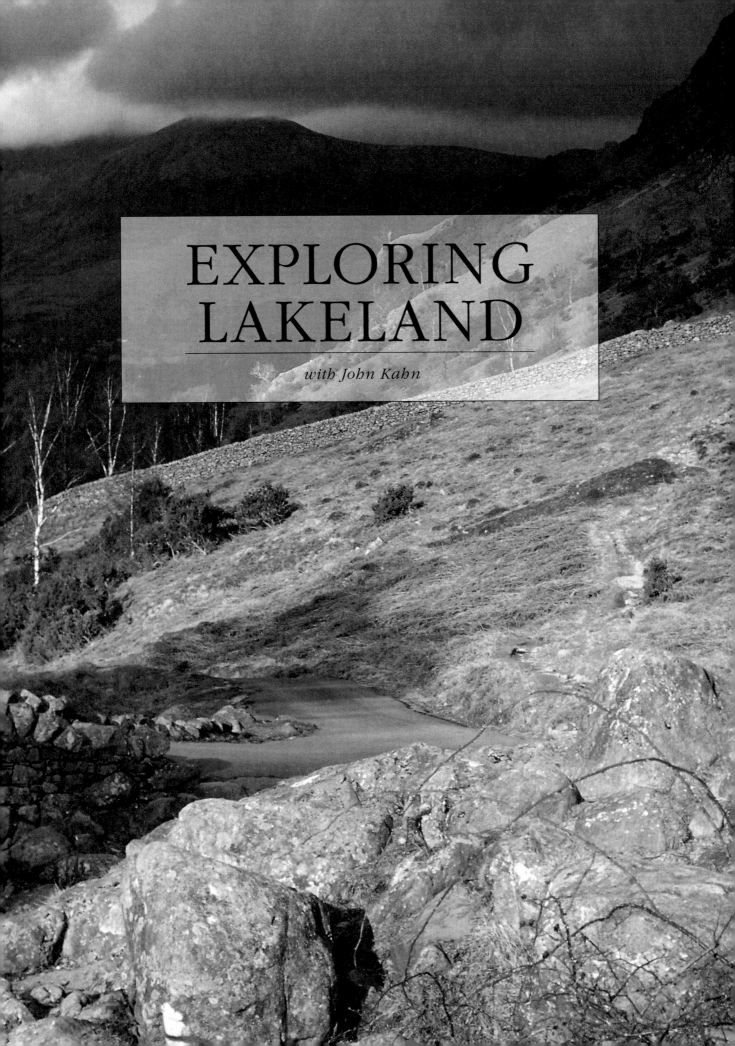

EXPLORING LAKELAND

with John Kahn

LAKELAND

with John Kahn

T IME AND AGAIN it happens: you crest a steep rise on the road, or turn a bend on the footpath, or emerge suddenly from the woods, and a vista spreads out before you that takes your breath away. For a moment, time comes to a standstill. Silence descends, and a sense of serene unity too. Everything holds together in a perfect composition: mountains, lake or waterfall, trees, clouds, shadows.

My mind goes back at once to some of these timeless Lakeland moments that have descended on me in recent years. At the summit of Orrest Head, after a ten-minute stroll and five-minute scramble up from Windermere station, gasping at the sweep of the lake below. At Castlerigg stone circle, near Keswick, at sunset, with the layers of glowing mountains in the background. In the gardens both of Wordsworth's house at Rydal Mount and of Ruskin's at Brantwood, glimpsing the shimmer of Rydal Water and Coniston Water respectively through the trees…

The spell soon passes. The bleating of a sheep on the valley floor, or the flash of a yacht's sails perhaps, or the sight of a rambler thwarted by a snaking dry-stone wall, restores you to reality. But it remains a slightly different reality from the familiar, modern, workaday world. It somehow shuts out that world's bustle and worries, as if residing on another plane. One commentator after another has tried to convey this idea—the kind of 'otherness' that pervades the Lake District. Wordsworth's poems hint at it continually; those of his fellow 'Lake poets' Coleridge and Southey too. The 19th-century novelist Mrs Eliza Lynn Linton referred to the region as 'a dream of Eden'.

A DIFFERENT WORLD

For those who visit rather than live there, the contrast is particularly vivid. Thomas Gray and J. M. W. Turner; Byron and Sir Walter Scott; Shelley and Keats; Dickens and Charlotte Brontë and Tennyson—they all recorded the strange relief and lifting of the spirits that they experienced during their pilgrimage.

My own most recent excursion into this magical domain took place in a mild mid-April, a fairly quiet time in Lakeland, between the boisterous fortnight of the Easter school holidays and the protracted invasion of summer tourists. Late daffodils were still parading on sunny banks, and early bluebells on shady slopes. A wet spring had swelled the rivers, and the waterfalls were in unusually fine spate. My intention had been not so much a holiday as a field trip: to 'decode' the region and master its layout and history and geology, rather than just to bask in its

splendours and meander aimlessly and enraptured as on my previous visits. I should have known better. Wordsworth had warned against such a dry approach:

> *Sweet is the lore which Nature brings;*
> *Our meddling intellect*
> *Mis-shapes the beauteous forms of things:*
> *We murder to dissect.*

Sure enough, my scholarly agenda and efficient schedule hadn't reckoned with nature's beguilements. The magic was not going to be denied. A ramble would turn into a hike, as some fine mountain view held out the promise of an even finer one just half a mile further along the ridge. An hour-long drive from point A ('interesting rock structure') to point B ('village with Hugh Walpole associations'), or from C ('Beatrix Potter setting') to D ('Quaker graveyard'), would take three hours, as unfamiliar side roads beckoned irresistibly, and remote valleys or gardens demanded lingering inspection.

As the dawdling and the detours accumulated, they made a mockery of my timetable. A village shopkeeper gave me directions, then recommended a more

scenic route, then queried my destination anyway and suggested a preferable itinerary, and then regaled me with anecdotes about the old days… My earnest resolutions wavered, and then gave up the struggle. In this northerly land of the lotus eaters, you can't stay in a studious frame of mind for long.

A good reason for learning something about the place *before* you go there, or go there again.

SURVEYING THE TERRAIN

Where does this magical domain begin and end? It lies entirely within Cumbria, covering parts of the old counties of Cumberland and Westmorland and a former enclave of Lancashire. The heartland is easy enough to identify: the scattering of fifteen or sixteen main lakes, together with their sentinel mountains and satellite tarns. But the periphery is not so easy to establish. The Lake District National Park, with its boundaries tracing a badly drawn circle thirty-five to forty miles across, is one thing; the Lake District itself is arguably another. Tourist Boards and guide-books usually make a more generous allocation of territory. They tend to include the 'gateway' towns of Kendal, Cockermouth and Penrith; additional stretches of the west coast, including the old ports of Whitehaven and Workington; and much

ABOVE *Presented with the magical panorama of the Lakes, the traveller soon forgets his worldly cares.*

of the Morecambe Bay or 'Lake District Peninsulas' region, such as Grange-over-Sands and even Barrow-in-Furness. By widening their reach in this way, they tend to embrace such attractions as the topiary gardens at Levens Hall and the magnificent ruins of Furness Abbey. But they tend to exclude Eden Vale in the east, and stop short of the Carlisle vicinity and the upper Solway Firth area in the north.

However broadly you draw the boundaries, the striking thing is how *compact* the Lake District seems, considering the vast variety of natural attractions it contains. Everything is so closely juxtaposed that your sense of scale falters: the most modest lake looks impressively expansive; the mountains—a mere four being of 'Munro' height, 3,000 feet or more—somehow concentrate their power to match the Alps in majesty. So numerous are these natural features that they seem almost to have outstripped the available supply of names. There are several Mosedales and Grisedales scattered about the region, and several unrelated cliffs and waterfalls called Ravens Crag or Sour Milk Gill. (Human settlements as well: two Granges, two Ulphas and two Seathwaites.) If Lakeland wanted a motto, the obvious choice would be *Multum in parvo*—a great quantity in a small space.

When it comes to orientating yourself, or mapping the core Lake District in your mind, the easiest way is to memorise the layout of the lakes themselves. Serious hikers and climbers may prefer to classify the region by its groups of mountains, or 'fells', while amateur geologists, as we'll see, partition it according to its rock formations. And tourist organisations and local authorities subdivide it in various ways, partly for administrative convenience. But for most casual visitors, it is the main lakes that constitute the dominant landmarks.

The usual image is of a wheel, with the individual lakes spreading outwards like spokes. (It was Wordsworth, in his guide to Lakeland, who first used the image—applying it to the river valleys in which the lakes lie, rather than to the lakes themselves.) Alternatively, the structure might be seen as two overlapping wheels, the hub of one lying near the peak of Great Gable perhaps, and of the other near Helvellyn.

The simplest way of grouping the lakes is by compass points: to the south, the group dominated by Windermere and Coniston Water (with Wordsworth's beloved Grasmere and Rydal Water, both much smaller and more central, included); to the north, the group dominated by Derwent Water; in the west and northwest, an untidy spread of five lakes, including Buttermere and Wast Water; in the east or northeast, Ullswater and Haweswater. One other compass point merits a particular tribute, despite having no major lake to offer: the southwest, where both Eskdale and the Duddon Valley, two of Lakeland's most unspoilt valleys, wind their scenic way.

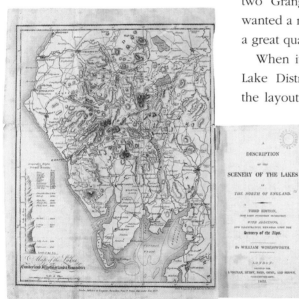

ABOVE *Wordsworth's* Description of the Scenery of the Lakes *was a best seller in its day, helping to make the area popular as a holiday destination. It was in this book that he famously likened the layout of the Lake District's river valleys to the design of a wheel.*

THE BEDROCK OF THE REGION

'There are the lakes, of course,' the tourism official conceded, in tired tones. I was consulting him while still forming the detailed plans (never properly carried out!) of my trip. 'But the really interesting thing here'—his voice had perked up now—'is the *rocks*...' It turned out that he was an amateur geologist ('So is everyone who spends enough time here,' he insisted—including Wordsworth and, especially, Ruskin), and his priorities were clear. Know the rocks, and you have the key to understanding the region. They determine the looks and land-scaping of the various sectors—rugged or rolling—and even the appearance of the villages, since the cottages tend to be built in local stone.

Broadly speaking, the region has three main bands of rock, running roughly east to west: blue-black Skiddaw slate in the north Lakeland fells, some of the most ancient rock on the planet, formed in layers in a shallow sea 500 million years ago; Borrowdale volcanic rocks, red or pink or green, in the centre, from a turbulent geo-logical era about 50 million years later; and softer sedimentary slates and shales in the south, from the Silurian era another 50 million years later still. There are various outcrops of granite, too, and three other important formations: limestone (from an era of flooding), forming a thin diameter and a fragmented circumference round the region; the west Cumberland coalfield in the north (from an era of swamp vegeta-tion); and various strips of New Red Sandstone (from an era of drought), clearly discernible in the walls of Furness Abbey and the seaside cliffs at St Bees alike.

BELOW *The variety of landscapes in the Lake District has been determined by the area's geology. Here, soft, red sandstone cliffs at St Bees, on Cumbria's west coast, are gradually eroding, while elsewhere solid granite and hard volcanic rock rigorously defy the elements.*

Presented with this raw material, nature's sculptors set about shaping the land-scape over the aeons. Subterranean pressures pushed the land northwards, and kneaded and raised and fissured it, and in a final paroxysm about 30 million years ago lifted the great dome higher still. The elements continued to erode the surface of that dome, which in time came to radiate a series of drainage valleys. Earthquakes lent a hand, running a fracture line down the middle (today linking Thirlmere and Windermere—hence the dislocated two-wheel impression of the lakes' layout, as mentioned earlier).

When the ice ages descended 1.5 million years ago, glaciers deepened and smoothed the existing valleys. They also dug, chipped or scraped the fells, dales and lake floors of today, and littered the valleys with debris—and meltwater: the lakes themselves are, geologically speaking, last-minute after-thoughts, presumptuous newcomers a mere 15,000 or so years old.

The landscaping has continued slowly over the millennia since then. Bassenthwaite Lake and Derwent Water were once a single lake; Buttermere and Crummock Water likewise. And it continues still: Elter Water is silting up, and will soon disappear. (Human intervention is at work too: Thirlmere was originally two lakes, now united and raised to form a reservoir to pipe water to Manchester; the popular beauty spot Tarn Hows was formed from three smaller swampy tarns.)

The end result is one of nature's finest sculpture gardens, a varied yet harmo-nious whole. The rounded and weathered slate hills in the north, such as Skiddaw itself. The dramatic central peaks, such as Scafell Pike (the highest mountain in England) and Helvellyn; together with high twisting ridges, and hanging valleys with ravines and cataracts, and soaring sheer cliffs such as Pillar Rock and Dow Crag. Then, in the south, the gentler irregular hillocks and wooded slopes, and the limestone surprise of Arnside Knott rearing above the expansive sands of Morecambe Bay and the River Kent estuary.

And the lakes, of course—the upstart lakes, large and small, with their distinct personalities: modest Buttermere, wooded and reclusive; grand and dignified Derwent Water; remote and austere Wast Water, the deepest lake in England, with its harsh scree backdrop; sprawling Windermere, the largest lake in England—sometimes urbane, sometimes rumbustious, with its powerboats and car ferry; and its diminutive sisters Rydal Water and Grasmere, somehow placid even in the midst of the summer crowds.

THE ONE GREAT INESCAPABLE SUBJECT

The varied geology and terrain of Lakeland result in a comparable variety of vegetation and of wildlife. And even of weather. Weather! The Lake District does have an abundance of it, and of discussion about it. 'We suffer more from bad jokes and a bad reputation than we do from bad weather itself,' the tourism officer told me resignedly. (Picture a cartoon postcard of a sorrowful sheep being pelted by heavy rain and hailstones, above a caption reading 'Lakeland in midwinter/midsummer—delete as appropriate', and you get the idea.)

OPPOSITE Ice, frost and sun have fractured ancient volcanic rock into dramatic crags and pillars, such as Napes Needle on Great Gable fell—an old favourite with climbers.

'If the weather were really as bad as it's painted,' he pointed out, 'the visitors would keep away. Well, that's not something I've noticed.'

Certainly it rains in the Lake District—though *not* incessantly, and not equally voluminously in *all* parts—but that is the price one has to pay for all the waterfalls and rainbows, and the bewitching morning mists on the mountaintops, and the dappling of grassy dales as the clouds chase one another across the sun.

In fact, Cumbria has a greater variety of climate than any other English county. The seasons are quite out of step from district to district. Daffodils and bluebells, as already mentioned, can coincide. Lambing can occur as early as February in the lowlands, and as late as May on the hills. Penrith averages just thirty-four inches of rain a year, the coastal stretch from Morecambe Bay up to Whitehaven gets forty to fifty, whereas the central lakes approach a hundred, and the higher central fells such as Sca Fell can reach as much as a hundred and eighty-five. But even on those notoriously drenched fells, it rains properly (that is, more than one millimetre, or one twenty-fifth of an inch) on only two hundred days a year.

Altitude affects the weather greatly, of course. Hunter Davies, in the book that follows, vividly recounts the contrasting weather conditions experienced by his family when they diverged on Skiddaw during a hike: freezing mist on the upper slopes, warm sunshine on the lower.

But altitude is only part of the story. The undulating terrain creates microclimates in one district or another, producing strange disparities in rainfall. In Borrowdale, Keswick averages fifty-eight inches a year while, eight miles away, Seathwaite averages over a hundred and thirty inches, though the difference in altitude is just 160 feet.

Seathwaite (the tiny farming settlement in Borrowdale, not the Duddon Valley village ten miles due south) has the distinction of being the rainiest inhabited place in England, if not the entire United Kingdom. I drove there on my latest trip. It was raining. I'd hoped to take a brief hike into the fells beyond, but no let-up looked to be in prospect, so I doubled back and continued my drive, over Honister Pass—with the sun beaming benignly overhead. That's how Lakeland weather typically works, and that's how it should be. 'Sunshine with showers' (or often, admittedly, 'showers with sunshine') to show the scenery in its changing moods.

Just two days of my six-day trip deviated from this pattern. Day Two (spent mainly in the 'Lake District Peninsulas', a precinct that prides itself on having the best weather in northern England) served up *cloud* rather than clouds, and almost unrelieved rain and dullness with it. I was denied the promised pleasure of a promenade through that stately Edwardian watering place, Grange-over-Sands. And as for the famous view from Arnside Knott, sweeping over the tidal race of the River Kent estuary and across the southern Lakeland hills up to the Old Man of Coniston, it amounted to no more than a hazy impression of distant mountain shapes, like some early black-and-white film set.

By contrast, the final day of my trip served up unrelieved sunshine. It was almost alarmingly cloudless from dawn until very late afternoon, a rare consistency for that

ABOVE *Seathwaite farmers accept the dubious distinction of living in the wettest place in England with an air of stoic resignation.*

time of year. At Whitehaven, where I'd spent the night, the sea sparkled with a Mediterranean radiance. In the woods around Ennerdale Water and later in Eskdale, it became uncomfortably warm. Driving up Hardknott Pass, dazzled on turning a rocky bend, I was put in mind of a mountain pass I had once had to negotiate in Greece. Beyond Wrynose Pass, the town of Ambleside seemed to have fallen asleep while sunbathing, and Windermere languished under a light haze. It was glorious. Yet it was also somehow wrong. The windsurfers and lakeside ramblers were no doubt elated. For my part, I *missed* the clouds, and the customary teasing alternation of showers and sunshine.

Wordsworth, as always, hit just the right note in his guidebook:

> The rain here comes down heartily, and is frequently succeeded by clear, bright weather, when every brook is vocal, and every torrent sonorous…clouds, cleaving to their stations, or lifting up suddenly their glittering heads from behind rocky barriers, or hurrying out of sight with speed of the sharpest edge, will often tempt an inhabitant to congratulate himself on belonging to a country of mists and clouds and storms, and make him think of the blank sky of Egypt, and of the cerulean [sky-blue] vacancy of Italy, as an unanimated and even a sad spectacle.

LANDSCAPE AND HUMAN LANDSCAPE

Once the series of ice ages had drawn to a close, and the last glacier had disappeared from Lakeland about 15,000 years ago, the region turned its attention from geology to biology, and started experimenting with flora. First it assumed a modest covering of tundra vegetation and alpine shrubs, then a more ambitious birch and pine woodland, and finally an oak forest. Into this fine habitat it lured elk, bear, wolves… and eventually human beings. With the arrival of that last creature, the Lakeland landscape began undergoing a new round of changes.

Stone Age and Bronze Age tribesmen took to felling or burning trees to free tracts of land for pasture or crops. Forest clearance continued over the millennia at the hands of later farmers, or raiders and soldiers, and in more recent centuries charcoal burners, road builders, timber merchants, quarrymen, miners and factory owners, until 20th-century reforestation began to reverse the trend at last.

That measure, together with other conservation projects, has helped to salvage or reinforce many of the region's threatened species. If not quite the magnet for amateur naturalists that it is for amateur geologists, the Lake District still has a great deal to offer by way of plant and animal life. Ferns and mosses grow prolifically,

ABOVE *Harebells and field scabious are among numerous wild-flower species that flourish in the Lake District.*

and the wild flowers come in a dizzying variety thanks to the diversity of the terrain. So too with the indigenous animals. In the lakes, trout, pike and eels; and dippers and herons. Coots, grebe and mallard too. Elterwater takes its name from the Viking word for 'swan'. In the woods, red deer and roe deer, red squirrels and badgers. And foxes: John Peel, the ebullient huntsman, was a Caldbeck man, as Hunter Davies relates. Kittiwakes and guillemots on the sea cliffs at St Bees; woodpeckers in the woodlands; moorland merlins and short-eared owls. And on the fells, the now resurgent buzzards and peregrine falcons (and even a few golden eagles)—the delight of birdwatchers, though not of shepherds anxious for the welfare of their lambs.

ABOVE *Whooper swans (named after their trumpeting call), along with numerous other water birds, find the Lake District an ideal habitat.*

To most observers, the 'human landscape' is defined not by what has been taken away—the bulk of the ancient forest—but by what has been added. In that respect, it can surely claim to be an unusually benign and engaging one here. Prehistoric Castlerigg stone circle; dry-stone walls winding laboriously uphill; tidy riverside villages such as Grange in Borrowdale, approached by mossy hump-backed bridges built in the same local stone: they all blend into the natural landscape.

Modern buildings are meant to aim for this ideal, too. It was partly to ensure such concordance that the Lake District National Park (still the largest National Park in England and Wales) was established in 1951. (One wonders, though, how some of the tourist developments—on the shores of Windermere, for example, or on the edge of Hawkshead—managed to secure planning permission.)

Still, on the whole, the human imprint does not jar. It plays its part in making Lakeland the famously *varied* place it is. The invigorating wildness of the fells or the loneliness of a remote lakeside glade is brought into even sharper relief by a sudden reminder of some ancient resident or wayfarer. The long sequence of the region's inhabitants has left its mark in myriad traces. Apart from the 3,500-year-old stone circle at Castlerigg in the north, there are prehistoric monuments around the tarn known as Devoke Water and at Swinside near Broughton in the south. When the Romans moved into the region, they concentrated their defensive resources further to the north, at Hadrian's Wall, but they did maintain a local military presence in Lakeland proper, and its remnants are still visible and visitable: the fort high on Hardknott Pass, for instance, and the garrison bathhouse near their naval base of Ravenglass.

ABOVE *Remnants of the Roman occupation are still visible nearly two thousand years on, in these bathhouse walls near Ravenglass.*

The Celts who preceded and outlasted the Romans left forts of their own, near Mosedale and Threlkeld in the north, but their long occupation of the region is more clearly memorialised in many of the place names: Penrith or Derwent, say, or Cumbria itself (compare the Welsh word for Wales, *Cymru*). The Vikings, too, left their linguistic stamp on the region, not only in place names this time but in local geographical features as well, such as beck, tarn, fell, gill or ghyll (ravine, or stream) and force (waterfall). Among the more tangible Viking mementos, one in particular impressed me on my recent trip: the famous fourteen-foot-high sandstone cross in the churchyard of Gosforth, with carvings of a crucifixion alongside scenes from Norse mythology featuring gods such as Odin and Thor. Presumably the theme is the displacement of paganism by Christianity, but could it be that the Viking sculptor was actually still hedging his bets?

As for the Normans, many specimens of their early architectural skill remain: a 12th-century church in Millom, for instance, and the imposing red sandstone ruins of Furness Abbey, founded in 1123 by King Stephen.

The later Middle Ages are especially well represented architecturally. Think of the maze-like village of Hawkshead, for example (excluding the modern development, that is!). One distinctive type of building dating from this period, surviving in considerable numbers, is the peel tower: a box-like three-storey fort developed in the 14th century to withstand Scottish marauders. Stoutly built, these towers have proved appropriately resilient, and today are often found incorporated into later castles, manor houses, or even farm buildings. You can see interestingly contrasted specimens at Broughton-in-Furness, Ravenglass and Kentmere.

The industrial age, finally—surely it passed Lakeland by? Far from it. Arcadias, being rich not just in beauty and pasture but in natural resources too, invite exploitation. Slate quarries, and lead and copper mines; iron mining near Dalton and Coniston, and the related steelworks and shipyard at Barrow; bobbin factories, to supply the textile mills of Yorkshire and Lancashire; graphite mines near Keswick; gunpowder mills near Elterwater.

ABOVE *Exhibits at the Museum of Lakeland Life and Industry include this punching-in clock from a local factory.*

Multifaceted Whitehaven has been through phases as a fishing village, a commercial port (in the 18th century it was the third largest British port after London) and a mining town: some coal seams extended under the sea, and were diligently pursued there. The relics are an industrial archaeologist's delight: the mighty harbour, now virtually redundant though being redeveloped; the disused mineheads still masquerading as medieval castles; the Georgian and Victorian town houses still proclaiming a long-gone prosperity, and perhaps heralding a new one.

THE CHANGING ECONOMY

With the mills and mines now silent for the most part, the region's industrial heritage is accessible mainly through its excellent array of museums, exhibitions and so on. Relic mills at Wythop, Boot and Caldbeck, and the Stott Park Bobbin Mill museum near the southern tip of Windermere. The Steamboat Museum on the opposite side of the lake, and the Florence Mine Heritage Centre at Egremont in the west. The fine trio of west-coast museums at Maryport, Workington and Whitehaven. Best of all, perhaps, the Museum of Lakeland Life and Industry in Kendal.

Not that recognition by a museum necessarily amounts to a memorial service. Some industries survive museum status: together with the perennially popular Pencil Museum in Keswick, a prestige pencil industry still flourishes in the vicinity.

And near the summit of Honister Pass, tourists can visit a working slate quarry which has recently reopened.

The region's current industrial and economic profile has obviously, however, changed beyond recognition from that of a century ago. The prominent industries today include 'K' shoes in Kendal, Kangol hats at Cleator Moor (the largest manufacturer of headwear in Europe) and nuclear reprocessing at Windscale on the coast. (Don't miss the Sellafield Visitor Centre if you're passing that way: a high-tech and hands-on attraction that deftly combines education, fun and public relations. And take the free coach tour, too, of the vast industrial complex itself, if time allows.)

But the two most pervasive and conspicuous industries are sheep farming and tourism, the old and the new foundation stones of the economy. Sheep farming is omnipresent, and contributes greatly to the sense of a bygone age that the region evokes. The old ways persist: picture a lone shepherd and his dog, high on a hillside of walled, patchwork fields, keeping watch over their hardy Herdwick flock. Unhurried, uncrowded, resolutely unmechanised, thoroughly free-range.

If only the same could be said of tourism. The popularity of Lakeland—especially for motorists—threatens to become self-defeating. When Thomas Gray and other 18th-century travellers referred to the 'dreadful' aspect of a mountain pass, or the 'horror' of the road ahead, they were actually awestruck at the deserted and wild character of the scene. When their counterparts today draw on the same vocabulary, it is in appalled dismay at what they see: a beauty spot throbbing with idling holiday coaches, perhaps, or a convoy of Range Rovers approaching on a single-track mountain pass.

ABOVE *The bleating of sheep accompanies almost any Lakeland walk. Local Herdwicks, and Swaledales from neighbouring Yorkshire, are the breeds best suited to life on the rugged fells.*

It has come to the point where dedicated Lakes-lovers shun the region in July and August. Where is the joy of the open road if your car is immobilised in a traffic jam in some remote valley? What is the use of seeking the solitude and serenity of the fells and dales if you are hemmed in by countless others intent on doing the same? What is there to rejoice at if your jocund companions, 'stretched in never-ending line/Along the margin of a bay', are not Wordsworth's daffodils but raucous day-trippers out on a picnic?

The figures are striking—impressively or shockingly so, according to taste. The Lake District National Park, an area with fewer than 50,000 permanent residents, receives 14 million visits a year. More than half are crammed into the Easter and summer school holidays, it seems, and journeys are made by car in the great majority of cases. (If Wordsworth had foreseen the 'horseless carriage' and the

ABOVE *Holidaymakers seeking the freedom of the open road all too often wind up bumper to bumper, in traffic so slow-moving that there's even time to pop out of the car for an ice cream.*

menacing tourist surge it made possible, he would have championed rather than opposed the spread of railways through Lakeland.) The network of buses is quite extensive, but people still far prefer the independent mobility afforded by private cars. I am as guilty as anyone. Apart from one trip twenty years ago, when I spent the entire five days on a damp sailing boat on Windermere, I have always used the car extensively on my visits—probably spending more time overall in driving than in walking. There's simply so much to *see*.

And it's not as if the visitors neglect alternative means of transport. Cycling seems to be as popular as ever, and hiking or rambling too. (Public-right-of-way footpaths exceed 1,500 miles.) Lake cruises on Windermere, steamer rides on Ullswater and pleasure trips on the two steam railways (based at Haverthwaite and Ravenglass) all feature in the top ten most popular chargeable attractions in Cumbria.

For many Lakeland enthusiasts, it is not just the motorists but the hikers and climbers, too, that present a threat. Footpaths crumble, and erosion results. The fad of 'gill-scrambling'—scaling the sides of narrow ravines, usually next to a waterfall—has been banned in many places, to prevent further damage to ferns and mosses.

It's a difficult balance, my tourism-officer informant had acknowledged. Environmental and traffic controls on the one hand, economic considerations on the other. He had spoken of 'sustainable tourism' (the emphasis still being on *tourism*, perhaps), and felt that it was being maintained, more or less. 'Sustainable tourism—that's what we want,' a National Park official told me later (the emphasis this time being more on *sustainable*, no doubt). I was visiting Brockhole, the magnificent National Park visitor centre on the shores of Windermere. It was reassuring to note a meeting of minds between the tourist authorities and the conservation groups. It's no secret that relations between them have been strained in the past. They need to work in harmony, to keep the Lake District's magic from wearing thin.

The challenge perhaps is to spread the tourist influx more evenly over the year and over the region. So: don't miss the Lakes, but do miss the peak season if you can. (In Wordsworth's opinion, the best time to visit is early September to mid-October; alternatively, mid-May to mid-June.) And do spend more time in the National Park's remoter corners. That's, after all, where it's quickest and easiest to fall under Lakeland's spell.

INTRODUCING *A WALK AROUND THE LAKES*

In the book that follows, Hunter Davies brings a rare double perspective to bear on Lakeland. As one who has spent much of his working life away from the region, he could see it with a fresh eye and take nothing for granted. At the same

time, he wrote as a resident of the region rather than as a visitor to it, and so could view it steadily and see it whole. He *lived* there, in all senses (indeed, he lives there still, at least part of the time), and saw facets of Lakeland life that the casual traveller is unlikely to see: the slow change of the seasons, fairs and festivals, neighbours, champion wrestlers and fell runners, local labourers and characters, some who depend on the tourist trade and others who are virtually oblivious to it. In the years since he wrote the book, changes have inevitably occurred. Mountain-rescue volunteers nowadays carry electronic pagers at all times; Francis Coulson, founder of the Sharrow Bay hotel and restaurant, is now mastering the cuisine of nectar and ambrosia in the kitchens of Paradise, having passed away early in 1998; and that great hiker and guide-book author, A. Wainwright, now goes striding the Elysian Fells. But the Mountain Goat minibus service still plies its invaluable whimsical routes among the mountains, and the ubiquitous sheep are still painted with coded markings to identify their owners.

For the author, the fascination of the region remains undimmed. He has gone on to write acclaimed biographies of two of its greatest sons, Wordsworth and Wainwright, and continues to update *The Good Guide to the Lakes*, which he not only compiled but actually published and marketed himself. But the book that remains closest to his heart, I suspect, is the one reproduced here in an edited version, *A Walk Around the Lakes*. It shines with affection and admiration for the magic kingdom that is his homeland.

ABOVE *The National Park visitor centre is at Brockhole. With its gracious gables, this glorious house merits a visit on its own account.*

A WALK AROUND
THE LAKES

A condensation of the book by Hunter Davies

CHAPTER ONE

THE GATEWAY
TO THE LAKES

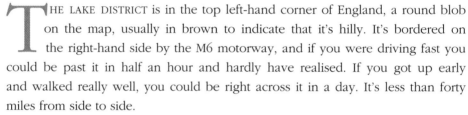

THE LAKE DISTRICT is in the top left-hand corner of England, a round blob on the map, usually in brown to indicate that it's hilly. It's bordered on the right-hand side by the M6 motorway, and if you were driving fast you could be past it in half an hour and hardly have realised. If you got up early and walked really well, you could be right across it in a day. It's less than forty miles from side to side.

The hills are hilly for England, but Scotland has more and bigger; and compared with the Alps or the Himalayas they're just wrinkles in a rather small rug. The lakes are large for England but only drops compared with lakes in the United States. So what's all the fuss? Why do millions come here for their holidays each year?

It is the extraordinary variety. In one small plot you have everything of England: lush pastures, twee cottages, stately castles, romantic valleys, lakeside resorts, hidden tarns, smooth hills, wild fells, sudden waterfalls, open heather, rough moorland, frightening crags, dramatic, snow-clad mountaintops. It's nature's miniature kingdom. The peaks rarely get above 3,000 feet, but enough people fall off them each year, finding them not as cuddly as they may look. Because of the unusual geological and climatic conditions, you can experience almost everything in a very short space and in a very short time, and feel as though you have gone sometimes from a Mediterranean heat to subarctic conditions in just a two-hour climb. Yet the scale is all so manageable. There is no place you can't escape from and be in complete isolation in half an hour, even on the busiest bank holiday.

This is the record of one year, wandering around the Lakes. The nicest year I have ever spent.

ENGLAND'S LARGEST LAKE

It was early January when I got off the InterCity and got on the local train at Oxenholme, the second day of a new year. We trundled through Kendal, climbing all the time, and in half an hour had reached Windermere.

ABOVE *The author, Hunter Davies, who spent a year exploring the 'miniature kingdom' of the Lake District.*

You have to start at Windermere for any tour of the Lakes. Even before the railway, it was the way into the heartland. Windermere is the biggest lake in the Lake District, some ten miles long and a mile wide, and by far the best known and most glamorous. Glamour in the North of England? Several other lakes are more beautiful, some are more mysterious, many are more hidden and undiscovered, but Windermere has definite Hollywood appeal. Wealthy 19th-century industrialists built palatial summer houses on the slopes of the lake, many with private piers and landing stages; today it looks a bit like Beverly Hills. And there is still a lot of money around. Down on the lake, especially on the eastern side, the bays and promontories bristle with smart yachts. Even in winter, enough lie at rest to make you think you're at the seaside.

The small town called Windermere, where the railway ends, is not on Windermere itself. (You have to go down the hillside for about a mile in order to reach the lake.) Until 1847, when the Kendal and Windermere line was opened, it was a little hamlet called Birthwaite. But it burst into commercial life with the arrival of the railway, becoming a booming holiday resort, full of hotels and guesthouses; it now has a population (with its lakeside neighbour Bowness) of 8,000.

The steamers weren't running yet, the ones that go up and down the lake, from Ambleside in the north to Lakeside at the southern tip, taking in Bowness as the halfway mark. They run from Easter to October and have been a feature of Windermere for the last hundred years.

In the middle of Windermere is an island called Belle Isle. On the island is a unique stately home, the first truly circular house in the country. The furniture was especially built and fitted so cleverly that you were hardly aware that all the main rooms had a curved side. (The house has recently undergone careful restoration following a devastating fire.)

ABOVE *Picture-postcard Windermere, biggest and best known of all the lakes, was the starting point of the author's journey.*

The Romans are thought to have used Belle Isle, and there was a house of sorts there during the Civil War, when the owner was a Royalist and got himself blockaded on the island by the Roundheads for ten days. The present, circular house was built by a Mr English in 1774. The locals of the time were not impressed, hating the new house and the way the island was being laid bare to give maximum views. Mr English got fed up with all the moans and in 1781 sold the island to Isabella Curwen, a member of an ancient Cumbrian family which had made a fortune out of the west Cumberland coal mines. She put back the trees and appeased the locals.

Belle Isle is not open to visitors, so I walked slowly round the lake shore, heading for the ferry right across the lake. This ferry runs all the year round, except Christmas Day. It's such a vital link for those who live on the west of Windermere, connecting them with the civilised world, that they must feel rather isolated when it's not running. In the height of the season it must be even more annoying, having to queue up to get across. The ferry has always been one of the arteries of the Lake District, connecting the old county of Westmorland, on the east of the lake, with the northwest tip of Lancashire, on the west. Since 1974 it's all been Cumbria.

The water was calm and the ferry hardly seemed to move, which isn't surprising as it's not a conventional motorboat. It pulls itself across the lake on two chains.

On board was a minibus, a twelve-seater which had emblazoned on its sides 'Mountain Goat'. It was empty but for the driver who said he was called Chris Taylor and was the operator of a minibus service round the Lakes.

The Mountain Goat man offered to drive me to a pub just up the road: the Tower Bank Arms. It was unusual as pubs go, in being owned by the National Trust. We sat round a huge log fire and had real ale from the wood. Chris talked about his herd of Mountain Goats. He was from Sussex, and had come to the Lakes five years before when his parents retired up here. His grandparents had their holiday home on Windermere, part of that very grand industrial squirearchy who knew how to holiday, back in the good old days. His grandfather was a director of a chemical firm that went to form ICI, and in the twenties he would take two coaches on the train up from Liverpool, one for his family and one for the servants. They would get off the train at Lakeside, at the foot of Windermere, and then go up the lake by steamer to where their family coaches would be waiting to take them all to the big house for the whole of the summer.

Chris had come back to the Lakes to try to recapture some of his family's memories. When he heard that Ribble Buses were giving up one of their routes from Windermere to Glenridding, he applied for the licence. He bought a secondhand minibus, christened it Mountain Goat, and drove it himself for six months. Now, five years later, he had seven Mountain Goat minibuses, three large buses, a staff of sixteen and a newly formed holiday side of the business.

The Mountain Goat holidays seemed an excellent idea. Anyone who has ever walked in the Lakes knows the drag of getting to the starting point of your walk. Getting back afterwards is even worse, thanks to the poor local bus service. The ideal is to plan a round walk, but very often you have to come back almost the way you went. Mountain Goat holidays provide guides and minibuses to take you to the beginning of the good walks, guide you across if so desired, and then pick you up at the end.

The bus side of the business, running a scheduled service, had proved very hard work. But the holiday side looked a winner, after only one season. Like so much of Lakeland, such developments big and small are often run by outsiders, people attracted for a variety of reasons to live and work or just retire to the Lakes—like Mrs Heelis.

THE TALE OF BEATRIX POTTER

Mrs Heelis is better known as Beatrix Potter. No visitor to the Lakes, especially one who has just come over on the Windermere ferry, should miss her home.

Hill Top is an unpretentious farm cottage in the village of Near Sawrey, less than two miles from the lake. Around seventy thousand visitors come to Hill Top every year, despite the efforts of the National Trust, the owners of the property, who are trying to restrict numbers (it is open only from April to October). The cottage is just too small to cater for all those who want to see where the creator of Peter Rabbit once lived. It is also the farm where Jemima Puddle-Duck lived, and the setting for *The Tale of Tom Kitten*, *The Tale of Pigling Bland* and *The Roly-Poly Pudding*. Beatrix Potter set all of these books in Hill Top, but many others contain views of Sawrey or are in some way connected with this gentle, rolling corner of the Lakes. No wonder there is such a scamper there every year.

LEFT *Beatrix Potter used the royalties from her children's books to purchase Hill Top Farm. She had fallen in love with the local village of Near Sawrey while holidaying there with her parents.*

ABOVE *Beatrix Potter (left), photographed with her brother Bertram and their nanny, Annie Carter.*

RIGHT *Holidays at Wray Castle provided the young Beatrix with an escape from her closeted London life.*

Beatrix Potter was born in London in 1866. Both her parents had inherited Lancashire cotton fortunes. Her grandfather had been a self-made cotton tycoon, and was at one time Liberal MP for Carlisle, but Beatrix's parents considered they had moved away from such things as trade and industry, never soiling their hands with any actual work. Beatrix's younger brother, Bertram, went away to school but it wasn't considered proper in their circle for girls to be educated; so Beatrix was kept at home, living her life in the nursery quarters, under the care of governesses.

The one bright spot in the year was their annual holiday. Mr Potter, complete with family, tons of luggage and lots of servants, would decamp for three months to a rented house in Scotland or the Lake District. They didn't take little country cottages but grand residences such as Wray Castle on the shores of Windermere. Beatrix would bring back pet animals from her summer idyll, rabbits and hedgehogs, and keep them with her in her bedroom in Kensington. She gave them names, like Peter Rabbit or Mrs Tiggy-Winkle, and would draw them and observe them and they would be her friends, her only friends, in the long days and nights spent in the nursery.

Apart from her pet animals, her only refuge was a secret diary where she recorded her private thoughts and impressions. This was not discovered until after her death (it was found in an attic in Sawrey). She had secretly written 200,000 words, from the age of about ten until she was almost middle-aged, which give minute details of her everyday life, a life that was silent and lonely, highly privileged, yet completely impoverished. Through her secret journal we see her aspirations, trying naively to find a career for herself, hoping that her interest

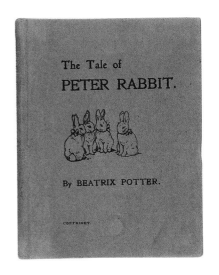

LEFT *Beatrix Potter created miniature illustrated letters and letterboxes to entertain the children of friends and relatives. Marrying late, she never had any children of her own.*

RIGHT *After* The Tale of Peter Rabbit *(above right), Potter went on to write over 20 further books. Still popular with children today, they have changed very little from the earlier editions (see below right).*

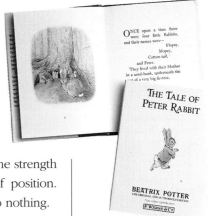

in drawing animals would somehow turn itself into a proper job. She gets an introduction to the Royal Botanic Gardens at Kew and hopes that on the strength of some delicate drawings of fungi, she might be given some sort of position. But she has no education, no scientific training of any sort. It all comes to nothing.

So life creaked on in Kensington, till she was well into her mid-thirties. One summer, during their stay at Wray Castle, they became family friends of Canon Rawnsley, then vicar of Wray, one of Lakeland's earliest and greatest activists. He was endlessly waging war against people who were ruining Lakeland, such as developers and railway companies. He wrote countless books, including several on the Lakes, became a Canon of Carlisle, and a great organiser of bonfires. In 1887, for Queen Victoria's Jubilee, 148 of his Lakeland bonfires could be seen from the top of Skiddaw. But his greatest action was the founding of the National Trust.

Canon Rawnsley was one of the few people in Beatrix's family circle who enthused about her interest in nature and animals and actively encouraged her to draw. It was he she turned to for advice when she thought of printing, at her own expense, a book for children called *The Tale of Peter Rabbit.*

For many years she had entertained the children of friends and relations by sending them drawings and stories about the doings of her pet animals. These were so popular that the idea eventually struck her of printing them as a book. She sent *The Tale of Peter Rabbit* off to Frederick Warne, a well-known publisher of children's books, but it was returned. Six other publishers also said no. So in 1901, with Canon Rawnsley's encouragement, she found a printer herself and he produced 250 copies at a total cost of £11. She sold them, price 1s 2d, to doting

ABOVE *Canon Rawnsley, himself an enthusiastic conservationist, encouraged Potter's interest in nature.*

aunts and uncles for their nephews and nieces, and then by word of mouth to friends of friends. The book sold so well that she did a second edition and then brought out a second book, *The Tailor of Gloucester*. By now, however, Warne had come back to her, saying they would, after all, do *The Tale of Peter Rabbit*. They became her publishers from then on.

Her third book, in 1903, was *The Tale of Squirrel Nutkin*; then came *The Tale of Benjamin Bunny*, *The Tale of Two Bad Mice* and, in 1905, *The Tale of Mrs Tiggy-Winkle*. By now Beatrix Potter was approaching forty.

In 1905 she was proposed to by Norman Warne, the son of her publisher, who had shown great interest in her books and whom she had consulted on every detail. He too loved children and made dolls' houses for his favourite nieces and nephews. But in the summer of 1905, just a few weeks after their engagement, Norman Warne fell ill and died of pernicious anaemia. In that same summer of 1905 Beatrix bought Hill Top Farm.

Beatrix Potter had seen Hill Top on holidays with her parents. She now had a bit of money from her books and she needed a bolt hole, a little place to escape to from London and her parents.

ABOVE *Potter often used her pets as models for the illustrations in her books. Mrs Tiggy-Winkle was inspired by a pet hedgehog of the same name.*

For the next eight years she remained the dutiful daughter, based in London, still spending the main holidays with the family, only managing to spend a few months every year at Hill Top. She had a manager living in one part of the cottage, running the farm, while she lived in it herself when she could get away from London and her family. It was in these eight years, in stolen weeks at Hill Top, that she wrote the bulk of her books.

The thirteen books produced during these eight years were all good sellers, being translated into French and produced in America in pirate editions. Right from the beginning her creations were merchandised—Sandersons brought out a nursery frieze, based on Peter Rabbit and her other animals, which has sold steadily, in revised versions, ever since.

With her growing income Beatrix started buying up chunks of Sawrey, adding to Hill Top Farm and acquiring cottages and increasing her stock of animals. In 1909 she bought Castle Farm, a property just across the road from Hill Top, and in so doing used the local Hawkshead solicitor, W. Heelis. William Heelis was about her age, a tall, quiet bachelor. He kept an eye on her Sawrey properties and kept her in touch with local affairs. They became engaged, got married in October 1913 and moved into Castle Farm. It was a bigger and more convenient farm cottage than Hill Top.

Castle Farm became her home for the next thirty years. She left Hill Top as it was, with the farm manager in one end. Her part of the cottage was unlived in, but kept full of furniture and possessions, exactly as she had had them. Every time she bought old plates or oak furniture or other local relics, she moved them into Hill Top. The farm became a personal museum—and in fact her life as Beatrix Potter, spinster author of children's books, became a museum piece. On moving into Castle Farm she became Mrs Heelis, woman farmer. She did write a few more books over the next thirty years, mainly emptying old sketchbooks, but to all intents and purposes she had ceased to be a writer. She said she had no ideas. She didn't have the time. The latter was certainly true. She gave herself to her property, which grew enormously as she bought up farm after farm, not just around Sawrey but throughout the southern Lakes.

In 1923 she bought an estate of 2,000 acres around Coniston. She became a passionate conservationist and, spurred on by the example of Canon Rawnsley, she gave generously to the National Trust. Whenever a parcel of land came up for sale which the Trust needed to complete a section, she often bought it and gave it to them, usually anonymously.

Her speciality as a farmer was Herdwick sheep, Lakeland's own breed. She became one of the best-known breeders of Herdwick sheep in the Lakes, as well as a judge and successful exhibitor. She would talk about sheep but not of her life as Beatrix Potter, refusing interviews and trying to avoid admirers who arrived at her cottage. Her life as Beatrix Potter was really over. It had been a means of

ABOVE *Beatrix Potter won many prizes with her Herdwick flock, including this cup from the annual Penrith Agricultural Show, and was in her element as a sheep farmer.*

LEFT *Looking not unlike Mrs Tiggy-Winkle, Potter casts her expert eye over entries in the Herdwick sheep class at a local show.*

escape from her overpowering parents and her highly restrictive upbringing. Now she was fulfilled as a farmer and a solicitor's wife and was able to live her life completely in her beloved Lakes. As is so often the way with strangers, offcomers as they are called, she became more passionate about preserving the Lakes than many of the natives.

She spent a lot of time at sheep fairs, with her shepherds and her sheep, and walked the fells in all weathers—looking as if she walked the fells in all weathers; for as she grew older, she became more and more like Mrs Tiggy-Winkle in her old, poorly fitting clothes. She wore several layers of old tweed, a battered bonnet on her head, metal-shod clogs on her feet and carried a stick in her hand. On several occasions she was mistaken for a potter, the local term for tinker or gypsy.

She died in 1943, aged seventy-seven, spending her last nights sitting up in bed interviewing her shepherd. Her flock of Herdwick sheep went to the National Trust, as well as 4,000 acres.

Today at Hill Top, once through the souvenir shop you go up a little garden path to the front door. The outside is rather dull, with its murky grey roughcast

ABOVE *Hill Top today is a museum, where visitors will instantly recognise images from Potter's books, such as the longcase clock made famous in* The Tailor of Gloucester.

walls and its dark slate roof. Inside, the house is much more attractive. The kitchen, the first room you enter, has a stone-flagged floor and a large fireplace, complete with roasting spit, spinning wheel and rag rug. (The house dates back to the 17th century.) By the fireplace are a pair of clogs, as if laid out for someone's return. The clogs were once worn by Beatrix Potter.

It's when you go upstairs, passing through the bedrooms full of her stuff, her cups for her prize-winning Herdwicks, the longcase clock she drew in *The Tailor of Gloucester*, that you come perhaps to the biggest attraction for all Potter lovers—the originals of her books. These are in a special gallery in which all her watercolours are on display. It's a lovely sight.

I left the house and was walking in the fields beside Hill Top Farm when I came across an old man who said his name was Tom Storey, and that for eighteen years he'd worked for Mrs Heelis as a shepherd and then farm bailiff. He was aged eighty-two.

In 1943, on her death, she instructed that, though the farm was to go to the National Trust, he should take over the tenancy. This he did, farming Hill Top Farm till he retired—handing the tenancy over to his son. He's eternally grateful for her kindness, though being a true Lakelander, there was no trace of sentimentality about his memories of her.

In the standard biography of Beatrix Potter by Margaret Lane, it says her fellow farmers sought her opinion on Herdwicks at sheep fairs and that she was 'one of the shrewdest farmers in the Lake Country'.

'Just a fallacy,' said Mr Storey. 'What could she know about farming, coming out of London? She liked Herdwicks, right enough. She'd look at no other, but she could make mistakes when judging them.

'I told her many a time that she'd be better off having some cattle instead of all Herdwicks. She was losing money by having just Herdwicks and I once got very worried. "Don't you worry, Storey," she told me. "It's only a hobby." '

After she died on December 22, 1943, Mr Storey was having his Christmas dinner when Mr Heelis walked into his house. 'He said, "Here's the ashes; you'll know what to do with them." I'd promised her I'd scatter them. Nobody else was to know the place, not even her husband. We'd discussed it several times. I talked to her the night before she died.

'So I got up from my dinner and went off and scattered them, in the place she'd chosen. I've never told anybody where the place is. She wasn't daft. She knew folks would go and look at the place if they knew.'

WORDSWORTH'S HAWKSHEAD DAYS

William Wordsworth used to take the ferry across Windermere every term when he went from home in Cockermouth or Penrith to school in Hawkshead. So I was now on the trail of Lakeland's best-known resident. On this pilgrimage around all the lakes, I wanted to visit most of the places associated with famous people and famous events, but Wordsworth and his circle would, I knew, provide the main fascination, as he has done ever since people first came specially to the Lakes to gape at him.

Wordsworth was born in Cockermouth on April 7, 1770, the second eldest in a family of five. His father, John, was a lawyer who worked for Sir James Lowther, one of the richest landowners in the North of England. The Wordsworth house, on Main Street in Cockermouth, was, and still is, the handsomest house in that very pretty west Cumbrian town. You can go round it today and admire its beautiful Georgian front and imposing gate piers, inspect the fine rooms and furniture, much of it owned by Wordsworth himself. There's even a landscape by Turner, who once stayed at Cockermouth Castle with his patron, Lord Egremont. But the

ABOVE *William Shuter's portrait of Wordsworth, aged 28, is believed to be the earliest painting of the poet.*

BELOW *This handsome house on Cockermouth's Main Street was Wordsworth's birthplace.*

'CLOTH IS MY BREAD'

BY THE TIME RICHARD LIONHEART was imprisoned in Austria in 1190, Kendal was already a well-established wool town, and paid two woolsacks (1,200 fleeces) towards his ransom. Natural assets for wool production in the area included numerous streams for driving 'fulling' mills, and bracken on the fells for burning into potash-rich ash. Wool from the local mountain sheep, described in a royal statute of 1390 as 'the worst wool within the realm', made a coarse cloth which, after fulling (pounding in a lye of dissolved ashes) and being stretched out to dry on tenterhooks, shrank into a tough duffle. With the nap brushed up with teasels and cropped to an even pile by the shearman, this made a warm, hard-wearing, almost weatherproof cloth.

Clothiers organised production of the cloth, getting it dyed, finished and marketed. 'Kendal Green' cloth was famous enough to be mentioned by Shakespeare in *Henry IV, Part I,* when Falstaff claims that 'three misbegotten knaves in Kendal-green came at my back and let drive at me'. This green was produced by combining yellow from dyers' greenweed, a yellow-flowered shrub, with blue from indigo or woad.

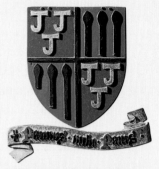

ABOVE *Kendal's coat of arms was designed c. 1610. The quarters show three pack hooks and three teasels. Pack hooks represent the carrier's trade, and the teasel is the sign of the Worshipful Company of Clothmakers.*

LEFT *Swaledale sheep are herded down Kendal high street back towards the fells, after overwintering in the valleys. This relatively new Yorkshire breed is now dominant in north and west Lakeland.*

Legendary outlaw Robin Hood is also said to have worn Kendal Green.

In its heyday, Kendal cloth was sold untaxed to 'poor and mean people within the realm', and exported to Europe through Hull and, via one of the longest packhorse routes in the land, Southampton. As competing cloths took over, it found an outlet as clothing for slaves in the West Indian plantations. Linsey-woolsey manufacture then developed, using the local wool woven into a linen warp, but by 1800 a hand-knitted hosiery trade had expanded, using fine-spun wool imported from other parts of the country, and supplying a nationwide market. Fancy waistcoats, tweed, horsecloths and carpets were the main products of the 19th century. Reminding visitors of Kendal's

medieval trade are pubs in the town's main street, named after the industry: the Fleece, the Woolpack and, once the dyers' watering-hole, the Rainbow. And over the town-hall door are the pack hooks and teasels of the town arms, with its motto *Pannus mihi panis*—'Cloth is my bread'.

BELOW *A local hand loom is now a museum piece, on display at Kendal's Museum of Lakeland Life and Industry.*

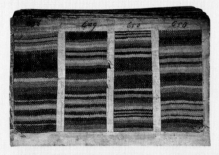

ABOVE *This Kendal clothier's pattern book from 1769 contains samples of linsey-woolsey cloth, used for making petticoats.*

RIGHT *In the 1800s, Kendal cloth was used to make fancy waistcoats: these gentlemen model the latest fashions of 1831.*

house itself was never owned by the Wordsworths. The precise financial relation-ship between John Wordsworth and the Lowthers has never been made clear. From the records it looks as if John Wordsworth never paid any rent. At the same time, he didn't get much of a salary, if any. He worked himself into an early grave for the Lowther family and got very little for his trouble. Sir James Lowther controlled nine parliamentary seats and one of Wordsworth's father's jobs was to go round at election time, keeping the voters sweet with money and other favours. He had a small property of his own which brought in a small income. He was also coroner of Millom, a position he got through Lowther influence.

Wordsworth's mother was Ann Cookson, daughter of a linen draper in Penrith, on the east side of Cumberland. The Cooksons lived over the shop in the market square. They had some landed relations and considered themselves as belonging to the 'Penrith upper classes', despite being only shopkeepers. Penrith, then as now, is a little market town with a decided lack of upper-class folk, though the surrounding area is still rich in squirearchy.

William went for a time to school in Cockermouth, where one of the pupils was Fletcher Christian, of mutiny on the *Bounty* fame. The Christians were neighbours of the Wordsworths in Cockermouth. Wordsworth later attended Dame Birkett's school in Penrith, his mother's home town. At this school William and Dorothy, his only sister, who was twenty-one months younger, became close friends of the Hutchinson children. From his mother, Wordsworth learned his love of the countryside and they went on picnics and expeditions to places like Penrith Beacon, the local landmark. His father is a more shadowy figure, forever travelling around Cumberland on his master's business, but he taught his son to learn chunks of Milton and Shakespeare by heart.

Wordsworth was unhappy with his Penrith relations, with whom he was forced to spend many of his early years. They had aspirations to gentility and considered him wild and unruly, too full of animal spirits. Even his own mother found him a handful and predicted that William would be memorable—'either for good or evil'. Dorothy, in later years, remembered many tears being associated with their time in Penrith, and how their uncles disliked William.

In 1778, when Wordsworth was almost eight, his mother died. It looks as if she caught pneumonia, which had been caused, so the family thought, by sleeping on a damp bed while on a visit to London. Dorothy was sent away to live with other relations, firstly in Yorkshire, and was very upset to be separated from William. In 1779 he and his brothers were sent away to school at Hawkshead, on the other side of the Lakes, where he was free at last of his Penrith relations and where he found himself a substitute home. They boarded with Ann Tyson, a joiner's widow, who looked after the motherless boys with great love and affection.

Hawkshead was in those days a prosperous market town, a centre for the wool and cloth trade. This local industry, which was based in Kendal, had been flour-ishing since the 12th century. Though the Industrial Revolution was eventually to move the factories south to Lancashire and Yorkshire, industry as a whole was booming in Cumberland and Westmorland. The west coast was in at the beginning of the coal and shipping and early industrial boom. In 1780, Whitehaven was the third port in the land, coming after London and Bristol, but before Liverpool and Newcastle.

The little grammar school in Hawkshead had been founded in 1585 and was noted for its scholarship. There were a hundred boys in the school in Wordsworth's time.

Wordsworth was now living in the heart of the Lake District—Penrith and Cockermouth are on the fringes—right beside Esthwaite Water, but also within easy walking distance of Windermere and Coniston. Even at the age of ten, in his first winter in Hawkshead, he was out roaming the fells half the night. It was during these school years at Hawkshead, between the ages of nine and seventeen, that he first started to have his visions. On his long walks up the valleys and over the fells, he often entered dreamlike trances in which he felt himself at one with nature. He started writing poems at school, encouraged by the headmaster, and his first known verses were written in 1785 to commemorate the school's bicentenary.

Hawkshead is probably as prosperous as ever it was in Wordsworth's day, thanks to tourism. It's the most beautifully preserved small town in the whole

WHITEHAVEN: FROM SLAVES TO TOURISTS

WHITEHAVEN, located in the northwest corner of Lakeland, owes its existence to a rich natural resource: coal. In the 17th century a local family, the Lowthers, discovered the mineral on their estate and began mining it and shipping it to Ireland.

Soon, more exotic commodities began to pass through Whitehaven's harbour. Ships plying the Atlantic and Indian Oceans brought back spices, tea, rum, tobacco—and slaves. During the 1700s, Cumbrian merchants bartered wares for people in Africa, exchanging them in America for luxury goods. In the dining rooms of Cumberland, well-to-do families drank and smoked, with scant regard for the misery that the trade produced.

In its heyday, Whitehaven was one of the most important towns in the North of England. But it began to lose its pre-eminence during the 19th century: the harbour was not deep enough to accommodate the bigger ships that were now being built, and Whitehaven was

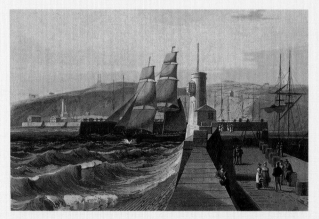

rapidly overtaken by ports such as Liverpool and Glasgow.

Today, Whitehaven's harbour is regaining something of its former glory, more for the benefit of tourists and yachtsmen than merchants. Visitors will find much to admire in the elegant Georgian architecture and to wonder at in its industrial archaeology. In 1997 the Millennium Commission gave the harbour redevelopment programme a great boost in the form of a generous award.

ABOVE LEFT *William Daniell's engraving* Whitehaven, Cumberland *shows the town's harbour as it appeared c. 1814.*

ABOVE RIGHT *This enamelled goblet, made in 1763, commemorates the launch from Whitehaven of the slave ship* King George.

Whitehaven can now enter the new millennium confident of having secured the future of its harbour, while also celebrating its past.

of the Lakes, with interconnecting little squares, over-hung 17th-century timber-framed buildings, narrow cobbled streets and some very handsome houses, formerly the homes of the wool merchants. There are several old coaching inns, where the horses were watered and rested after their ride up from the ferry, and a host of olde-worlde tea shoppes and gifte shoppes, all in genuinely olde buildings, but selling the usual Lakeland tourist tat.

I went first to look for the grammar school and was amazed by its smallness. It's largely as Wordsworth knew it, yet it seems impossible to believe that a hundred boys were ever taught there. The ground floor is one huge classroom, with the original pews laid out as they used to be. Wordsworth's desk is still in its old position, carved with a mass of initials of long-since-forgotten pupils. The room is dark and scholarly and it takes time to get accustomed to the gloom.

ABOVE *The Hawkshead of medieval times is still visible in its narrow streets. From the 15th-century court house and church to the 17th-century timbered buildings, this well-preserved town remains an unspoilt part of 'olde England'.*

There are fine collections of contemporary books, the ones Wordsworth read and was taught from, and details of the school work of himself and his brothers. The classroom looked as if Wordsworth and the other pupils had only just popped out, perhaps gone away for the holidays.

I went next to the parish church, St Michael and All Angels. Wordsworth described it in 1788: 'I saw a snow white church upon a hill, sit like a throned lady sending out a gracious look all over her domain.' There is still a fine view over the countryside, though the church has now been un-whitewashed.

My last visit in Hawkshead was to Ann Tyson's cottage. It is well signposted and most shops have postcards that say that Wordsworth lived there. Alas for the postcard buyers, Wordsworth didn't live in that house. The cottage in Hawkshead marked as Ann Tyson's was at one time lived in by Ann Tyson but, by the time Wordsworth came to live with her, she had moved to another cottage, in the nearby hamlet of Colthouse. Interestingly, it was Mrs Heelis who found the evidence for this in Ann Tyson's ledgers in a barn that she happened to be clearing in the 1930s. References in Wordsworth's vast autobiographical poem, *The Prelude*, fit the Colthouse cottage much better than they do the Hawkshead cottage—such as a brook running through the garden and Wordsworth catching hold of a tree on his way to school. Hawkshead, then and now, is very much a built-up town.

In 1783 Wordsworth's father died. From then on, not only was Wordsworth an orphan but he was also beset with money problems. His father had died with Sir James Lowther (who became Earl of Lonsdale in 1784) owing him £4,700 in legal and political fees. Various uncles took over the guardianship of Wordsworth and his brothers, and they tried hard, with no luck, to get the money from the Lowther family.

In 1787 Wordsworth went up to Cambridge, but returned to Hawkshead in the holidays, going back to Mrs Tyson and his old digs, the only real home he had. His Uncle Richard advanced £400 for his education at Cambridge, a debt that Wordsworth worked for many years to repay, not finally settling it till 1813.

A FRENCH AFFAIR

Wordsworth got his degree in 1791, but couldn't face the thought of the church or the law, both of which had been vague ideas at one time, so he bummed around London, doing nothing in particular. Then, in November 1791, he decided to go to France. This brings us to one of the most intriguing incidents in Wordsworth's life, one that never became public till over a hundred years later, one that you never hear about when you're learning Wordsworth at school.

Most of his friends thought he was mad. France was in the first heady stages of revolution. The Bastille had been destroyed and the monarchy put to rout, but, like all students, Wordsworth approved of the Revolution and its aims. He went first to Paris, and then in December moved to Orléans, which in pre-Revolution days had been a popular city in which young Englishmen could learn French. He had very little money, but he found some cheap digs in Orléans and got a young French girl to give him French conversation lessons—for free. The girl was called Annette Vallon, aged twenty-five, four and a half years his senior, and they fell madly in love. She became pregnant.

In December 1792 Annette had a child by Wordsworth, a girl called Caroline. Two months before the birth Wordsworth had gone back to England, perhaps hoping the Lonsdale money had come through, planning to return and marry her when he could support her. But for the fact that war soon broke out between England and France, and continued for twenty years, he would certainly have returned.

For the next two or three years, Wordsworth travelled around the country, did a lot of late-night talking, wrote away at his poetry and other bits and pieces. His first poems were published in 1793. They sold badly, but several young men of taste were impressed by Wordsworth's talent. Some even helped with loans and gifts, just when he needed them. His best bit of luck was when he was left a legacy of £900 in 1795 by Raisley Calvert, a young friend from the Lakes whom he had helped to nurse during an illness.

In 1795, disappointed at the reception of his poems, he felt the call of the countryside, to live simply and get back to nature. He didn't head for the Lake District, but to the West Country, because that was where he was offered some cheap accommodation. He went with Dorothy, his only sister, and they set up house together.

It was here that Wordsworth met Samuel Taylor Coleridge and formed a friendship that is one of the legends of English literature. They came together, dazzled together, shone together like two bright stars, brought out the genius in each other and had an effect on English poetry that has probably never been equalled.

Coleridge was born in 1772, two years after Wordsworth, in Ottery St Mary, Devon. Like Wordsworth, his home life was disrupted, and he was sent away

ABOVE *Annette Vallon, from whom Wordsworth became separated by war, gave birth to the poet's illegitimate child in 1792.*

ABOVE *Dorothy was William's devoted sister and lifelong companion. This silhouette is the only known portrait of her as a young woman.*

to school at Christ's Hospital in London, not returning home for eight years. He was brilliant at Greek, captain of the school; then he went up to Cambridge and won awards and medals.

During his last long vacation, Coleridge went to Oxford and met Robert Southey, and they moved together to Bristol, writing poems, discussing philosophy, making plans for a new and better life. Their big scheme was called Pantisocracy. They intended to go to America and start a commune on the banks of the Susquehanna River, based on mutual love and mutual ownership, all very idyllic, living off the land. There were twelve young men, all of good education, and they were taking a suitable number of young ladies. There was some argument about whether marriages should be lasting. But marriage seemed the most sensible system, at least to Robert Southey, who was planning to marry one of five sisters, the Fricker girls, who were also going on the voyage. He married Edith Fricker and Coleridge married Sarah Fricker. However, the proposed Susquehanna scheme never got going. They couldn't get the money and they started to fall out, all blaming each other. It was at this moment that Coleridge met Wordsworth.

William and Dorothy decided to move to Alfoxden in Somerset to be nearer Coleridge and all three of them as good as lived together, talking all day, writing and reciting, walking half the night. Coleridge was of course married, and had a child, Hartley, but Mrs Coleridge tended to get left behind. It was always William and Dorothy and Coleridge who were out on nocturnal tours.

Coleridge had been as fortunate as Wordsworth with his friends. He had a pension of £150 a year from Tom and Josiah Wedgwood, of the pottery family. It enabled him to devote himself to poetry so that he would not have to go into the ministry as his family wanted.

The major result of the friendship between Wordsworth and Coleridge was the appearance of *Lyrical Ballads*, first published in 1798. *Lyrical Ballads*, though it created little fuss at the time, is now considered to be one of the turning points in the history of English poetry. All but four of the poems were Wordsworth's. Coleridge's main contribution was *The Rime of the Ancient Mariner*.

Wordsworth explained that the poems were experiments, trying to use the language and conversation of ordinary people, writing about ordinary topics, especially the humble and rustic. It was a complete breakaway, in subject matter and form, from the heavy, metrical poems of the 18th century. Wordsworth had been influenced by other contemporary poets, people like Burns, but he was showing genuine originality in linking the spiritual with nature, writing personal poetry which had its origins in his own 'emotion recollected in tranquillity'.

Wordsworth now decided to return to the Lakes—so many of his poems had sprung from his Lakeland memories—and he and Dorothy came back to Hawkshead in November 1799. He was now aged twenty-nine. He had seen a great deal of the world, but he had never spiritually left the Lakes. He was to live there for the rest of his long life—trailing just a little cloud of glory at this stage, but a whole host of golden friends and followers who were soon to make up what the world came to know as the Lake poets.

ABOVE *Samuel Taylor Coleridge first met Wordsworth in the 1790s and established what was to prove an enduring friendship.*

ABOVE *The poet Robert Southey lived in the Lake District and was an old friend of Coleridge's, yet he rarely met his fellow poet, Wordsworth.*

AMONG THE MOUNTAINS

I LEFT HAWKSHEAD, heading for Coniston, and very soon there were signs everywhere urging me to go to Tarn Hows, so I decided to follow them. Tarn Hows is a beauty spot. It's so beautiful it doesn't look real—and technically it isn't real. It's a stretch of beautifully sculptured parkland with a sensationally pretty tarn in the middle. There are pine trees around the edges, smooth fells rising behind and terrific views from every point. I later took my children to see it in their school holidays; they loved it, racing round the little peninsulas

RIGHT *Brilliant sunshine brings an icy winter's day to colourful life at Tarn Hows.*

and inlets, wading to the pine-clad islands, throwing fir cones at each other.

It was created in the 19th century by damming a stream and joining what were three rather swampy pools. The National Trust looks after it very efficiently, providing excellent car parks and a nature trail with a well-written guide, but in a good year the park can get over three-quarters of a million visitors and the human erosion is now becoming a big problem.

Before heading down to the slopes of Coniston Water, I spent some time exploring Grizedale Forest, which lies between Coniston and Esthwaite

LEFT *From 1969 concerts, exhibitions and dance and drama performances were staged amid the trees in the Theatre in the Forest at Grizedale. The theatre closed in 1998.*

Water. Grizedale Forest used to have a German prisoner-of-war camp at one time—officers, of course—and they were always trying to escape. They rarely made it. I bet they were confused by the maps. As in many instances in the Lakes, you get different places with similar names. Grizedale Forest, for example, has no connection with Grisedale Pike (which is miles away, near Keswick) or with Grisedale Tarn (which is miles the other way, near Helvellyn).

The Forestry Commission are trying hard these days, welcoming visitors and laying on nature trails. There's a wildlife centre and a big camping site, and, most surprisingly of all, a Theatre in the Forest which attracts internationally known musicians. Even so, I was glad to leave it and hit open land on the shores of Coniston.

RUSKIN'S RETREAT

I was aiming for Brantwood, on the eastern side of the lake, the home of John Ruskin for the last twenty-eight years of his life. It was February, and out of season, but I had been told the house could be seen by appointment; so I had rung up and arranged to be shown round. I knocked at the door of the lodge, as instructed, and it was opened by a tall, gaunt-looking man.

He was Derek Phippard, manager of Brantwood, and he took me round. The Pre-Raphaelite paintings and furniture are stark and uncomfortable, but I enjoyed noticing Ruskin's hair, handkerchief, tie, baby chair and other personal delights. In Ruskin's bedroom, Mr Phippard pointed out a little turret which Ruskin had built in the corner, providing excellent views of the lake. 'This bedroom gave him nightmares; so he moved.' I nodded my head wisely in reply, saying that of course Ruskin did go mad in the end.

'Who said he went mad,' declared Mr Phippard, turning on me. 'I go mad if I hear people saying Ruskin went mad.'

'Well, several books say he went mad,' I said.

'He wasn't mad. He just did so much writing in this house that he had a mental blockage. He was a bit eccentric, that's all.'

John Ruskin was born in London in 1819 and first visited Coniston as a young boy of five. His father was a successful wine merchant in partnership with Domecq, the sherry people, and it was his custom in the early days of his business to take his wife and family on his tours with him. He would stay at local hotels or houses with his family and servants and visit local houses and beauty spots. A great lover of the arts and the countryside, he encouraged his son to paint and to write poems about his travels—which soon took them all over Europe.

Ruskin went up to Oxford in 1836 and it was while at Oxford that he started to collect paintings by Turner, who was then under attack because of his abstract style. This led to the first volume of Ruskin's great work, *Modern Painters*, which appeared in 1843, when he was only twenty-four. It was a great success, though Turner was slightly embarrassed by the passionate defence from such a young man.

Ruskin was a great patron of the arts and a champion of many social and economic causes. He wrote books, gave lectures and encouraged painters, using his private wealth to buy their works when the world at large was against them, as with the Pre-Raphaelites. He was a great friend of Rossetti, Burne-Jones and Millais, and was an eminent artist in his own right.

In 1848 he married Effie Gray, the pretty young daughter of a Scottish friend of his family. It sounds a strange marriage. On their holidays, Ruskin took lusty young men with them, such as the young Millais. The marriage ended in 1854 with Effie running off with Millais. London society was shocked when she gained the annulment of her marriage to Ruskin on the grounds of her husband's impotence. Ruskin maintained he could prove his virility, if need be, but didn't want her back anyway.

In 1871 he bought Brantwood, little more than a large cottage at the time. He admitted in letters to friends that it wasn't that pretty, calling it 'dilapidated and rather dismal', but it had been famous for its views for almost a century, and it was the views he'd bought it for. 'Here I have rocks, streams, fresh air.'

Ruskin moved into the house with his cousin Joan Severn (he never remarried) and began rebuilding, putting on twelve rooms and his fancy bedroom tower, and adding to the estate till eventually it covered almost five hundred acres, including Fir Island in the lake. He was fifty-three when he moved in and it was his home till he died, aged eighty, in 1900. He wrote many books there, and was visited by many other eminent Victorians, such as Holman Hunt, Charles Darwin, Coventry Patmore, Marie Corelli and Kate Greenaway. He filled the house with paintings, by himself and his contemporaries, including many priceless Turners. His final years

ABOVE *Effie Gray's marriage to Ruskin was unsuccessful. She left him for the Pre-Raphaelite painter John Everett Millais, who painted this portrait of her.*

LEFT *Looking elderly and frail, Ruskin poses for a photograph on a country walk at Brantwood in 1889.*

CHARCOAL: BLADES, BOMBS AND BARBECUES

PICTURE AN 18TH-CENTURY charcoal burner, or 'collier'. It's early summer and he has set up camp in the woods, built his tepee-shaped, turf-covered hut, and perhaps brought his family along. In a nearby clearing, or 'pitstead', he starts to assemble a dome-like pyre. Around the 'motty-peg', a central supporting stake, he tightly packs seasoned logs and branches, and covers the structure with turf and bracken, cemented with damp earth and ash. Once the motty-peg is removed, a central flue remains. It is now that the charcoal-making process begins. The collier throws red-hot charcoal down the flue, tops it up with cold charcoal and plugs the hole with turf. For the next week or so he will carefully monitor his slow-burning fuel factory.

This meticulous method, and variations on it, has been used to produce charcoal for millennia. Charcoal has been a valued product since the Iron Age, when its ability to burn at temperatures high enough to smelt metal enabled this early civilisation to make tools and weapons. In medieval and Tudor times, charcoal was a commodity as precious as gas and oil are today. The production of both glass and glazed pottery relied on it, and charcoal,

mixed with sulphur and saltpetre, was the vital ingredient in the manufacture of gunpowder. Thanks to the charcoal burners of the 16th century, Britain had sufficient supplies of iron cannonballs to fire at the Spanish Armada, saving the country from invasion.

A wealth of local iron ore made the Lake District a prime site for charcoal burning, and the ancient forests provided an abundance of the all-important timber. Vast quantities of wood are required: it takes seven tons of this raw material to produce a single ton of charcoal. The charcoal from different types of trees has different uses. From juniper trees comes savin

LEFT Trees are coppiced each year to grow the maximum number of branches for burning.

BELOW The various stages in charcoal-burning have hardly changed since this early woodcut was made.

charcoal used for gunpowder; from willows comes the artist's charcoal of choice. Modern products reliant on charcoal include sugar, penicillin, deodorants and, of course, barbecue fuel. From crude Iron Age knives to char-grilled steak, charcoal has made its distinctive mark on British industrial and domestic life.

ABOVE Summer evenings have become synonymous with the appetising smell of charcoal barbecues.

LEFT Colliers can still be found in Lakeland woods, practising their craft in a tradition that dates back to the Iron Age.

were overshadowed by mental illness and depression, a sad ending for such an original spirit. 'One of the most remarkable men,' so Tolstoy described him, 'not only of England and our time but of all countries at all times.'

He left the house to his cousin Mrs Severn and her husband—and this is where Brantwood's troubles began. He wanted the Severns to 'accord thirty consecutive days in every year to strangers to see the house and pictures as I have done in my lifetime', but they refused, putting up a notice saying they were not open to the public.

They also started to sell off the treasures of Brantwood, including the Turners. All the best items from the house—paintings, furniture, books and manuscripts— were individually sold. Luckily, a wealthy collector and disciple of Ruskin, John Howard Whitehouse, went round buying back all the Ruskin possessions he could find. He had founded the Birmingham Ruskin Society and a boys' school in Bembridge, Isle of Wight, in 1919, which he ran on Ruskin's educational principles.

The Bembridge connection is where Mr Phippard, my guide, comes into the story. He was educated at Bembridge School before the war and had lectures by Whitehouse about Ruskin. 'The education was considered very progressive for those days. We had woodwork and printing which boys' schools didn't do then. I remember being taught that in life you should use your head, hands and eyes— that was a Ruskin principle.'

One of Brantwood's big problems is putting over exactly who Ruskin was. The general public, even the educated public, are a bit confused. If only Ruskin had done only one thing, and not involved himself in so many activities, he would have been easier to identify.

'Did you know Ruskin thought up green belts, smokeless zones, free schools, free libraries, the National Trust, Rent Restriction Act, town planning?' said Mr Phippard.

I queried his founding of the National Trust, as it was Canon Rawnsley and two others who are generally credited with doing that, but Mr Phippard would have none of it.

The walk round Coniston was delightful. At the head of the lake there's a most tremendous view. You see right up the lake at almost water level, as if you are swimming, with the water stretching for ever into the distance. Wordsworth loved the view from this end, and there used to be near Brantwood a Wordsworth Seat, so called because he was always recommending friends to use the spot for the best views of Coniston. The Old Man of Coniston towers over the lake, and in February it was snow-clad and most dramatic.

Coniston Water is now much quieter than Windermere, but in its day it was a veritable highway. From Norman times there was considerable charcoal burning in the area and iron ore was often brought up the lake to be smelted. There were copper mines around Coniston for centuries, the last ones closing after the First World War. You can still see little rows of miners' cottages around the village. There was a railway line from Furness to Coniston, opened in 1859,

ABOVE *Uninhabited Peel Island on Coniston Water was the childhood playground of Arthur Ransome. It appears in the guise of Wild Cat Island in his famous children's novel* Swallows and Amazons.

which brought crowds of trippers before the coming of the motor car, but it is now closed.

Most of the shores of the lake are open to the public, thanks to such large tracts being owned by either the National Trust or the Forestry Commission. There are three islands, in the care of the National Trust, and one of them, Peel Island, appears as Wild Cat Island in Arthur Ransome's *Swallows and Amazons*.

Coniston village's Ruskin Museum is part of what's known locally as the Institute—though more properly it should be called the Coniston Mechanics Institute and Literary Society. It was founded in 1852, part of that sudden splurge of educational and cultural institutes that spread across the country in the mid-Victorian age, designed to bring cultural and intellectual facilities to the workers. In those days, Coniston had a population of 1,300 (a third more than it has today), of whom 600 were employed in the copper mines. John Ruskin, naturally enough, became a pillar of the Institute when he moved to Brantwood and helped its expansion. On his death, it lost its most eminent patron—and with the Severns being so bolshie about opening Brantwood to the public, it looked as if Coniston could lose its Ruskin connection completely. W. G. Collingwood, Ruskin's secretary, worked to set up a Ruskin Museum at the back of the Institute as a place to preserve any Ruskin mementos they could get their hands on, and in 1901 the new building was opened by Canon Rawnsley—who else?

It gets almost as many visitors as Brantwood, yet it's little more than a village hall, an endearing if rather amateurish collection of bits and pieces that once belonged to Ruskin. There's a lovely collection, made by Ruskin himself, of local geological specimens, all carefully polished and arranged, a nice thing to have in a village that has such a stirring mining history. There's also his birth certificate, his Bible, his painting box and his funeral pall. Ruskin had encouraged the local linen trade, so the local linen ladies decided they would stitch his pall themselves. It took some months, as they hadn't done one before, but, having got the hang of it, they then went on to do Tennyson's when he died, stitching that one in three days flat.

In the middle of the little Ruskin Museum is what at first sight seems an incongruous intrusion—a set of photographs of a motorboat disaster on Coniston Water. They are a memento to the other great name for ever associated with Coniston, a gentleman who has nothing at all in common with Ruskin, apart from the fact that he too happened to die there. Donald Campbell made his last attempt on the world's water-speed record on Coniston in 1967, when he somersaulted at a speed of some three hundred and twenty miles an hour. He had been a frequent visitor to Coniston over the years. The lake is five miles long, without the curves and bays or pleasure craft of Windermere and Ullswater, and therefore ideal for speeding.

Ruskin is buried in Coniston churchyard and his grave is marked with a large decorated cross, carved out of Coniston stone from a local quarry. Donald Campbell has no grave. The disaster happened in the upper reaches of the lake. His body and most of the wreckage have never been recovered. Coniston is a very deep lake.

DONALD CAMPBELL: BORN TO SPEED

BORN IN 1921, Donald Campbell grew up in a household obsessed with speed. Throughout his childhood he was surrounded by talk of the record-breaking exploits of his father, Malcolm, who had become a national hero for his constant world speed attempts. It's not surprising, therefore, that Donald was bitten by the racing bug. From an early age he and his sister would race pedal cars and bikes up and down the driveway of their home. By the time he was twelve, Donald had progressed to riding a motorbike. During the 1930s, his riding skills were put to good use in the local police force's voluntary 'flying squad', set up to deal with car thieves.

Later in life, Donald emulated his father by making several successful attempts on both land and water-speed world records. Wherever the ground was flat enough or the water still enough, he would set new targets. He reached speeds of 276.33 miles per hour on water and 403.1 miles per hour on land. Following the tradition started by his father, his cars and boats were always named *Bluebird*, after Maurice Maeterlinck's play telling of the fabled bluebird of happiness which, when strived for, remains out of reach.

Thus it was when Donald Campbell's record-breaking life came to an end on

ABOVE *All the Campbells' vehicles, including Donald's 1955 model, seen here, took the name* Bluebird, *starting with Malcolm Campbell's first hydroplane.*

LEFT *Donald Campbell gives the thumbs-up as he prepares for a speed trial on Coniston. In a spectacular accident, Campbell was later to die on this very stretch of water.*

January 4, 1967, as he attempted to become the first man to reach over 300 miles per hour on water. His boat somersaulted spectacularly on Coniston Water, and sank; Campbell's body was never retrieved from the depths, and remains to this day in its watery grave.

LOST IN THE MIST

From Coniston I set off, in the rain, on my first long walk, heading for the Duddon Valley and the Langdales. So far I'd been wandering mainly round the Windermere–Coniston area, but now I was approaching the high fells.

I started climbing very steeply up a little road behind the village, past the Sun Hotel and the old railway station, heading for the Walna Scar Road. This isn't a road, despite its name, but an old packhorse route which climbs up and round the Old Man of Coniston. On a clear day, you can see Morecambe Bay from the top of the Old Man. On an even clearer day, you can see Blackpool Tower. Old Man is 2,633 feet high and, as the southernmost major fell in the Lakes, it does command terrific views, but not on a rainy day.

This was mining country and the Old Man itself is like an old cheese, full of holes and mounds where man has been hacking it about over the centuries. Today the copper mines are closed, though the spoil heaps are still there and names like Coppermines Valley linger on.

As I climbed higher, I could see the dark, volcanic rocks above, the craggy, spiky outcrops that are so typical of the southern fells—so different from the smooth slopes and rounded tops of the north. The red bracken and the rocks mingled in the mist and rain before my eyes. Then the mist completely descended and I could see nothing. The path had turned into a stream and I was walking up a torrent, picking my way over little waterfalls. I was glad, as ever, for my wellingtons.

Was it a path, I began to think to myself? All paths on steep hillsides become streams in rainy weather, so that didn't alarm me too much, but I couldn't believe that packhorses had ever climbed this way.

Suddenly I realised I had been following a line of cairns, definite little mounds of stones, planted at regular intervals beside the rough, streamy path. Every twenty yards they appeared—just the length of my vision. So I wouldn't fall down an old mine, which had been my worst fear.

The cairns kept going, though the path was now non-existent, until I realised that I was on the top of something, a plateau of some sort. Then at my feet there appeared water, deep water, not a stream this time. It must be flooding, I thought, or perhaps a little tarn. I explored the side of the tarn, climbing over large boulders, wading through the edges, but I could neither see the tarn's size nor shape because of the mist.

I struggled round the edge for fifteen minutes—and still the tarn went on. It must have been a known tarn, not a temporary bit of flooding, so I got the map out, had a quick fight with the wind and rain, and realised with horror that I'd gone completely off my route. A tarn this size must either be Blind Tarn, a most appropriate name, or Goat's Water. I got to the end of it at last, and found myself climbing again—this time up some sheer rocks. I realised from the map that, whichever of the two tarns I had just passed, I was very close to the edge of Dow Crag—which I knew to be one of the steepest and most dangerous crags in the Lake District, one of the spots where rock climbing in this country had begun. The range of climbs here goes from 'difficult' to 'severe'.

OPPOSITE *With its blanket of sunlit snow, the ridge of the Coniston group of mountains is a magnificent sight. In this aerial view, the much-climbed Old Man of Coniston and sheer Dow Crag form a distinctive horseshoe shape to the top left of the ridge.*

ABOVE *National Trust workers and volunteers take on the skilled job of repairing the Duddon Valley's dry-stone walls.*

RIGHT *As the storm clouds move away, the lush green fields of the Duddon Valley are revealed in all their glory.*

I concentrated on the cairns. I cursed them for leading me astray on the way up, but I should have been lost without them on the way down. I stumbled and slipped and it was almost a mile before I hit a definable path. Consulting the map, now the wind and mist had slackened a little, I realised that it must have been Blind Tarn I'd hit by mistake, the furthest away and more isolated of the two tarns on the west of the Old Man. I thought of continuing to retrace all my steps, right back to the village, but I was sure I was now on the real Walna Scar packhorse route at last. I came to a little stone bridge which gave me confidence that I'd hit civilisation. Then I came across a group of about ten schoolboys in the usual orange anoraks.

The leader, a bearded Irishman, said they were from County Durham, on some local authority adventure holiday, heading for a youth hostel. The Lakes are full of school and student parties. Most local authorities from the Northeast and Northwest seem to have some sort of residential centre in the Lakes, where they lay on climbing, walking and boating holidays for their pupils.

The descent was quick and grassy and suddenly I was into fresh air again, with a sky above and a view beyond. I came down a hillside stream above Seathwaite and so into the Duddon Valley, one of the most beautiful valleys in the Lake District. There's a narrow road right through the valley, which twists and turns and goes round little hummocks.

The road was deserted and for an hour I saw neither vehicle nor human being. Lakeland roads, the minor ones of course, are a pleasure to walk. You can look up and down and all around without having to bother to watch your feet the way you do on the fells. Fell walkers scorn roads of any sort—which is silly. It's traffic that is terrible, not tarmac.

The walls and houses of the Duddon Valley looked so different from the Coniston area. In a few hours, I'd left slates behind and was into stone, soft and rounded. The rain was still pouring down and I sheltered by a bridge over the

Duddon—before realising it was Birks Bridge. The river forces and polishes its way through a little rock gorge and the humpback stone bridge seems itself to be a work of nature, blending and melding with the rocks on either side.

The road started to flatten out and the valley became broader, which was a surprise. I was heading up the river, towards its source, so you would normally expect it to get steeper and narrower. But it was the fattening before the thinning. Wrynose Pass was getting near, my final haul up and over to the Langdales. Wrynose, one of the steepest and most difficult roads in the Lake District, was unsurfaced till 1945. During most winters, it can still be closed for many weeks because of snow.

I turned right at Cockley Beck Bridge for Wrynose—looking left towards Hardknott Pass, which loomed equally menacingly. I plodded on, thinking of the days Wordsworth strode this way. He wrote in his long poem, *The Excursion*, about 'Wonderful Walker', a 19th-century parson who lived in the Duddon Valley for sixty-six years, managing on a stipend of £5 a year, yet feeding the poor, treating the sick, bringing up his own large family and dying at ninety-two. But I was getting a bit too tired for such reveries.

ABOVE *Birks Bridge, at one with the rocks that surround it, straddles the crystal-clear waters of the Duddon River.*

Then a Mini sneaked up behind me and suddenly stopped. A door was opened and a little puff of confetti blew onto the road, sucked out by the gale-force wind and rain. It was a honeymoon couple. They said they'd give me a lift to Little Langdale, wherever that was. They had been to Ravenglass for the day to look at the steam railway and were heading back for their hotel. They were from Blackburn, Lancashire. On the top of Wrynose, right at the very summit beside the Three Shires Stone—which marked the meeting point of the three old counties, Cumberland, Westmorland and Lancashire—we got a sensational view down the other side of the valley and the first glimpse of Little Langdale Tarn.

ROOM AT THE INN

At the Three Shires Inn, close by the tarn, the welcome was warm, the tea was hot and the bath was scalding. What more can one ask after a day in the rain on the fells? My sodden garments were whipped off silently to an airing room. No doubt, I thought, years of wet walkers had taught the owners the way to their hearts.

Later that night I discovered that Mr and Mrs Price had opened only two days previously. It was their first hotel. For the previous three years they had been in the Middle East. John Price was a civil engineer by profession, and during his three years with the Arabs they had accumulated enough money to come home, buy a small hotel and start a completely new life. His wife Mavis had always liked cooking, but neither had any previous experience of running a hotel.

There were only four other guests in the hotel, and the Prices joined us for coffee and drinks by the log fire in the sitting room after they had served us dinner. All seven of us sat boozing, cut off from the outside world in a remote little valley, the rain lashing outside, telling our life stories. All that was missing was an Agatha Christie villain to bump one of us off.

Next day I set out for Great Langdale. You can see the Langdale Pikes for miles around. They're perhaps the most impressive-looking crags in the whole of the Lake District, and Great Langdale has long been one of the country's chief climbing centres. This is where the professionals come, loaded down with their hardware. The National Trust and the National Park people are worried that some paths in Great Langdale, even on the high crags, will disappear under the weight of numbers, and they're making great efforts to redirect the hordes.

The valley starts gently at Elter Water. I didn't notice any swans on the strangely shaped little tarn, though I looked hard through the reeds. (The name comes from the Viking and means 'swan'.) I headed up the valley side to Stickle Tarn. There are some terrific waterfalls on the way up Stickle Ghyll, all nicely fenced in, the paths laid with poles, viewing stations beaten flat by generations of gapers. The Victorians loved waterfalls and these and the nearby Dungeon Ghyll waterfalls were an enormous attraction.

ON TOP OF THE WORLD

ABOVE *Victorian climbers reach the summit of Napes Needle on Great Gable in 1896. The pinnacle had been climbed for the first time only 10 years previously, by W. P. Haskett Smith.*

THE LAKE DISTRICT, condensed into an area less than forty miles across, contains the highest concentration in England not only of lakes but also of mountains, or fells. Of all these fells, Scafell Pike is king, laying claim to the title of highest peak in England, at 3,210 feet. Abundant crags of igneous rock, limestone and sandstone, slate and granite exert a magnetic pull on climbers eager to pit their wits against some of the toughest climbs in the country.

The earliest climbers were shepherds in the late 18th and early 19th centuries, but the poet Coleridge was also somewhat of a trailblazer, recording in his journals and letters the difficult routes he climbed at the turn of the 19th century. With the arrival of the railways came tourists: the first outsider to come to the Lake District to make an ascent purely for sport was one Lieutenant Wilson, who climbed Pillar Rock in 1848. The Pillar climb became a popular goal, and in the next eighteen

years twenty-eight people completed it. In 1870 the first women began climbing in the area, clad in (and probably hindered by) the long dresses required to maintain ladies' modesty.

Since the early days of the sport, the advent of new materials and equipment—grippy rubber-soled shoes rather than hobnailed boots, nylon ropes instead of hemp—has led to great advances in climbing and made more peaks accessible to more people. Similarly, increased leisure time, better transport, and the provision of training facilities such as gyms and

RIGHT *Climbing equipment and clothing have come a long way since the turn of the century. Lycra leggings have replaced long skirts and restrictive corsets for ladies, and rubber-soled shoes have taken over from heavy hobnailed boots.*

The path beside the Ghyll climbs steeply and I was soon into rough scree and rocks. All the way up, the beck roars and screeches as it throws itself over rock faces, and I was grateful for the times the path veered away, just to give my ears a rest.

Stickle Tarn came as a beautiful surprise. Such calm, still water, so smooth and inviting, with behind, rising sheer out of the tarn, the tremendous rock face of Pavey Ark. They all have such strange names, the Pikes in the Langdales. To my left I could see Harrison Stickle, a great block stuck on the end of Pavey Ark. Then there's Pike of Stickle and Gimmer Crag. I stuck to my plan of walking round the tarn and not attempting anything too clever. I'd leave the real rock climbs for the professionals.

I crossed the beck on some steppingstones and hit a path along the side of the valley which brought me out above Old Dungeon Ghyll Hotel, at the end of Great Langdale. This is where the road stops. After that, you have to walk, though there is still some easy walking ahead up two smaller valleys, till you're completely surrounded by the towering fells and crags, the sort that true climbers dream about: Bow Fell, Crinkle Crags, Rossett Pike, Scafell Pike, Great Gable.

LEFT *The Langdale Pikes, seen here from Great Langdale, attract climbers from all round the country. The tall, central crag is Harrison Stickle, 2,414 feet high.*

BELOW *A climber gets to grips with the route known somewhat ominously as Bludgeon, on Shepherd's Crag. His reward will be an unparalleled view from the top.*

indoor climbing walls mean that thousands of climbers pour into the Lake District every year to attempt the old, classic routes as well as tackling new ones.

Indeed, climbs that were once thought exceptional are now easily achievable by those who travel to the area to experience the unparalleled thrill of grappling with the rock and conquering a forbidding crag—not to mention seeing the magical beauty of the valleys and lakes laid out below them once they reach the top.

Old Dungeon Ghyll Hotel is owned by the National Trust, as is much of the Great Langdale valley, most of it being left to them in 1928 by G. M. Trevelyan, the historian. As seaside hotels boast a sea view in their brochure, so the Old Dungeon Ghyll Hotel has its own very Lake District attraction: 'A large Drying Room is available in the cellar.'

There's a regular Ribble bus service right to the front door of the hotel from Ambleside, via Skelwith Bridge and Elterwater, four times a day. How nice to think that such an isolated place should have a bus service—all thanks to its being a mecca for climbers.

I turned left and headed across the valley towards the little winding road that climbs up and over into Little Langdale. At Wall End, just as I started the climb, I inspected a lovely dry-stone barn, made of stone and layers of slate. I could see no trace of cement, even where it had been repaired. Dry-stone walls are commonplace, but I hadn't seen a dry-stone building before.

On top of the road, which is usually impassable in winter, you catch the first sight of a lonely tarn called Blea Tarn. It has a pretty setting amid pine trees.

The road down into Little Langdale was rather marred by a succession of empty polythene bags, the sort that contain feeding blocks. Farmers open one side of the plastic bags, exposing the blocks, and leave them in the fields, especially at lambing time. When the blocks are eaten up, the bags just blow away, unless the farmer goes round again and collects them.

Back in the bar of the Three Shires in Little Langdale, I met a Co-op delivery man called Tom Wilson. His little van was outside and he said he was collecting orders from local farmers' wives for the Co-op in Chapel Stile. Wouldn't it be easier if they rang their orders through? He said no. It was a tradition round here. Farmers' wives liked to be called upon. Most of them didn't have a car and were stuck at home all day. Anyway, he wasn't really a proper Co-op salesman. It was just a temporary job. 'I'm a dropout from the rat race, that's what I really am.'

Four years before, he had been working as the manager of a wallpaper machinery factory in Cheshire and had a good salary, a nice semi, and he and his wife ran two cars. Now they had a rented cottage in Great Langdale and for a year he'd been trying to set himself up as a full-time potter.

They lived a very simple life, he and his wife and twelve-year-old son. 'We have no fuel bills because we only use wood for heat and we gather all that ourselves from the fields and the fells. You're allowed to pick up any fallen branch under six inches in circumference. We do our weekly wood-gathering session on Sunday afternoon. In the morning we go for our weekly swim at Windermere.

'Socially, we have a terrific time. You think at first there must be nothing happening in Langdale, just a few cottages, but there's endless dances and lectures. We've had a Windscale scientist to talk to us, someone on red deer, how to make furniture, how the mountain-rescue teams work. All fascinating. And all free. Then there's cheese and wine parties. My wife is very active in the Young Wives and puts on plays in the school hall. It's a more social life than in Cheshire. We just didn't have the time then. We were too exhausted working.'

LEFT *The cottage at Town End, Grasmere, as the Wordsworths knew it. Although Grasmere has expanded, Dove Cottage remains much as it was in the early 1800s, when it was the poet's home.*

WORDSWORTH AT DOVE COTTAGE

Dove Cottage, Grasmere, is known around the world as the home of Wordsworth—yet the Wordsworths never knew it as Dove Cottage. It didn't have a name when they moved there from Hawkshead in December 1799, and they never gave it one. Their address was simply Town End, Grasmere, which was the collective name for the group of cottages at the southern end of the village. The cottage had at some stage previously been an inn called The Dove and Olive, and this is where its present-day name has come from.

It was a fairly humble cottage, and still is, with two rooms downstairs, plus a back kitchen, and four little rooms above. Dorothy and her brother lived here for eight years, and they had a constant stream of visitors. Coleridge almost immediately followed them up to the Lakes. He stayed with them and then Dorothy found him a house to let at Keswick—Greta Hall—where he moved in with his family, to be followed not long afterwards by the Southeys. Coleridge and Southey had, of course, married sisters, and a third sister also moved into Greta Hall with them. Coleridge, however, seems to have spent most of his time in the first few years with the Wordsworths, walking the twelve miles or so to take tea, then staying for weeks.

Wordsworth's younger brother John, who'd gone to sea, stayed with them, too, for long stretches when he was between voyages. But the basic unit, in the early Dove Cottage years, from 1800 to 1802, was Dorothy and William. Together they built up the garden, creating a hut in one corner (still to be seen) which she planted with mosses and rock plants, found on the fells. There were no houses in front of the cottage at the time (now there is a hotel and a terrace), and Wordsworth could lie in bed and see the water rippling on Grasmere. Dorothy was his housekeeper, cooking and cleaning, and his secretary, writing his letters and copying out his poems. Wordsworth's habit was to compose aloud, out in the garden or on the fells, reciting as he walked, polishing and declaiming at the same time. Later he would recite it to Dorothy, who usually had the task of writing it all down.

ABOVE *Dorothy's journal contains the description of daffodils that inspired her brother's most famous poem.*

BELOW *On one of their many walks Wordsworth and friends left their mark by carving their initials on a wayside rock.*

Dorothy was also his inspiration. She kept notes and descriptions in her own journals, details of what she and William had seen and felt together, people they'd met on their walks, and he would make her read them out later, to remind him of what they'd done. 'I wandered lonely as a cloud', the Wordsworth poem best known to the general public, owes a great deal to Dorothy's original description, in prose, of daffodils they had seen by the shore of Ullswater.

While William shared many intimate times with Dorothy, there were other ladies in his life, especially Mary Hutchinson. She and her sister came to stay during the early days at Dove Cottage, and took part in expeditions. There would be William and Dorothy, Mary and Sarah Hutchinson, John Wordsworth the sailor, plus Coleridge. They all carved their initials on a rock by a road near Keswick—WW, MH, DW, STC, JW, SH. It remained there for many years, but was removed during road improvements. It now stands outside the Wordsworth Museum in Grasmere.

The engagement of William and Mary happened suddenly, at least that's how it appears in Dorothy's journal. They get up one day and Dorothy and William are off south, making for Dover. Now that he had become engaged William wanted Annette to be the first to know.

The trip to France lasted four weeks. It was now August 1802, and the Peace of Amiens had brought a temporary settlement between France and England. William hadn't been to France for ten years.

In his discussions and explanations with Annette, William possibly promised her some money. Lord Lonsdale, the bad 'un who had been so horrid to the Wordsworth family, had died earlier in 1802, without ever paying up any money, but they felt certain that the new lord would settle the scores. William felt he could now support a wife and family, and also Annette.

The marriage took place almost immediately after their return from France in October 1802. William now had two ladies to mop his fevered brow when the creative passions took him. And his creative passions were now at their height. A new edition of *Lyrical Ballads* came out, this time with only Wordsworth's name on it, and it sold quite well. He had a little money at last and some passing fame, with his poems becoming better known, and literary types of the day started coming up to the Lakes just to see him and his friend Coleridge down the road.

By 1808 the Wordsworths had three children: John, aged four and a half, Dora, aged three, and Thomas, aged one. Dove Cottage became too small for their growing brood, plus all the relations and friends who seemed permanently to be staying with them, and in May the Wordsworths moved out of Dove Cottage into a bigger house nearby in Grasmere, Allan Bank. It was a new house, and Wordsworth had watched furiously as it was being built. 'A temple of abomination,' so he'd described it, 'the house will stare you in the face from every part of the Vale and entirely destroy its character of simplicity and seclusion.' But as it was the only house available when he came to move, he ate his words and took it over.

When they moved out, Dove Cottage was taken over by a brilliant young writer, Thomas De Quincey, and he had the tenancy of the cottage for the next twenty-eight years. The son of a wealthy Manchester merchant, De Quincey was excellent with Wordsworth's children. He was also very good with the womenfolk, though the Wordsworths were upset by his addiction to opium.

He was very proud to be one of the literary Lakers, and thrilled by life in Grasmere. He wrote of the Wordsworths going skating, when the lake froze over in winter. They went as a family—Dorothy and Mary on chairs, holding a baby each in their arms, while William skated behind, pushing them across the lake. It's a sight you rarely see in the Lakes today. None of the lakes ever seems to freeze right over, the way they did in the early 19th century. Esthwaite Water, particularly, the one beside Hawkshead, was always freezing over in William's schooldays. Today, our winters are positively Mediterranean by comparison.

OPIUM—THE 'JOY PLANT'

THERE IS, THE SAYING GOES, nothing new under the sun. We may think of heroin addiction as a modern-day evil, but the euphoria-inducing effects of the resin found in the seed capsules of opium poppies have been known for 6,000 years. And opium and its derivatives, such as heroin, morphine and codeine, have been used in medicine as effective painkillers for centuries. But for all their benefits, opiates have one critical drawback: they are highly addictive.

One of the most renowned victims of opium's insidious stranglehold was the writer Thomas De Quincey. A colourful member of the circle that gathered round Wordsworth in the early 19th century,

BELOW *Ornate opium sets suggest that opium-taking was a rich man's pastime.*

LEFT *Opium dens in London's East End allowed 'respectable' gentlemen to indulge their habit secretly.*

RIGHT *The writer Thomas De Quincey's experience of opium-taking provided raw material for his work.*

De Quincey vividly portrayed the horrifying alternation between dream and nightmare that opium abuse could generate in his *Confessions of an English Opium-eater* (1821). Another eminent member of the circle, the poet Samuel Taylor Coleridge, was also an addict.

Many contemporary users first took opium for medicinal purposes but gradually became dependent on its unerring ability to numb the senses. In Coleridge's day, opium was a quasi-respectable drug of the well-to-do. Britain controlled a flourishing trade in opium

from India. Keen to expand this trade, the British set to exporting the drug from India to China—much to the anger of the Chinese authorities, who had banned its use. But the British government supported its traders, and twice took up arms against the Chinese in the infamous Opium Wars of the mid-19th century.

It is ironic, then, as attitudes to opiates have changed and heroin has become the scourge of modern society, that the British government now finds itself waging war on the drug trafficking it once advocated.

DOVE COTTAGE TODAY

Grasmere village is really in two chunks, with Dove Cottage in the east and Allan Bank in the other, bigger part of the village. If I were living in Grasmere today—which I'd rather not, as it's so popular and overrun and always seems to me to have a claustrophobic feeling, overshadowed by the towering fells on all sides—then I'd prefer to be in Allan Bank, Wordsworth's second Grasmere home. It's a handsome house on high ground, on the slopes of Silver How.

It was bought in 1915 by Canon Rawnsley, who left it to the National Trust. It was empty when I was there and the National Trust was currently advertising for a new tenant. I went on to Dove Cottage.

It's a small, whitewashed cottage in a little lane with no view today of the lake. Some cottages opposite, which include a book store, all belong to Dove Cottage.

A guide opened up, saying did I want to be taken round or would I walk round on my own? I said I wanted to be taken, so we waited for some more visitors. Eventually a young couple arrived and joined me on the guided tour.

Dove Cottage is a pleasure to go round, because it's been so beautifully preserved and furnished that you can almost believe the family is still living there. It is so much bigger and richer than it looks from the outside, though of course the feeling of richness comes from it being a preserved, period cottage. In its day, it was relatively humble. You enter immediately into the kitchen–parlour, which has stone flags, dark wood panelling, a fireplace and a window seat, all as they were in Wordsworth's time. The guide pointed out where Dorothy made the family's two meals a day—'both porridge'—and drew our attention to three chairs embroidered by the three poets' daughters: Dora Wordsworth, Sara Coleridge and Edith Southey.

The atmosphere is helped by the fact that so many detailed descriptions have been left to us about Dove Cottage, by Dorothy in her journals, by De Quincey and by Wordsworth himself; anyone who has done a little bit of background reading immediately recognises many of the objects. There's a little pair of balancing scales, perfectly ordinary in themselves, till you see they are marked 'T. De Q.' and you know he mixed opium on them. The newspapers have been replaced on the walls of the Newspaper Room, a bedroom Dorothy papered to try to keep it warm, but they are all genuine, contemporary newspapers from Wordsworth's day.

The garden has been equally carefully tended with plants and paths and little bowers arranged as far as possible as Dorothy described them. If, of course, you'd never heard of Wordsworth, most of the details would be wasted. It would just be another nicely preserved little 17th-century cottage.

ABOVE *The Newspaper Room at Dove Cottage, repapered in recent times with newspapers of the period.*

Dove Cottage attracts scholars from all over the world. Grasmere is always full of Wordsworth experts, students from Japan or America, writing yet another Wordsworth study or PhD. Dove Cottage, as scholarship goes, is big business and the library and the museum nearby, which contain priceless Wordsworth manuscripts, are always humming with intellectual activity.

George Kirkby, the guide who took me round, had been born in Grasmere. He couldn't remember learning much about Wordsworth at school. It was wartime and his schoolday memories of Grasmere were of utter freedom. Since coming to Dove Cottage he had made it his business to teach himself everything he could about Wordsworth. 'The day I stop reading about Wordsworth is the day I stop this job.'

I met many academic experts on Wordsworth over the year, but few I talked to had more *breadth* of knowledge about Wordsworth than George. His conversation was full of quotations from Wordsworth poems, and opinions from all the leading Wordsworth scholars, backed up with a few of his own personal views. He corrected me when I called Southey 'Suthy', saying it should be 'South-y', to rhyme with mouth. The clue to the correct pronunciation is in a Byron poem. He even refuted my suggestion that the vital element missing in Wordsworth as a person was a sense of humour.

ABOVE *The garden at Dove Cottage is well tended, with layout and planting closely resembling those of Wordsworth's time.*

'You must read *all* Wordsworth again,' said George. 'He has a dry, putting-down humour which you can miss at first glance. It has a cruel streak to it. Very Northern.'

In the height of the summer, he and the other guides showed round 600 visitors a day, doing up to twenty tours between them. School parties could be tough, especially the ones who hadn't prepared the children first but came in at the last moment to get out of the rain.

He lived in one of Dove Cottage's ten tied cottages. 'If it wasn't for the National Trust, the Council and Dove Cottage, Grasmere would lose its indigenous population. They wouldn't be able to stay. We're part of the continuity. I look around the fells and I look at the stone walls and I think of the lives that my forefathers put into building them. If the real locals go, Grasmere becomes a green desert.'

CHAPTER THREE

THE WESTERN LAKES

ABOVE *Toughened by the rigours of hill farming, Joss Naylor is a champion at the arduous sport of fell running, and is still competing in his sixties.*

I MOVED ON TO WAST WATER, home of one of Lakeland's best-known living residents, Joss Naylor. He held many world records—records that most of the world has never heard of. Joss Naylor was a fell runner.

Fell running is not just long-distance running—it's long-distance obstacle running. World-class marathon runners have failed to beat Joss, not aware of the variety of terrain that has to be covered, the complexity of pacing yourself, of knowing how to run over swamp and rocks, how to avoid hidden peaty holes and leap over bracken, what sorts of grass and moss to trust.

Joss Naylor was not just well known in the Lakes—he was well liked. He was known for doing something that requires that much-admired quality, hard graft. He ran hard and he worked hard, combining a tough life as a sheep farmer on the high fells with running up and down peaks.

His home was in Wasdale, overlooking Wast Water. It's probably the most dramatic valley in the whole of the Lake District. It starts off soft and rather lush, till you reach the lake itself, when life and nature narrow and become tough and unrelenting. It's an isolated, hidden valley with a one-way road. You have to work your way round the coast to get in, so most tourists never see it.

Almost at the end of the lake, on the left-hand side, I came to an isolated farm called Bowderdale, Joss Naylor's home. The road itself petered out in another mile or so at Wasdale Head, a little tundra of no-man's-land, like an Alpine oasis, with, towering behind the peaks of Scafell and Great Gable, the highest mass of mountains in the whole of the Lakes.

Joss weighed only nine and a half stone, yet he was not much short of six feet high. His face seemed to be all bone with deep-set eyes. Most surprising of all was his walk, as if every step was agony. It was only on the fells that the speed of his walk was apparent, his long legs eating up the yards. For most of his life he had indeed been in agony. He'd had disc trouble since the age of nine, for which he had undergone an operation and worn corsets and special straitjackets.

ABOVE *Wasdale Head opens out onto Wast Water, the deepest lake in England at 260 feet. Surrounding Wast Water are the fells that Joss Naylor farms—the perfect environment for a fell runner.*

He was born in 1936 in Wasdale Head, just a mile from his present house, where his father was a tenant farmer. He went to school at Gosforth, the village some eight miles away towards the coast, the school his two younger children now attended. He left at fifteen and became a shepherd, working for his father and on other farms. But for his fell running, which had taken him on trips around Britain and as far away as Colorado, he'd lived and worked in Wasdale.

His wife Mary was from Newcastle, a city girl who had come one summer to work for two months for Joss's mother, who took in paying guests in the holiday seasons as Joss and his wife did now. They got married in 1963 and the same year Joss applied to be the tenant of Bowderdale, which had just become empty. He offered £166 a year for it, the same rent as the previous tenant had paid. There were higher offers but they decided to let a local shepherd have it.

For his £166 a year he got a farm of 140 acres, only eighteen acres of which were workable, though even those were only good enough for hay, not arable. The sheep grazed almost entirely on the open high fells, some two thousand acres of Red Pike, High Fell and Scoat Fell, which go up to 2,700 feet, most of it owned

THE SHEPHERD'S YEAR

L OOK UP towards the Lakeland fells in late autumn and you are likely to see large flocks of Herdwick and Swaledale ewes—some flocks numbering over 1,000 sheep—being gathered in preparation for the breeding season. Neighbouring farmers often join forces for the 'autumn gather', each with their lean, hard-working sheepdogs tirelessly herding the flocks from the high fell grazing to lower pastures.

The ewes are placed with the ram—which is kept on lower ground—and then returned to the fell early in the New Year. Fell winters are long and hard, but Lakeland sheep are robust animals, and only in the harshest weather will they need hay. When food is scarce in late winter, concentrated hard blocks of feed are available for them to nibble at, and these provide essential nutrition to sustain the developing lambs.

In the lengthening days and warmer weather of late April, shepherds bring the ewes down to the sheltered, lower-

lying pastures round the farm for lambing. This is a hectic period for the shepherd, who has to keep a close eye on his flock in case any ewes need a helping hand. Shepherds will check every newborn lamb, and a bottle of ewe's-milk replacer will be on hand to give weakly lambs an extra feed.

Ewes and lambs spend the summer on the fell, but return to the farm in July to have their warm wool fleece, or 'jacket', sheared. Before going back to the fell, the shorn ewes will be dipped in a chemical solution to protect them from insects and parasites. The next time the flocks visit the farm is in early autumn after the lambs are weaned. Some ewe lambs stay in the flock while the rest, including the castrated male lambs, or wethers, go for sale at the great autumn sheep fairs—the highlight of the sheep farmer's year. These are the main source of annual income for many Lakeland fell families, who depend on lowland farmers with kinder pastures to buy their sheep and produce prime lambs for the butcher.

With the darkening days of November, which naturally trigger ewes to come into breeding condition, the cycle begins all over again.

LEFT *A shepherd, with his trusty dog and crook, gently carries a small Herdwick lamb down from the fell.*

BELOW *After shearing, Herdwick fleeces will be treated and spun for use in tweeds and carpets.*

ABOVE *Sheep have little chance of finding much sustenance after heavy snow, so the hardy sheep farmer has to brave the elements and carry hay to his flock.*

BELOW *Fleece marks and ear clippings serve to identify different flocks. The first Shepherd's Guide for all the local flocks was compiled in 1817 by a Lakeland farmer.*

BELOW *Crooks are prized objects among sheep farmers, and are even judged at sheepdog trials. The intricately carved heads are made from sheep's horns.*

by the National Trust. For his £166 he also got 150 stock sheep, all Herdwick. If and when he ever gave up the farm, he would have to leave the same number and type of sheep. It had taken him ten years to build up his own stock to over a thousand.

He was a one-man sheep farmer, having no help, even at the height of the shearing and lambing seasons. He had three children. The younger two went on the school bus from the end of the road to Gosforth. The eldest had to go to the secondary modern school at Keswick, where she boarded during the week.

Depending on the time of year, he spent most of each day on the fells. He had six dogs, all curs, who worked with him.

He had mainly Herdwicks, which are most suited to the rough land, plus some Swaledales and cross-bred Rough Fells. A Swaledale ewe comes dearer than a Herdwick, because a Swaledale is 90 per cent sure to produce lambs while a Herdwick is only 60 per cent sure.

He had about four hundred lambs a year, and sold all but six of the males, which were kept as rams for breeding. The rest of the males were castrated, then fattened up and sold. All the ewes were kept for breeding, eventually replacing the older ewes that had got too old to withstand life on the high fells. He knew all his sheep individually, and could tell you sagas about almost all of them, accidents and births and parentage.

I had slowly come to recognise a Herdwick from a Swaledale. Herdwicks are thickset and white-faced, and only the males have horns. Swaledales are finer-bodied, dark-faced (with a light nose) and both males and ewes have horns when fully grown. Herdwicks have been on the Cumbrian fells for 400 years. They're supposed to owe their origins to Spanish sheep shipwrecked on the Cumberland coast during the defeat of the Armada, but this is a matter of contention. It is a breed that is special to the Lake District, and they are supposed to be the hardiest sheep in the world. When they have absolutely nothing else to eat, they eat their own wool.

The government gives a subsidy to encourage sheep farmers to keep sheep on the fells. Otherwise, most would give up. Certainly Herdwicks don't make a lot of money, never growing big and fat, which is why it was an indulgence of Beatrix Potter's to keep so many of them down in her lush, lowland pasture. The money comes from the wool. It was the tough Herdwick wool that laid the foundations of the wool trade in places like Hawkshead. Local farmers would do their own spinning, having little spinning galleries where the wool was hung out to dry. (There's one at High Yewdale, near Coniston.)

Joss had his own identification mark on each of his sheep, a mark that went with the flock he had inherited. Each area has a shepherds' guidebook, listing all the local marks, and big occasions in a shepherd's year are the annual shepherds' meets which always take place in the same pubs. Traditionally this is the time to hand back stray sheep, but it's also a big social evening, with dialect songs and poems being performed. The other big social occasions are the sports.

ABOVE *A sheep farmer in the 1920s shears one of his sheep outside his cottage. The wool would later be washed and hung out to dry from the spinning gallery upstairs.*

Joss never ran as a lad. It wasn't till he was thirty-one that he started to be any good. He told me that that was when his circulation improved and he stopped having cramp. Now, at forty-one, he'd been ten years at the top in fell running and didn't expect to get any better, despite his back giving him less trouble than it had ever done.

He set the first of his twelve records in 1970. They included the Lakeland classic, the Lake District 24 Hours Fell Record, in which he had done seventy-two peaks of over two thousand feet in twenty-four hours, covering a distance of 108 miles and climbing in all 40,000 feet.

Outside the Lakes, he held the national record for the Three Peaks—the three biggest in England, Scotland and Wales: Scafell Pike, Ben Nevis and Snowdon. You're allowed to drive between them, though when Joss set his record it was before the M6 was built, which lost him time. He did the three in eleven hours, fifty-four minutes.

Not only is fell running growing, it's becoming overcrowded. Some of the popular races are now like processions. Every year there's a 30 per cent increase in entries for almost every race. In 1950 the Three Peaks Race in Yorkshire had fourteen runners. In 1977 they had to limit it to 450.

Although genuinely retiring and unpushy, Joss would help any local organisation out when they were stuck for a speaker. He could be out three or four nights a week round Cumbria, travelling long distances, just to chat to a handful of people, always about fell running. He'd just been to talk to the Wigton Round Table in Caldbeck—a trip right round the Lakes. In 1976 he was awarded an MBE.

Joss's wife Mary loved the life of fell farming, though on the outside it might look lonely and deprived, stuck in the back of beyond, with so few modern conveniences. The nearest neighbour was over a mile away. They got no newspapers and they had to go eight miles to the nearest village. But there was a great social life among sheep-farming folk. They could have been out every night if they wanted.

DOWN IN THE FOREST

The Lake poets were the first of the fell walkers—that's if you count a fell walker as someone who walks the fells purely for the pleasure of walking the fells, as opposed to shepherds like Joss Naylor who have to walk the fells to get their work done. Wordsworth, being a local lad, walked the fells from his childhood and continued walking throughout his life, but he preferred low fells and paths to the hard stuff. Southey had a very brief spurt of fell walking when he first came to the Lakes, but it didn't last long. Of the three poets, Coleridge was by far the champion. He only did it seriously for three years, but managed some amazing climbs.

Wordsworth first took Coleridge on a walk in 1799. They climbed Helvellyn and visited Ennerdale and Ullswater. They inspected Castlerigg stone circle near Keswick, and found the famous stones had been defaced with white paint. Vandals in 1799. (I always quote that incident when people moan about the present generation's hooligan tendencies.)

When Coleridge moved up full-time to the Lake District the next year, he started going off for long walks on his own. He used to take in Helvellyn, on his way from Keswick to visit William and Dorothy in Grasmere. He climbed Helvellyn one night by moonlight, which sounds a rather foolhardy thing to do, arriving at the Wordsworths' cottage when William was in bed. William put on his dressing gown while Coleridge read to him the latest part of his poem 'Christabel' and Dorothy cooked him a chop.

Coleridge later climbed Scafell Pike, an ascent that is thought to be the first recorded climb of that mountain by an outsider. He carried, as always, a portable inkhorn with him, and he wrote a letter on the spot. 'Surely the first letter ever written from the top of Scafell.' It probably was, as only shepherds had ever climbed it before, as far as is known. He then came straight down, scrambling over a ridge, ignoring the easier ways.

Coleridge was particularly fond of Ennerdale, which was where I was now heading. In 1799, when Wordsworth was giving him that introductory tour, a farmer told him how some eagles had stolen a live goose. In 1802 Coleridge went there again, and he heard tales of a pair of foxes and their five cubs who had managed to kill eight lambs.

Ennerdale Water is the most westerly of the Lakes and the valley that leads from it is one of the most remote and hardest to explore. It's the only lake without a road. Every other lake has at least one side with a road running along it. You can take your car to the edge of the lake, near Bowness Knott, but then the next ten miles of Ennerdale has to be walked.

Ennerdale would be unrecognisable today to Coleridge and Wordsworth, even to anyone who was there only fifty years ago. It is now a forest. The barren rough fellsides and tumbling scree slopes that Coleridge walked have been dramatically transformed by the Forestry Commission into a sea of dark green.

ABOVE *Foxgloves bring a splash of colour and a touch of wilderness to rows of conifers in Ennerdale Forest. It is only a few decades since this area was merely barren scree and fell.*

The Forestry Commission is all over the Lakes, with forests in many areas, and it has in all about forty thousand acres. The Commission's property at Ennerdale includes parts of Great Gable, Pillar Rock and a lot of higher fell, which is leased to the National Trust and unforested.

There are two youth hostels, one beyond the lake and the other, Black Sail, right through the forest at the end of the valley. It's six miles from the nearest road, and is the most cut-off hostel in the Lake District. You could easily miss it, dismissing it as a shepherd's hut, which is what it was. It has only three small rooms—in one the shepherd slept, in another his horse and in the third he kept his wool clippings. Somehow, they now get in eighteen hostellers. There's no public phone and it's a ten-mile walk to the nearest shop in Ennerdale Bridge.

ABOVE *The remote location of the very basic Black Sail youth hostel ensures solitude for those who choose to stay there.*

You get the best views from the end of the valley, once you hit open skies again—especially of Pillar, the 2,927-foot-high fell that dominates the valley, and, most of all, Pillar Rock, which can be seen best from Ennerdale. This is a vertical chunk of rock, almost six hundred feet high, which is said to be the tallest vertical crag in England.

At one time Pillar Rock was thought unclimbable, till a local shepherd, John Atkinson, did it in 1826. It's now done regularly, but only with the aid of ropes and all the tackle.

Ennerdale Water has been used as a reservoir for Cumbria for 130 years, without much affecting the environment. The water is incredibly pure—you just have to walk round it to see how clean it is, with no vegetation in sight, no reeds, little plant or bird life, little variety of fish, though it's always been popular with fishermen because of the trout. The water authority has had to do no more than put a small weir over the outlet river, the Ehen, and pipe down what they need to Workington and Whitehaven.

I walked round the edge of Ennerdale Water, looking for any signs of spoiling by the water people, but could find very little. There is a small retaining wall, about four feet high, along the western shore, where the Ehen runs out, but this is the cultivated end anyway, with farm land going down to the water's edge. The weir looks as if it's always been there, and the pump house is small and insignificant.

It was a calm soft evening in early summer and there were many fishermen around, all local lads, judging by the accents of the ones I talked to. Ennerdale, because of its situation, is very much a local, Cumbrian lake. I watched one young lad almost cycle straight into the lake, then throw his bike down just as he got to the water, and take out his rods. He'd come straight from work on a building site and was from Frizington. Frizington is perhaps the least attractive of a little string of left-over mining villages in Cumbria, an area where it's almost impossible to believe lush Lakeland is only a few miles inland. It's not just the natural scenery, which is flat and boring, but the houses and the people who seem deprived and left behind. I asked him what life was like in Frizington. He looked at me thoughtfully and replied: 'Desperate.' Then he walked into the water and started casting.

Life would be even more desperate in west Cumberland today if it wasn't for the handful of thriving new industries, many of them begun by refugees from Nazi Germany just after the war. They took great chances, moving into fields dominated by giant firms, such as chemicals and clothes, yet they succeeded and have given back much to the local community, in the way of theatres and cultural activities as well as employment.

The biggest employer, however, is the atomic plant at Sellafield, which employs over seven thousand. The site includes the first full-scale nuclear power station in the world, which was opened in 1956. It is a nice coincidence that the father of atomic theory, John Dalton, should have been born not far away—in Eaglesfield, outside Cockermouth. Sellafield is just two miles outside the National Park boundary, but it dominates the view and the minds of many throughout the

LAKELAND'S MODEST SCIENTIFIC PIONEER

JOHN DALTON was one of science's unlikely heroes—solitary and awkward, careless in his experiments, and colour-blind. But with his insatiable curiosity, independent thinking, and deftness at meshing diverse ideas into ambitious theories, he revolutionised the study of chemistry.

He was born in 1766 in Eaglesfield, of humble Quaker stock, and began his working life as a schoolteacher. His scientific interests included astronomy and biology (so extensive were his investigations into his own red–green colour blindness that the condition became known as Daltonism), and above all, meteorology—the varied weather of the Lake District being a fertile source for his observations and discoveries.

From studying the atmosphere, he turned to studying gases, and thence to matter in general. Several crucial

scientific laws or theories ensued, on such questions as how gas pressure increases as the temperature rises. In about 1801, he began developing his famous 'atomic theory'—reaffirming that all matter consists of indivisible particles or atoms, of different fundamental kinds or elements, and maintaining that chemical compounds consist of elements linked atom-to-atom in defined proportions. Many of the details were mistaken, but the outline still holds good. Similarly with his crude classification table of the elements, which prefigured today's standard periodic table.

Later in life, Dalton emerged from his Quaker austerity and obscurity. Fellowships of learned societies, awards and honorary degrees, and even a royal pension came his way. When he died in Manchester in 1844, the funeral was on a grand scale, with a procession over a mile long— a fitting tribute to the modest herald of the atomic age.

LEFT *The Cumbrian chemist John Dalton is known as one of the fathers of modern physical science.*

RIGHT *Dalton devised a table of chemical symbols which was the forerunner of today's periodic table.*

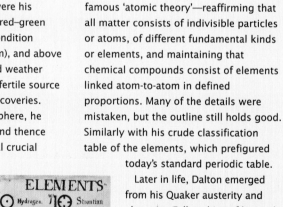

ELEMENTS·

Hydrogen.	1	Strontian	
Azote	5	Barytes	
Carbon	54	Iron	
Oxygen	7	Zinc	
Phosphorus	9	Copper	
Sulphur	13	Lead	
Magnesia	20	Silver	
Lime	24	Gold	
Soda	28	Platina	

LEFT *Sellafield was built in the aftermath of the Second World War to make plutonium for nuclear bombs, and is now a large-scale nuclear power plant. To comply with a decision taken by the European convention on marine pollution in July 1998, Sellafield must cut its radioactive emissions to 'close to zero' by 2020 if it is to avoid closure.*

Lakes. The scientists are now part of the community, manning mountain-rescue teams in their spare time, joining village drama societies. They end up being Cumbrians by adoption. In 1998 new international guidelines were introduced; Sellafield will have to cut its radioactive emissions or face closure.

UP THE PIKE

In early June I decided to climb Scafell Pike from Borrowdale, the longest way to climb it but the most exciting and scenic. You can make it a round trip, if you do it from Borrowdale, going up one way and coming down the other.

There is a separate mountain called Sca Fell, which is very confusing. It's part of the same massive range, but there is no argument about Scafell Pike's claim to fame. At 3,210 feet, it is the highest place in England.

I was with Jake, my eleven-year-old. Also setting off with us were my wife and five-year-old-daughter Flora, though they were only aiming to get halfway.

We got to Seathwaite at the end of Borrowdale at ten in the morning. Seathwaite's claim to national fame is that it is the wettest inhabited place in England. It's not that Seathwaite gets many more rainy days than some other places but that, when it does rain, it puts a lot of effort into it. They still talk about the terrible floods of 1966 when the head of Borrowdale became a lake with bridges damaged, roads ruined and the valley bottom littered with rocks washed down from the fells.

The Lake District has a bad name for climate, especially rainfall, but what people don't realise is that, inside the Lakes, there are huge variations. While Seathwaite gets more than a hundred and thirty inches a year, at Keswick, only eight miles away, the rain decreases dramatically to fifty-eight inches. And if you go, say, twenty miles away, down the coast or the northeastern fells towards Carlisle, the rainfall drops to around thirty inches a year. It's the high bits at the heads of valleys, such as Seathwaite, that give the Lakes a bad name for rain.

'There can be very few pieces of country in the world where such variety from place to place, from day to day, can be found in a short distance.' So Professor Gordon Manley, the country's leading expert on weather, has written about the Lakes. It's not just day to day but hour to hour that you get such changes. Within half an hour's drive of anywhere in the Lakes, you can run out of rain and into shine. When I lived in Carlisle, I was always amazed to go to Silloth, or Caldbeck, or Keswick, and have a rainy afternoon, yet come home and find the streets dry and everyone in the garden.

Wordsworth always recommended that people come to the Lakes in May and June or in September and October, which are still the best two times. May and June are the driest months, and September and October are the most colourful.

So, off we set for Scafell Pike. The sun was hot and the sky was unbelievably blue. Eventually we came to Stockley Bridge, a little old packhorse stone bridge over the River Derwent. We rested for a while, looking into a little pool so perfect it seemed a mirage. It was deep and rounded with a flat bottom, and the water was ice green.

PREDICTING THE UNPREDICTABLE

As THE FIGS RIPEN at Sizergh Castle south of Kendal, an arctic squall may be battering the summit of Great Gable or Helvellyn, only twenty miles away. At one end of Borrowdale the annual rainfall may be three or four times greater than at the other. Lakeland, thanks to its varied geography, boasts Britain's most varied climate. The Met Office issues its Lakeland forecasts regardless—fairly broad brush and tentative—and farmers, fell walkers and day-trippers alike welcome their guidance.

Weather-forecasting must be almost as old as human life itself, and represents one of the earliest forms of science. Proverbs such as 'Rain before seven, fine before eleven', and habits such as counting the berries on a tree, are the distillations of millennia of observations on the elements' behaviour. A proper scientific approach began in the 17th century, when Galileo and others designed instruments for measuring moisture, air temperature and pressure, wind speed and so on—the basic data for compiling forecasts. Modern technology has allowed ever more sophisticated data-gathering and from a far wider range of locations: oil rigs, dedicated weather ships and planes; buoys, balloons and remote, unmanned polar-monitoring stations; and satellites, beaming their photographs of cloud patterns back to earth.

Meanwhile, supercomputers around the world are sifting, swapping and analysing the millions of data streaming in, refining their predictions of both short-term local weather and long-term global climate changes. Dalesmen and fell-side shepherds may still pay regard to intuition and ancient proverbs, but they tune into the weather reports as well.

ABOVE *In a typical Lakeland scene, Coniston Water is swathed in mist while the surroundings are completely clear.*

RIGHT *Satellite images showing cloud patterns are the latest weapon in the weather forecaster's technical armoury.*

As we got higher, other climbers became fewer. They'd either turned back or taken different paths. We had come straight up Grains Gill and were now at a little plateau at the top of the ravine.

The thing about Scafell Pike, and why you must allow six hours to get up and down from Borrowdale, is that, unlike Skiddaw or Helvellyn, Scafell Pike is a mountain stuck behind other mountains. You have to do a lot of climbing, up and down and over and round, before you actually get to climb it.

We turned left, heading for Esk Hause, the topmost part of the plateau, and then we turned right, climbing up again. In effect, we were working our way up and round the huge chunk that had been in front of us. It turned out to be called Great End. Ahead we could see snow, large splinters of it, stuck fast in some deep crevices. I could also see mist, swirling down from where Scafell Pike must lie, but going the other way.

The Esk Hause route had opened up beautifully, and we soon seemed to be striding through so many summits. Then came the wonderful moment when we saw the top of Scafell Pike for the first time, just as we got on the slopes of Ill Crag. We were now up among the snow enclaves.

The grass had given out and it was now all rocks, but good-sized rocks in the main with only a little scree. We bounded to the top, racing to the cairn, but when we got there, we found a queue. It's a very large circular cairn with flat slab steps up to it. We had to wait till someone came down before we could get up. We inspected the cairn dedicated to Lord Leconfield for having given over the land, and then studied the view. Wast Water looked incredibly near, as if you could dive into it. Derwent Water also looked quite close. There was a large, long lake, much further away. I decided it must be Windermere as, from that angle, the Old Man must obscure most of Coniston Water. Despite the brilliant sun, I couldn't see the Isle of Man. It must have been the heat haze.

We bounded down the scree-ridden summit slopes towards Styhead Tarn, making for what's known as the Corridor Route. The Corridor was a path between rocky summits, very safe and easy to walk, though I did lose it at one time, finding myself looking down a huge ravine which I worked out was Piers Gill.

You get a terrific view of Great Gable, coming down to Styhead Tarn, a beautiful, moulded, mountain-looking mountain, going straight up into the sky, the path beckoning up its classical slope, the sort of hill you see in a child's painting.

Just below Styhead Tarn, we came upon the rest of our party, Margaret and Flora. They'd had a marvellous day, going up to Sprinkling Tarn and then round to Styhead Tarn. They'd climbed well over two thousand feet, which wasn't bad for a five-year-old.

ABOVE *Climbers attempting to reach Scafell Pike's 3,210-foot summit (on the left, in the background) have first to scale the other peaks that hem it in.*

LEFT *The Hon. Augustus Hope, as he styled himself, was a rogue and a bigamist, and was finally hanged for fraud.*

RIGHT *Mary Robinson was the local beauty, and was working in her father's inn when she met Augustus Hope.*

ABOVE *The marriage deed of Augustus Hope and Mary Robinson, but one of many such deeds Hatfield fraudulently signed.*

THE MAID OF BUTTERMERE

Here is a true tale about Buttermere, the next stage in my journey, which captivated the attention of the nation back in 1802.

A gentleman calling himself the Hon. Augustus Hope arrived in Keswick and took lodgings at the Royal Oak, the smartest place in town. He rode about in an elegant carriage, dined with the quality, flashing his impressive visiting cards, telling everyone he was the brother and heir to Lord Hopetown. He became very friendly with the local wealthy. Surprisingly, he didn't seek out the company of Mr Coleridge, Keswick's eminent man of letters, who was then living at Greta Hall, though he became a welcome guest almost everywhere else in the Keswick area.

He decided to take a few days' respite from his hectic social life and went for a short fishing holiday on Buttermere, taking accommodation at a little inn by the lakeside. There he was served by a young woman of eighteen years of age, daughter of the house, who acted as a waitress. She was a noted beauty in the Buttermere valley, and Mr Hope, entranced, soon desired her hand in marriage. Permission was given. After all, he was the brother of a lord, had a smart carriage and his letters franked with his own name—a Post Office privilege that in 1802 was granted only to the great and the wealthy. He married Mary Robinson, as the Beauty was called, on October 3, 1802, and off they went on a round of the smart hotels in the Lake District, moving mainly between Buttermere and Keswick.

One day, the police arrived at the place they were staying. All was then revealed about the Hon. Augustus Hope. He was no more than a confidence trickster—not a lord's brother, but a failed commercial traveller who had left abandoned wives and countless fatherless children all over England.

He was in due course tried at the assizes in Carlisle and the case was a sensation, splashed over every newspaper. Among his belongings were found

LEFT *J. C. Ibbetson's painting (1813) of Buttermere, tranquil again after the local scandal had died down.*

BELOW *The Fish Hotel, as it is now known, profited from the public interest in its serving girl's misfortune.*

heartbreaking letters from the ladies he had left. Wordsworth and Coleridge, who happened to be near Carlisle at the time, both asked to see him, agog to see the letters and the man who had caused such anguish. He agreed to see Wordsworth and they had a long chat, but for some reason he wouldn't see Coleridge.

The man's identity was never conclusively revealed, but his original name was thought to have been Hatfield, and it was believed that he had come from the West Country. De Quincey hazarded the guess that he feared that Coleridge, coming from the same area, might recognise him, which was why he had avoided him in Keswick. Anyway, Coleridge did eventually read the juicy correspondence and what particularly struck him about the case was that though the man was a blackguard, 'with the litany of anguish sounding in his ears from despairing women and famishing children', he could still find it possible to 'enjoy the calm pleasures of a Lake tourist and deliberately hunt for the picturesque'.

The crime he was accused of was not bigamy, but defrauding the Post Office. In those days it was a capital offence to frank your own letters without authority. The Carlisle jury weren't all that keen to hang someone just for cheating on a few postage stamps, but when they heard what he'd done to poor Mary, and countless others, he was sentenced to death and duly hanged on September 3, 1803.

The melodrama of the Beauty of Buttermere passed into popular legend, and several plays based on the story were performed on the London stage. Wordsworth used the incident, calling her the Maid of Buttermere, in the seventh book of *The Prelude*…'unfaithful to a virtuous wife, deserted and deceived, the spoiler came and wooed the artless daughter of the hills, and wedded her, in cruel mockery'.

In a fictional Victorian melodrama, she would have been ruined for ever, but Mary of Buttermere turned out to be not so artless after all and made the most of her encounter with the wicked spoiler. Hordes of tourists rushed to Buttermere just to see the Beauty, and stayed at the inn where she remained for some time, a figure of national attention. De Quincey, being a true rubberneck, went to stay there, in the company of Southey.

Buttermere is the only valley in the Lake District with three lakes. I approached it deliberately from the Cockermouth end, wanting to take them in order, never having been there before. Loweswater is the first lake and it opens up like a secret valley, a watercolour of a lake, the sort of idyllic sylvan scene that smart antique shops in Cockermouth try to sell you, for a large sum, yet which you never seem to see in real life. There are houses around it, with TV aerials, and fields going down to the lakeside, yet it still seems unspoilt. The surrounding hills look isolated, independent, acknowledging no connection with any other. Normally in the Lake District the lakeside fells are in ranges, making it hard to see where one starts and the other ends, despite the map throwing individual names over every bump.

BELOW *Buttermere valley is awash with lakes: in this view, Buttermere itself is in the foreground, followed by Crummock Water and then Loweswater. Top left is Ennerdale Water.*

Crummock Water, the next lake, is very different. It's wild and Scottish-looking, which suits its name, with no fields in sight and the bare fells going straight down to the water's edge. It's over two and a half miles long, twice as big as either Loweswater or Buttermere.

Then there's Buttermere, star of the show, top of the bill, head of the vale, which has a mixture of the prettiness of Loweswater and the wildness of Crummock. All three lakes are owned by the National Trust, which probably helps the whole valley to have a uniformity of spirit, a natural tranquillity, despite the tourists. It's a place loved by knowledgeable walkers, and is fortunately missed by many of the car-bound day-trippers, who stick to the Windermere–Keswick race track.

Buttermere would be an easy valley to seal off, should you be in the business of sealing off valleys, and it's not surprising that the Beast of Buttermere thought he would be safe here to go about his wicked ways. Quite a few centuries before him, the English made it their secret headquarters when they were being overrun by the Norman conquerors. They manned a counterattack from the valley, and Buttermere was one of the few northern valleys the Normans never managed to capture.

The village is in a little alluvial plain between Crummock and Buttermere lakes, and you have a choice of walking round either, a choice made easy by the excellent walking leaflets that the National Park provides. I had my family with me, and as we set off, following the arrows for the lakeside, it seemed as if the whole world and his family were taking the same route that bright summer day.

However, most people soon turned towards Crummock and Scale Force, the highest waterfall in the Lake District, said to drop 172 feet. We were set to walk round Buttermere, a five-mile walk. The path went quickly into some sweet-smelling pine woods where the kids gathered fresh pine cones.

BELOW *Impressive Scale Force drops without interruption for 172 feet.*

HAY STACKS IN HASTE

We had our picnic at the end of the lake beside a stream, and sunbathed. As I lay there, I realised that the craggy silhouettes above us at the dead end of the valley looked strangely familiar, so I got out my map, and identified the crags as Hay Stacks. It's just a minor fell, not one with any great height; in fact I'd never even heard of it until, a few days previously, I had read Wainwright's *Memoirs of a Fellwanderer*. He came out at the end with the surprising statement that he wanted his ashes scattered on Hay Stacks. As Mr Wainwright had climbed and written about every fell in the Lake District, he had to be heeded.

'I'll just be a couple of hours,' I told my wife. 'Up and down, no messing; you lot wander back round the lake and I'll catch you up. I've just got to see it.' There was a lot of moaning. But I was off, haring up the hillside towards Scarth Gap Pass, a modern Beast of Buttermere, selfishly neglecting his family, all for the sake of a mysterious beauty on the horizon.

I stopped at the first brow on the pass for a rest, had a quick drink from a tumbling beck beside the rocky path, and a quick shout down to the valley bottom where I could see the family like little matchstick men, moving jerkily through some bright green fields, past some bright orange tents, towards Gatesgarth. To my amazement, they must have heard my shouts for they all stopped and looked up. They were waving their arms, and probably shouting as well, but I could hear nothing.

I was soon on a ridge, with Hay Stacks on my left and High Crag on my right, but I could see no way up Hay Stacks, though the map I had with me clearly had a dotted line going straight up this side.

I headed straight up, sliding straight down again. I hadn't realised the scree was so loose. I did another run up and quick grab, looking for some bracken that would take my weight, and eventually got going. I managed to find some zigzag sheep tracks, running in parallel lines along the sides of the fell, dragging myself up to the next one every time they started to go down. The fell side was more like a spoil heap, a leftover mining tip, than a wonder of nature. Wainwright must be a nut, I thought, to want to get buried up here. The surrounding views were terrific, but how can you see them if you have continually to watch every footstep?

Far below me, the forest of Ennerdale looked enormous, with the Liza River snaking through it, like an Amazon jungle where no man had ever been, except of course it was full of Forestry Commission men, calculating the fire risks. It was strange to see it from the air. It looked much wilder than it had done from ground level. Across the valley were the heights of Pillar and Kirk Fell with not a flash of orange anorak between them, just as nature intended. I suppose it's this remoteness, the lack of any lush little Beatrix Potter roly-poly fields or little cottages that appealed to Wainwright, though I still couldn't share his enthusiasm.

At long last I pulled myself over the final stretch of scree and almost fell onto a hidden plateau, a secret land of its own with strange tarns and paths, patches of heather and thick bracken, marshes and rocky outcrops. After the monotonous grey of the scree it seemed to be in technicolour, deep purples and browns, bright greens, sparkling rainbow waters. I had thought the views down to Ennerdale had been good but these new views were magnificent—enormously extensive, down and over other plateaus and fells, and still with no signs of civilisation. They weren't valley views, looking down a dale with a lake below, the normal pretty fell-top views, but horizontal views. I'd got so used to climbing to a top and looking down. The subtlety of Hay Stacks is that you climb up—and then keep looking up and over. It's surrounded by much higher fells, such as Great Gable and Pillar, each a good thousand feet higher than Hay Stacks, which is a mere 1,927 feet.

I'd meant to come straight down again, having got to the top, to rejoin the family, but I found myself being drawn along its mysterious, broad ridge towards a strange gleaming tarn which seemed to have three little islands on it, stepping-stones for giants. This is Innominate Tarn, so called because it hasn't got a name (old Cumbrian joke).

I moved on to another tarn, Blackbeck Tarn, and just to the left, in a gap between the crags, I caught a glimpse of a magnificently framed view, sheer down the valley sides to Buttermere and Crummock. Very picturesque. I went nearer to savour it, thinking I might go back that way, but the view that hit me was so stunning I had to sit down. I felt suddenly dizzy. I'd almost wandered over a sheer drop. It was the view I'd seen from below, the sharp silhouette of the ridge of Hay Stacks. It had been hard enough scrambling up the scree from the other side, but from this side, up the rock face, it would have been impossible. Later, when I got home, I read Wainwright's notes. 'The only advice that can be given to a novice lost on Hay Stacks in mist is that he should kneel down and pray for safe deliverance.' Thank goodness it was a sunny day.

It was a great walk down, with waterfalls and ravines, sudden grassy paths, then rocky climbs, screes and streams. The family were waiting in the nearby Croft Farm tearoom. I might have guessed. I took my wellies off, and my socks steamed like kettles, but the ladies in charge of the tearoom didn't seem to mind. I had two cups of tea, and two enormous slices of homemade gingerbread.

ABOVE *Famous fell wanderer A. Wainwright found Hay Stacks' summit so beautiful that he asked that his ashes be scattered there.*

THE HEART
OF LAKELAND

As I HEADED for Keswick and Southey's Greta Hall, I thought how surprising it was of Southey, coming to gape at the Beauty of Buttermere. The impression I had of him was of a stodgy literary gent, forever stuck in his study in Keswick with his millions of books.

Robert Southey, when he's thought about today, which is rarely, is presumed to have been a close member of the Wordsworth set. In fact he ran a powerhouse of his own, a rival literary factory, with its own characters and fringe figures, relations and hangers-on.

But it was the combination of the two of them, Wordsworth and Southey, that for almost fifty years turned the Lake District into a centre of English poetry, where young poets and writers went to worship, and hopefully meet, the Greats.

The London smart set might have turned rather scornful of them, when they became disgusted by the changes in once-radical and brilliant men, but the new poets tended to die young, like Shelley and Keats, while Southey and Wordsworth ploughed on, still dominating their profession. Sir Walter Scott's poetry sold better and Byron pleased the intellectuals, but it was Southey and Wordsworth both being in the Lakes and both being prolific for so long that made the Lakes synonymous with poetry throughout most of the century.

It's surprising they were so successful, managing to live on their writings and support huge families, while resolutely living 300 miles away from London. The railways arrived late in their lives. Until then, the 300-mile coach journey to London could take four days—forty-eight hours at best, if you got the right coaches and the right weather. They were never flush, never without a need to watch the pennies, but they survived and in turn took all the honours. Most surprisingly of all, Southey took the honours first.

ABOVE *The engraving Breakfast at Samuel Rogers' by C. Mottram is a veritable 'who's who' of contemporary literary life, depicting an imaginary gathering of Southey, Wordsworth, Coleridge and other greats of the day.*

LEFT *The rural surroundings of Greta Hall, as Coleridge and Southey knew it. The area soon changed when the railway came to Keswick.*

THE GREATS OF GRETA HALL

It was Coleridge who first took on Greta Hall in Keswick. He moved in with his wife and children in 1800, but almost immediately he was rushing across to Grasmere, neglecting his family, to be with William and Dorothy.

In 1803 Coleridge persuaded his brother-in-law Southey to come up and share Greta Hall with them, though he warned him not to bring the third Fricker sister, the widowed Mrs Lovell, but to pension her off. Southey, ever the gentleman, ignored the advice. When he arrived, he soon found he had all three sisters to look after—his own wife, Mrs Lovell, plus the abandoned Mrs Coleridge and her family. For the rest of his life, Southey made his home in the Lakes.

Southey had been born in Bristol in 1774, four years after Wordsworth, and, like Wordsworth and Coleridge, he too had had a disturbed childhood, being brought up by an eccentric spinster half-aunt in Bath. An uncle paid for him to go to Westminster School, but he was expelled for an attack on corporal punishment in a radical and unauthorised school magazine, *The Flagellant.* He went on to Oxford where he met Coleridge—two years older—who was there on a visit from Cambridge, and they became young radicals and idealists together. It was with Coleridge that he had intended to drop out and form that utopian, agrarian community in the United States of America.

Coleridge, rather ungallantly, maintained later that he'd only married his Fricker sister for Southey's sake, that he had been conned into it when it looked as if they were all going off to America. Southey's own marriage wasn't all that romantic either. He left his Fricker sister at the church door and went off to Lisbon, presumably on the rebound from the abandoned American trip. It was on this trip that he started a life-long interest in Portugal and its empire. He then came back to his wife, made the marriage public, and looked around for a job, refusing family pressure to take holy orders, just as Wordsworth had done. Like Wordsworth, after several attempts at different jobs in different parts of the country, an old friend, Charles Wynn, impressed by Southey's literary talents, made him an annuity of £160.

The specific reason for Southey's decision to come up to Greta Hall was the loss of his first child, Margaret. Southey felt it would be a comfort for his wife to be with her sister, who also needed comforting.

For the next forty years, Southey took on the responsibility of supporting an ever-increasing flock of little Frickers. There were, for a start, the three Coleridge children—Hartley, a child genius, brilliant beyond his years at all academic subjects; Derwent, clever but more normal; and Sara, yet another gifted child, with a definite literary talent.

Then there were Southey's own offspring. He had eight in all, though two died in infancy. After a run of six girls, he had a longed-for son, Herbert, who was another child prodigy, but he died aged ten in 1815. They had a final child, a son, Cuthbert, in 1819 when Mrs Southey was forty-seven.

Southey also had adults to support—his wife and her two sisters lived full-time in the house and they were joined now and again by yet more Fricker sisters, two maiden ladies called Martha and Eliza. Southey himself had two brothers who were always leaning on him for money. Southey became poet laureate in 1813 (Scott

BRITAIN'S BARDS

LEFT *A richly bound copy of Southey's* Carmen Triumphale, *and a book of poems by Wordsworth, his successor as laureate.*

ABOVE *Andrew Motion, latest in a long and distinguished line of poets laureate, was appointed in May 1999 following the death of Ted Hughes.*

POETRY HAS for centuries been closely associated with the royal court, with monarchs traditionally employing a bard to sing before them of the heroic deeds of their ancestors. Elizabeth I's court in particular was the stage for a golden age of literature, and the Stuart kings who followed her supported their favourite poets with salaries. But the laureateship was not officially established until 1668, when John Dryden received a pension and a butt of wine in exchange for composing masques that flattered the king and satirised his enemies.

The early 18th-century laureate Nicholas Rowe was the first poet obliged to produce New Year and birthday odes for the sovereign; this became a tradition that continued until the appointment of Robert Southey in 1813. Southey found the writing of odes tiresome, and during his laureateship the custom lapsed and then gradually ceased altogether. Although now freed from this obligation, laureates still had to be politically aware: Southey gave offence with his depiction of Napoleon as a murderer and tyrant during the French Emperor's negotiations with the British government, and was forced to cut the offending lines from his *Carmen* verses.

On Southey's death in 1843, the laureateship was offered to an ageing William Wordsworth, who at first declined it. Reassured, however, that the post was now more of an honour than an office, with no attendant duties, Wordsworth accepted. The laureateship has continued in this spirit to modern times, with the holder now producing poems for occasions of national importance as the muse, rather than the monarch, dictates.

having declined), which brought in £90 a year, but it's little wonder he worked round the clock. His complete published works—poetry, history, biographies, book reviews, articles and translations—would fill a hundred volumes. He started on a history of the Portuguese Empire when he moved up to Keswick, though he only published three volumes of it. This was the *History of Brazil*, the first published history of that country.

Normally, Southey was at work on his writings from waking up until going to bed, except for an hour's exercise around midday. During this hour, he walked round Keswick and Derwent Water with a book in his hand, unless it was raining too hard. He and Wordsworth must have made strange sights—one poet walking deep in a book, the other walking and shouting his head off as he practised new lines.

Southey struck many outsiders as living only for his books, though he was courteous and kind. He gave time to help young writers, like Shelley, who came up to the Lakes and lived in Keswick during the winter of 1811–12 with his young bride. Shelley was just nineteen at the time. De Quincey says he found Southey the nicer person, but really rather uninteresting, compared with Wordsworth. Yet at home with his family he was full of jokes and awful puns. He referred to Greta Hall as 'the anthill', which it was in two senses, being a hive of industry and a place where every lady was addressed as Aunt.

ABOVE *Southey's second wife Caroline created this summery painting of her husband's study at Greta Hall.*

'Southey had a large collection of books,' so Shelley wrote later. 'The shelves extended over the walls in every room of his large, dismal house in Keswick; they were in the bedrooms and even down the stairs.'

Southey was always buying books, and once sent back nine hundredweight from a trip to Holland. In the end he had amassed 14,000 volumes, so many that they feared for the floors. He was jealous of them, and wouldn't think of lending them to someone careless, like Wordsworth, as De Quincey had once done, getting back a precious book all covered in jam. He got the children of the house to cover many of his books, cutting up their old dresses to do so, and his library was known in the family—and still is known to scholars today—as the Cottonian Library.

It's ironic that of all the millions of words he published, his only well-known work today is one he wrote for children. Even so, today's readers of *The Three Bears* are probably unaware that Southey was its author. In Southey's original version, it's an old woman who takes their porridge and sleeps in their beds. Goldilocks is a much later substitution by someone else.

Southey loved picnics and outings with his family. In 1815, to celebrate the victory at Waterloo, he organised a party on the top of Skiddaw to light a celebratory bonfire. Almost all the Southeys, Coleridges and Wordsworths were there.

There was an endless stream of visitors to Greta Hall. Charles Lamb and his sister were two of the first, staying three weeks and climbing Skiddaw. William Hazlitt came, and painted some portraits, but was driven out by irate locals after some amatory indiscretion.

Walter Scott made three visits to Southey, and one of the literary greats of the day, now hardly remembered, Walter Savage Landor, was also a visitor. The non-literary visitors included George Canning in 1814 and William Wilberforce in 1818. Sir Humphrey Davy visited Southey, as well as Wordsworth. John Stuart Mill found Southey a 'remarkably likable man' and so did Robert Owen, the Scottish social pioneer. Owen tried to interest both Wordsworth and Southey in his schemes but he got a poor reception from the Wordsworth household. 'He is a good man and a great enthusiast,' wrote Sarah Hutchinson, 'but must be a little cranky.' However, Southey was a bit more interested and went with Thomas Telford, the great Scottish bridge builder, to look at Owen's model factory at New Lanark, but his basic Tory principles made him suspicious of the socialistic overtones.

Southey's wife Edith had always had depressive tendencies, and in 1834 she began to show signs of insanity; three years later she died. Southey was much affected by this and became a recluse for a while and was very depressed, but in 1839 he surprised, and greatly annoyed, many people, including Wordsworth, by marrying for a second time. His new wife was Caroline Bowles, some twenty years his junior, who had been a friend of the family for some time. The new Mrs Southey became more of a nurse than a wife as Southey's mental and physical powers were fast beginning to fade. He died at Greta Hall in March 1843, aged sixty-nine, and was buried at Crosthwaite Church, Keswick. So ended the literary life of Greta Hall, for forty-three years one of the most fascinating houses in the history of English literature.

ABOVE *Greta Hall functioned until 1996 as a school, a fitting use for a building that had earlier housed such learned minds.*

Coleridge, its first literary inhabitant, had died some ten years previously in Highgate, London, where he had eventually ended up, after quarrelling with Wordsworth. His last years were in fact rather happy, since he was taken in by a doctor's family and worked again as a critic and essayist. He never had the discipline of Wordsworth or Southey, yet in many ways he had a better mind.

After Southey's death, Greta Hall passed through a variety of tenants, before being purchased in 1909 by Canon Rawnsley and then rented to Keswick School. In 1921 the governors of Keswick School bought the house. It's a simple but handsome three-storey Georgian building. Two plaques record that Coleridge lived there from 1800 to 1803 and Southey from 1803 to 1843.

I went to visit Greta Hall. It still had a homely, family atmosphere, with prints on the walls in the entrance hall, plus a letter from Southey and some visiting cards. The rooms were named after the original occupants: 'Southey's study' and 'Mrs Coleridge's bedroom'. There were thirty-four girls sleeping there, aged eleven and twelve. The chatter of their conversations echoed down the staircases, much as when all those Coleridge and Southey girls lived there.

The matron, Mrs Whitfield, said there had been talk in the past of the ghost of Mrs Southey haunting one of the rooms, but she had never seen it, nor had the girls. They still called a storeroom the 'apple room', as that's what the Southeys used it for, and a corridor outside Southey's study was always referred to as 'Duck Row', a name handed down from the days in which it had been completely lined with Southey's books, and you had to duck down to get past them.

SINGING STONES

Keswick today likes to think it's the heart of Lakeland, and it probably is. Windermere is bigger—population 8,500 as opposed to Keswick's 5,000— and it has the railway, which Keswick no longer does. But Windermere is a bit of a sprawl, eating up Bowness and spreading itself along the lake, and there's a feeling of being at the *edge* of the Lakes, rather than in them. Keswick has the better situation, surrounded on all sides by famous lakes, famous climbs and famous views. It appears on the map to be rather stuck away in northern Lakeland, but it is in fact a better centre for exploring it. Getting to those secluded western lakes, such as Wast Water, Ennerdale and Buttermere, is hell from Windermere but relatively easy from Keswick.

Both Keswick and Windermere, being the two major Lakeland tourist centres, are pretty awful in high summer, and you can hardly walk on the pavements or find a seat in a café, yet I've always been able to park in Keswick, which biases me in

LEFT *Keswick is the largest town in the Lake District. In Elizabethan times mining was its main source of wealth, but now, like so many Lakeland towns, it relies primarily on tourism.*

THE HOME OF PENCILS

COPPER, LEAD, SILVER...over the centuries, the Borrowdale region has yielded several mineral bonanzas. One of the most valuable is graphite, also known as 'black lead' or 'wad'. This crumbly silver-grey form of carbon originates in primeval forests buried millions of years ago under volcanic debris, and slowly transformed by heat and pressure.

The mining of graphite began in Borrowdale in about 1500. It proved a remarkably versatile and saleable commodity. Farmers used it to mark their sheep. Doctors recommended it for easing digestive problems. Although slow to displace chalk and charcoal for sketching purposes, it was being used occasionally by Italian artists as early as 1558. It was used, too, in pottery glazes, as a rust preventative and a fixative for blue dyes, and for casting cannonballs. Prices were kept high by rationing the supply, and by the 18th century robbers and smugglers began to show an unsettling interest. Laws were passed to protect it, and armed guards patrolled the mine and escorted the transport convoys.

At one end of the valley, near Seathwaite, miners might be toiling deep within the mountainside shafts, while at the other end, in Keswick, their

LEFT *Derwent Graphic pencils are made in varying degrees of hardness, from a sharp 9H to a soft, smudgy 9B.*

families would be working the precious substance into pencils in a thriving cottage industry. Among the many processes involved were grading the wad (separating hard 'H' from soft, black 'B' fragments), slicing it into slivers, and gluing these into the grooves of open cedar casings, ready for sealing and finishing by machine.

In 1832 the first factory opened, which was to become in 1916 the Cumberland Pencil Company. In the 1930s the first colour pencils were made at the factory, by a quite different method: the coloured 'lead' was not graphite at all, but a mixture of clay and pigment with gum to bind the mixture, which was then soaked in wax for smoothness. On the factory premises today is a pencil museum, where you can find a replica of the Seathwaite mine, see displays of old machinery, watch videos of manufacturing techniques, and admire the world's largest pencil—seven foot long, with an inch-thick 'lead'.

LEFT *The Cumberland Pencil Museum is based in a working pencil factory in Keswick. The museum displays the history of pencil making from its earliest days.*

RIGHT *Colour pencils come in a rainbow of shades. The clay and pigment that make up the coloured core are carefully weighed to ensure consistency of colour across batches.*

ABOVE *Graphite, which brought prosperity to Borrowdale, is a crystalline form of the element carbon.*

LEFT *Workers at the original factory in Keswick glue strips of graphite into the wood casing before sealing by machine.*

ABOVE *Raymond Briggs's famous book* The Snowman *was transformed into a magical animated film using pencils made by the Cumberland company.*

its favour. The Moot Hall in the marketplace provides a central focal point, a very handy meeting place if you have kids who tend to wander off, and it looks suitably olde and attractive. It's not really that ancient, having been completely rebuilt in 1813. Today it houses the Information Centre, where there are some good displays of local scenes and an excellent selection of National Park leaflets and booklets.

Culturally, Keswick definitely has the edge over Windermere. It's hard to think of any literary or artistic figures who settled in Windermere, but Keswick is packed with literary connections. The Royal Oak had a set of stained-glass windows in the dining room, each dedicated to a Lake poet—including Shelley, which is straining it a bit, though he did live in Keswick for a while.

Keats, Scott, Hazlitt and Ruskin all visited Keswick and were very impressed. Charles Lamb perhaps overdid it, remarking that 'we thought we had got into fairyland'. What writer, anyway, could resist a town that gave pencils to the world?

The world's first pencil production began in Keswick in 1566, using a rich deposit of graphite found in Borrowdale. Local graphite ran out in 1880, but the pencil industry is still going strong, and Cumberland pencils are used the world over. The factory of the Cumberland Pencil Company is about the biggest building in Keswick. There's also a pencil museum, a mecca for pencil lovers everywhere.

The town has always been very culturally conscious, as can be seen in the history of the Keswick Lecture Society, founded in 1869, which is itself a microcosm of Lakeland life over the last century. All the topics and arguments of the day, from the worthy to the positively dotty, from the national to the obscurely local, are reflected in its annals. It was founded for 'mutual improvement', with members reading prepared essays to each other, or listening to essays by eminent guests.

Perhaps their all-time star lecturer was our old friend Canon Rawnsley, as ever at the heart of Lakeland life. Crosthwaite is the parish church of Keswick, and he became vicar there in 1883 and was a staunch member of the Society until his death in 1920. He became President of the Society, and in all presented over thirty lectures. He delighted the members with Reminiscences of Wordsworth among the Peasantry of Westmoreland (later published), Some Royal Mummies, Memories of the Great Paris Exhibition, What I Saw of the Coronation of the Czar, The History and Reminiscences of the Jubilee Bonfires, The Excavation at Pompeii, German Miners at Keswick, Allan Bank, and the League of Nations. The last was on Ruskin.

The Keswick Lecture Society, over the decades, has not only attracted some eccentric lecturers but collected some eccentric objects. Most of them are today in the Keswick Museum and Art Gallery, one of the most amazing museums in the Lake District.

'Don't look at the musical stones,' shouted the curator from his little anteroom, as I entered the museum and was standing looking at the first exhibit, some musical stones. 'They're the least important exhibit! Start at the far end. Look at the Southey manuscripts first. They're the most important!'

I obeyed his command, though it was hard to drag myself away from such a fascinating object, and headed for the far room where, true enough, there were letters and manuscripts by Southey, Wordsworth, Ruskin, De Quincey and others.

ABOVE *Keswick's Moot Hall still maintains its original function as a meeting place for local organisations, although the ground floor is now occupied by the National Park Information Centre. The hall's unusual one-handed clock is a useful landmark, if somewhat less useful for telling the time.*

The Southey collection (most of which is not on show, but is available to scholars) is enormous. The manuscripts that are on show are in glass cases and are rather boringly presented, though they do try to capture passing interest by displaying a copy of *The Three Bears*. I watched as a party of school kids lifted the covers and then quickly dropped them, heading straight back for the musical stones, stopping on the way to climb on the edges of a massive relief model of the Lake District, which clearly asks visitors not to touch it. This huge model was built by a Mr Flintoft, an emigré who settled in Keswick in 1823. It took him sixteen years to build. The Keswick Lecture Society bought it at auction in 1878.

The museum also contains an etching of the Beauty of Buttermere, some pleasant Lakeland watercolours, geological specimens and a rather nice old English oak chest which has a notice on top announcing '500-Year-Old Cat—Lift Lid Carefully!'. Inside are the mummified remains of an ancient cat, preserved in a glass box.

And so back to the entrance, to the musical stones. The curator must get bored with their endless fascination for visitors, especially as everyone insists on trying to play a tune on them—and everyone is welcome to try. They're genuine stones, scoured from the Skiddaw area between 1827 and 1840, arranged in layers like a xylophone. When struck, each gives out a different note. In the 19th century they were trailed all over Europe and performed in public as a truly amazing oddity. They were played at a command performance before Queen Victoria at Buckingham Palace in 1848, but she wasn't particularly amused by them.

I had a go and played a scale, but they're hard on the knuckles. When they were played professionally, hammers were used, but the museum doesn't leave hammers around for kids to strike each other with. Almost every one of the museum's 15,000 annual visitors has a go and, according to the curator, 80 per cent of them play one of six tunes. The most popular of all was the 'Doh Ray Me' tune from *The Sound of Music*. 'John Peel' was also quite popular, with visitors no doubt trying to think of something Lakelandish. There are only six sets of musical stones in the world, all of them from this area.

ABOVE Even the least musical cannot resist trying out some tunes on Keswick Museum's unusual 12-foot-long stone xylophone.

Keswick has lots of easy walks, straight from the town centre, the most popular being along the shores of Derwent Water to Friar's Crag, the rocky promontory that sticks into the lake, one of the most photographed chunks of rock in the Lake District. There are two memorial stones, one to Canon Rawnsley and the other to John Ruskin, one definitely a founder of the National Trust and the other not so definitely, though don't say that if you visit Brantwood.

Cat Bells, along the western shore of Derwent Water, is my favourite little fell in the whole of the Lake District, and I have lots of boyhood memories of climbing it. It's not really a climb, more a dawdle. It's very popular with children and old people. The gentle, humpy slopes of Cat Bells stand out for miles around, a progression of easy heights. You get to the first top so easily, yet you get instant and terrific views. No wonder Beatrix Potter loved Cat Bells, and set *The Tale of Mrs Tiggy-Winkle* there.

OPPOSITE The leisurely hike up Cat Bells leaves walkers with enough energy to appreciate its vista of mountains and valleys.

Sir Hugh Walpole also loved Cat Bells. His novels made him a fortune between the wars but are now sadly out of fashion. He settled in the Lakes in 1923, buying a house called Brackenburgh, 'a little paradise on Cat Bells'. His early successes had been with stories of London life, but he turned with even more success to novels set in Cumberland—*Rogue Herries, Judith Paris, The Fortress* and *Vanessa*. He died at his home beside Cat Bells in 1941 and is buried in St John's churchyard at Keswick. 'That I wasn't born a Cumbrian isn't my fault,' he wrote; 'that Cumbrians in spite of my "foreignness" have been so kind to me is my good fortune.'

I went round Derwent Water to do the Lodore Falls, part of the Keswick tourist trail. In 1809, Southey wrote about the falls to his brother:

> Tell the people how the water comes down Lodore? Why, it comes thundering and floundering, and thumping and plumping and bumping and jumping and hissing and whizzing and dripping and skipping and grumbling and rumbling and tumbling and falling and brawling, dashing and clashing and splashing, and purring and roaring and whirling and curling, and leaping and creeping, and sounding and bounding, and clattering and chattering, with a dreadful uproar—and that way the water comes down at Lodore.

There was a special entrance you had to go through, behind the hotel, to get to the falls. You put 2p in a turnstile, and of course my family didn't have enough 2p pieces so we all had to jam in at one go, which led to a lot of cramming and damning, huffing and puffing, cursing and bursting, moaning and groaning, breathing and heaving, fighting and biting…

The Lodore Falls are well known for being disappointing. People go there in the height of summer and are furious to find only a trickle. We'd recently had rain so there was quite a bit of gurgling and splurging, pattering and nattering, etc, but nothing to roar home about. It was in the 19th century that they were so passionate about waterfalls, making pilgrimage places out of the best Lake District ones. Most of the old guidebooks have lovely engravings of places like Lodore, Aira Force, Dungeon Ghyll Force, Scale Force and the others, with little Victorian gentlemen at the foot, staring up in awe at the immense, all-powerful, white foaming cascade above their heads.

We climbed right up to the top, scrambling over wet rocks and under fallen trees and round crevices, but when we came down, we decided that the best view of all was from the bottom, where we'd begun. There's a spot between the bottom trees where you can stand back and have an uninterrupted view of all the tumbling cataracts above.

Back in Keswick, I went to see Crosthwaite Church, parish church of the town. The church is beautiful, and inside it has an affluent feeling.

The church's founder was St Kentigern, known as St Mungo in Scotland, the 6th-century bishop of Glasgow. He was in Carlisle when he heard about the awful paganism of the folks in the mountain region, so he made his way south, establishing churches on his way, as at Caldbeck, where the parish church

ABOVE *Two Victorian gentlemen, perched precariously on rocks at the foot of Lodore Falls, indulge the contemporary passion for waterfalls.*

is called St Kentigern, and at Mungrisdale (Mungo's Dale), and Crosthwaite. He planted his cross in a suitable clearing in the vale between the two lakes, Derwent Water and Bassenthwaite, which is where the name comes from—Crosthwaite. (*Thwaite* is Norse for 'clearing'.)

The Southey connection is the main attraction for visitors to Crosthwaite Church. There's a marble effigy of him, with a long inscription composed by Wordsworth, and arrows outside saying 'Poet Southey's Grave' to guide you to the gravestone. The use of the word poet is indicative, as if no one would know otherwise. Beside the grave a little plaque says, 'Restored by the Generosity of the Brazilian Government, 1961'.

BELOW *Crosthwaite Church, the resting place of Robert Southey, is the oldest building in Keswick. It was built in 1553 on the site of a much earlier church.*

THE SKIDDAW SLOG

Skiddaw is Keswick's mountain. It's so accessible that it's almost an extension of the main street. Southey, the Wordsworths and the Coleridges went up it to light their Waterloo bonfire, with the ladies in the party on ponies. Today, people have been up it on motorbikes. Poor old Skiddaw. It's a big mountain, one of that select band of four Lake District mountains that rise over three thousand feet, yet no one seems to treat it with dignity.

Skiddaw has graceful curves and smooth contours. It's Lakeland's oldest resident, having been there several million years before those volcanic upstarts in the southern Lakes. It has a whole geological formation named after it—Skiddaw slate—which is soft and malleable and gives to the touch.

Skiddaw is 3,054 feet high, only 156 feet lower than Scafell Pike itself, but you can climb Skiddaw and back in three hours, starting from the middle of Keswick. You just have to push the legs, bend the back and use a little bit of puff to get you up there.

I had the whole family with me, so I didn't subject them to walking through the streets of Keswick and having to cross the noisy ring road, though it was a shame to miss the walk round Latrigg fell. We drove instead up to Ormathwaite and along Gale Road to a car park, the beginning of the most popular way up Skiddaw. Even early in the morning there was a cluster of cars.

ABOVE *Mist hovers over Derwent Water, its tranquil surface mirroring sunlit Skiddaw beyond.*

We all raced through a gate, round a little mound, and came to the first landmark on the foothills of Skiddaw. It's a humble little cross to the memory of three shepherds.

Ahead, we could see the main path, stretching up the straight slopes of Jenkin Hill. It follows a neat fence and might easily have been transplanted from a suburban park, but it's surprisingly steep all the same.

I forced the others to keep stopping, to turn back and soak up the incredible views of Derwent Water. New views and perspectives appeared so quickly it was almost like being in a lift, then, alas, we started to hit pockets of mist. We got to the top of the steep stuff, and strolled along the wide path towards Skiddaw Little Man, but the mist was thickening and our view was disappearing fast, so the girls decided to have their picnic in the sun and not go any further. Skiddaw is not dangerous in the mist but it's not much fun. Jake and I decided to press on alone.

With the mist came the cold, so we sang to keep warm. We were singing so loudly that we almost knocked over an old man and his dog, coming out of the mist in front of us, fresh from the top of Skiddaw, judging by the mass of shining droplets clinging to his bushy eyebrows. You could tell he was a local, a real countryman, from the lack of anorak, boots or walking clothes. He wore an old suit jacket, in faded dark-blue stripes, grey unmatching trousers and a shapeless pullover. He turned out to be a retired storeman from Keswick who walked up Skiddaw at least three times a week with his dog. It made Skiddaw sound even more suburban.

During the war, he said, they really did have vehicles driving up Skiddaw when the army used it as a training area for Jeeps. In the old days, shepherds used to live out for several days at a time in Skiddaw House, an isolated building stuck out in the wild fells over the top of Skiddaw, but today's shepherds have cars and tractors and can get home of an evening. The building is now a youth hostel.

When we reached the final assault, there was thick snow all over the path; the mist was like freezing fog, the grass suddenly gave way to slippery scree and bits of slaty rocks, and the going was surprisingly steep. I half expected to see the Skiddaw Hermit, a gentleman called George Smith who lived in a cave on Skiddaw, using a boulder for a table and hay for a bed, earning odd pennies by painting people's pictures, except that he would be rather old by now as it was in 1875 that he was last seen.

We reached the final ridge at last, where we were chilled to the marrow by the most appalling blast of wild, freezing wind. The blast felt as if it had come straight across Scotland from the North Pole. We staggered along the ridge, trying to decide which pile of cairns was the top, then turned round and rushed back, desperate to get out of the wind. No wonder they categorise the mountaintops as subarctic.

We didn't stop till we reached an iron gate, much lower down, where we crouched and quickly gulped our coffee and sandwiches. That's another suburban touch—there are three gates and two stiles to go through on this route up Skiddaw. We were dried out by the time we reached the girls, with no signs of our ordeal against the elements. They'd been sunbathing all afternoon and didn't believe our terrifying tales about thick snow, arctic winds and sub-zero temperatures.

Back O'Skiddaw is what the locals call everything to the back of Skiddaw. It is a country in itself, a clearly defined area, a little region with exact boundaries. Behind its two dominant peaks, Skiddaw and Saddleback, are hidden away the Caldbeck Fells, remote, silent, almost as unknown today as they've ever been. Many guidebooks miss them out completely.

Bassenthwaite Lake is the moat that acts as their western boundary. Its claim to fame is that it is the only lake in the Lake District. This astounding fact is the sort

ABOVE *Fell ponies are a hardy native British breed. In mining days they were used as packhorses for transporting lead.*

of riddle you get in a Christmas cracker. The explanation is that every other stretch of water in the Lake District has either mere or water in its title and so doesn't require the word lake.

Bassenthwaite is a great sailing lake, and I began to get fine views of the yachts as I climbed along the road to Orthwaite. Derwent Water, the rival lake, is a bit rough, with fiendish crosswinds, so sailors prefer Bassenthwaite.

Once Bassenthwaite is left behind, and, with it, the last vestiges of tourism, the roads become much quieter, even in the height of the summer. Towards Uldale you come into open moorland, with the little roads unfenced. This is still the Lake District, still well inside the National Park, but it's a different sort of Lake District. For a start, there aren't any lakes, except for Over Water which is really a large tarn. The fells are low and rounded, rough with heather and bracken, with very little arable land around. It's all sheep with a few cattle on the better meadows, plus the distinctive dark Fell ponies which are allowed to roam all over the Caldbeck Fells.

FROM THE LAKES TO THE HIMALAYAS

Chris Bonington and his wife and two children live in a cottage among a huddle of four or five other cottages about a mile from Caldbeck. They can come straight out of their cottage and onto the open fell. The fell in question is one of the nicest in the whole of the Lakes, yet one of the least known—High Pike.

ABOVE *Chris Bonington has scaled the world's highest peaks, yet still enjoys the challenge of climbing local fells.*

When Jake and I first went to see them we hit one of those perfect winter days that, looking back, seems almost unreal. It had been rainy and misty when we left Carlisle, but as we approached the Caldbeck Fells we could see snow on the top, and the weather got suddenly sharper and clearer and a blue sky started to appear. It all happened in the space of ten miles, yet it was like crossing some climate date line as we went up Warnell. One moment we were on a wet grey road, the next the whole landscape was virgin snow. The snow had obviously fallen earlier that morning.

When we got to the Bonington cottage, his two boys were on their skis, tearing down the slopes beside their house. They gave Jake a sledge—and I never saw them again till nightfall. Chris and I decided to go up High Pike.

High Pike is a surprisingly big fell, occupying a complete corner of the northeast plateau of the northern fells. You sweep up and along its vast shoulders, climbing all the time, yet with nothing ever obscured, no pretend summits to make you lose heart.

On top there is an ordinary garden seat, which somehow doesn't make it look suburban, just a pleasant treat after a pleasant, unarduous walk. To the south, I could see a line-up of famous Lake District peaks, all clothed in white, majestic against the blue sky. The most prominent, of course, was Skiddaw.

Bonington was born in Hampstead and went to University College School, though his early school days were rather disturbed: his father, a journalist, and his mother, a copywriter, separated when he was only one. He went to Sandhurst, where he was an army officer for five years. He had started climbing at sixteen, after a relation had given him a book of photographs of Scottish mountains, and he kept it up in the army. After the army, he joined Unilever as a management trainee and became a margarine salesman, but gave that up after nine months. In 1962 he decided to go it alone and try to live as a climber. By then he had discovered that climbing was what he liked most in life.

He first hit the headlines in 1962 when he and Ian Clough were the first Britons to ascend the North Face of the Eiger. Since then he's become an expedition leader, and his best-known expeditions have been Annapurna in 1970, Everest in 1972 (which failed to get up) and Everest in 1975 (a success). He was also on the Old Man of Hoy climb, which thrilled the nation watching on TV.

Bonington was always good at rallying support, getting money out of people, and was very professional in presenting himself. But in order for him and his family to live when he wasn't up a mountain, he had to come back and talk or write about being up mountains. He's written best-selling books about his climbs and done a lot of photojournalism. He did radio and TV programmes when asked. But his main income came from lecturing. He did three-week tours, several times a year, complete with audiovisual devices.

He bought the Caldbeck cottage in 1971, using it at first as a weekend cottage. Wendy, his wife, hated the thought of living in London, though she is also a southerner, from Buckinghamshire, so they compromised on Manchester, where they lived, near a group of other young climbers, for five years. In 1974 they moved full-time up to Caldbeck.

Wendy was an illustrator of children's books when Chris first met her at a party in Hampstead, but now she was turning to pottery and did three days a week at Carlisle Art College. She was building a kiln in their garden—something they couldn't do in the suburbs of Manchester.

'I felt claustrophobic living in a town,' she says. 'Here I can live by just looking at the sky and the fields and the hills. There's as much social life as I want, more really than I can cope with. The only problem is having to be a chauffeur, driving the boys everywhere, but even that is bearable. The drive into Carlisle is beautiful. Every time I see something breathtaking.'

Bonington climbs High Pike almost every day he is at home. In the summer, he rings climbing friends, in either Carlisle or Keswick, and they arrange to meet on Great Gable. He can do a day's climbing in an evening, as the nights are so light in summer, after he's done all his other work.

'I get as much pleasure out of the Lakes as the Himalayas. It's a familiar beauty, and yet it is always refreshing. The very familiarity adds to the beauty. I could walk round the northern fells for ever.'

Although he's bored by writing about climbing, his love of climbing is no less strong. 'Basically, it's just tremendous fun, giving aesthetic and physical pleasure. There's an exhilaration about a long, hard climb. Most of all, I like being in mountains. That's why I could never live anywhere else but here.'

ABOVE *Those who make it to the top of High Pike are rewarded with a comfortable seat from which to take in the view.*

CHAPTER FIVE

EASTERN APPROACHES

C ALDBECK IS JOHN PEEL country, though you could pass through it and never be aware that John Peel lived and hunted and died in this area. Hunting dominates so much of Lakeland life, but native life, not the life the tourists see. Peel's name, and the song written about him, are known wherever hunting takes place, which means almost the whole world. Most English-speaking people could manage at least two lines of 'D'ye Ken John Peel?'.

His grave is in Caldbeck churchyard, and several hundred look at it every year. In the same graveyard is the grave of Mary of Buttermere, the Beauty, who later married (becoming Mary Harrison) and settled in Caldbeck.

John Peel's grave made the headlines in 1977 when it was desecrated by hunt saboteurs, protesting against blood sports, but now all is peace and quiet. Little attention is drawn to it, nor to the Caldbeck pub where the song was first sung, the Oddfellows Arms, nor to the farmhouse in nearby Ruthwaite where John Peel died.

John Peel lived from 1776 to 1854, almost the same life span as Wordsworth. He lived a life that was typical of the period, but one vastly different from Wordsworth's, and I'm sure they never met or even heard of each other, though Coleridge and Southey, during a stay in Caldbeck and a tramp across the Caldbeck Fells, might well have seen him on the horizon, blowing his horn, or heard him talked about in the pub in the evening. In his lifetime, Peel was a legend, if only a local one. He died without ever being known outside the immediate area—long before the tune we know today was even composed.

ABOVE *John Peel, painted by R. R. Reinagle. This romantic depiction has him wearing traditional hunting 'pink', rather than his usual grey coat.*

His parents were living at Parkend, Caldbeck, when he was born, the site now of a restaurant. They soon moved into an adjacent farm at Greenrigg which was where John was brought up. His father specialised in horses, breeding and selling them, the sort of Fell ponies still seen in the area. John Peel's own favourite pony, which he used to ride when hunting, was called Binsey, after the gentle solitary fell above Ireby.

John Peel ran away to Gretna Green in 1797 with a local girl, the daughter of a prosperous farmer at Uldale who didn't fancy John as a son-in-law, but they were later forgiven and were officially married in Caldbeck Church. They eventually moved into a small farm at Ruthwaite, which his wife's parents gave them. Peel was one of thirteen children, and he and his wife also had thirteen children, so there are lots of Peels still in the area, but he wasn't there for all the births. He lived only for hunting, closely followed by carousing in the local pubs after the hunt was over. In 1954, when centenary celebrations were held in Caldbeck, the then rector described him as one of Caldbeck's least worthy sons. 'Why make such a hero of one who neglected his farm and impoverished his family by his unrestrained pursuit of hunting?'

Peel had his own pack of hounds, getting friends and local farmers to feed and lodge those he couldn't afford to maintain himself, and he hunted the fox every possible day. When it was impossible, he and his hounds chased hares. He was by all accounts a brilliant huntsman, and the sound of his horn, when he and his hounds had got the scent of a fox, would drag farm hands from their work, disrupt weddings and upset funerals as people all chased off to take part in the excitement.

Many contemporary accounts of his hunts appeared in local papers, such as the *Carlisle Journal*, and the local quality as well as the humblest farm hand all joined in. A hunt could cover sixty to seventy miles, on foot on the high ground or on horseback on the slopes, and could last all day and night, with celebrations afterwards going on for as long again. Canon Rawnsley, that inexhaustible collector of titbits on all aspects of Cumbrian life, interviewed several locals who had known him personally. 'He wad drink, wad John Peel, till he couldn't stand; and then they would just clap him on't pony and away he wad gang as reet as a fiddle.'

He was six feet tall, weighed over thirteen stone, had a big nose and was probably a fairly disreputable character, without being downright wicked. He may well have been illiterate, apart from being able to write his name, but he was a character whose company all sporting men greatly enjoyed. He wore a grey coat (not a coat so gay as some versions of the song have it), knee breeches and a tall boxer hat, and carried a whip and horn. The grey coat was the traditional coat of local farmers, made from wool clipped from Herdwick sheep and woven in the Caldbeck area. The wool was undyed and still retained traces of the rancid butter that shepherds often plastered on the sheep in winter. Peel wore his like a blanket and hardly ever took it off. Those twee table and beer mats, in pretty hunting pink, purporting to be John Peel's image, bear little relation to the rather smelly, scruffy original.

ABOVE *John Peel's gravestone, ornately decorated with scenes of the chase, reflects his passion for hunting. Anti-blood sports activists desecrated the grave in 1977.*

ABOVE AND RIGHT
Carlisle United's club logo illustrates the tradition of hunting in Cumbrian life, as do their fans' renditions of 'D'ye Ken John Peel?'.

ABOVE *Forty years elapsed between Peel's friend John Woodcock Graves writing the words to 'D'ye Ken John Peel?' and William Metcalfe of Carlisle composing the tune in 1869.*

The words of the song were written in 1829, when Peel was fifty-three, by John Woodcock Graves, a hunting friend. He made up the John Peel verses on the spur of the moment, so he said in later life, when his young son asked him for the words of a Scottish Border tune his granny was humming.

Graves was a rather impetuous, though clever, young man, born in Wigton. Not long after writing the song he got involved in a court case, left his wife and emigrated to Tasmania where he hunted kangaroos instead of foxes and died in 1886.

The song became quite well known locally among the hunting people, but it didn't appear in print for almost forty years, long after Peel was dead, until a Carlisle bookseller published it in a book of Cumberland ballads. The song was read by William Metcalfe, choir master at Carlisle Cathedral, who rearranged it to new music (he told Canon Rawnsley that he used only the 'germ' of the original tune), and in 1869 he sang it in public with great success, first in Carlisle and then in London.

The Border Regiment adopted it for their regimental march and took it round the world. It was sung at the Relief of Lucknow.

It's a neat tune, and can bring tears to exiled Cumbrians in far corners of the world. Such a pity John Peel never heard it. At his funeral in Caldbeck in 1854, however, fifteen years before the song was first sung in its present version, over three thousand locals turned out to mourn the great huntsman. The *Carlisle Journal* reported that when the procession passed the kennels containing Peel's hounds 'they raised a deep-mouthed cry'.

It's on sentimental occasions, when Cumbrians are searching for an identity, that 'John Peel' usually comes out, such as in 1974–5, when Carlisle United had their one and only year of glory in the First Division. The symbol of the club is a fox, and their handful of supporters was heard, rather hesitantly if defiantly at foreign grounds, singing the words of 'D'ye Ken John Peel?'.

Caldbeck today has 700 inhabitants, a third of the population of John Peel's time, but is a thriving and lively farming community, off the main tourist track and therefore not dependent on visitors for a living. Only one of its original thirteen pubs now survives, though they have got a village clog maker. The old woollen industries have all gone, the bobbin and other mills now romantic ruins. In a ravine beside the village, known locally as the Howk, was once a water wheel forty-two feet in diameter, said at one time to be the largest in the country. Exploring its remains, hidden away in the depths of the gorge, is like discovering Atlantis. I'd passed through Caldbeck for thirty years without ever knowing it was there.

As for the hunting, that's as strong as it ever was in Peel's day. The foxes are said to be smaller than in the old days, but there seem to be more of them, judging by the figures that each hunt proudly produces at the end of a season. There are more followers, though many these days are in cars. There are six fell packs in all, which carve up Lakeland between them—Blencathra, Coniston, Ullswater, Eskdale and Ennerdale, Lunesdale and Melbreak. The Blencathra

BOBBIN·MILLING—A BYGONE SPECIALITY

AS THE LANCASHIRE cotton mills burgeoned two centuries ago, their hunger for bobbins increased in proportion. Without these simple wooden reels, the mills' spinning and weaving machines would soon choke on their own yarn. To appease this hunger, Victorian entrepreneurs envisaged mass-production 'bobbin mills', and lighted on Lakeland as the ideal location. Woodlands would supply the raw materials, and the fast local streams would drive the water wheels to turn the lathes.

Labourers came from near and far. Specialist skills were in demand for each stage of production: coppicing the birch stumps, sawing the poles and grading them according to diameter, cutting the thicker logs into blocks, boring holes into the blanks, drying and finishing and polishing them.

In the early days, the flanges and barrel of each bobbin were carved separately and then glued together, but in the mid-19th century technological

RIGHT *Stott Park Bobbin Mill was built in 1835 and continued to operate until 1971. It is now an industrial museum.*

BELOW *The Lakeland mills provided the textile industries of Lancashire with huge quantities of wooden bobbins.*

advances allowed the production of one-piece bobbins. Turbines and steam engines helped to increase output. There were dangers—from the dust as well as the erratic pulleys and drive-belts—but working conditions were probably better than in some of the 'dark satanic mills' to the east and south.

By the mid-20th century, plastics and foreign competitors had jointly rendered local bobbin-making obsolete. A few mills struggled on, producing specialised bobbins for wire, and continuing traditional woodturning sidelines such as pick-handles and axe-shafts. But the industry had reached the end of its natural life span, and so had a unique way of life.

RIGHT *Pink-coated huntsmen tramp the fells and dales, harrying their hounds to hunt out the fox.*

BELOW *The object of the chase, the fox, often has enough speed and guile to evade capture.*

covers John Peel's old stamping ground, and both it and the Ullswater pack pride themselves on having hounds bred from his original hounds. All of them now hunt on foot.

In Peel's day, a pack would depend very much on the personality of the man who organised it, a local farmer who called out other farmers with his horn. Most farmers kept a hound or two all the year round and joined in when they felt like it, especially when their own stock was in danger, or simply because they loved the hunt, as Peel did. Today, each of the six fell packs has a full-time huntsman (who wears pink, not grey, when hunting) who is in charge of the twenty or so couples of hounds each hunt maintains.

Each hunt has a master, but the position has little of the social importance of the mounted hunts in the South. It's a completely classless sport, which they boast about in their local hunting songs:

> *The brave pack o' Blencathra*
> *Is free alike to all;*
> *The peasant from the cottage,*
> *The lordling from the hall.*

I first heard the hounds one day in the Langdales when I was near Blea Tarn. (It must have been the Coniston hunt, now I look at the hunting map, though three packs overlap in that area.) I heard yelping high up on the topmost crags, then I heard the echoes, and the more I tried to pick out the crags in question the more it seemed to be everywhere. I gave up searching and just sat and listened to their ghostly, eerie crying. Eventually, I caught a flash of red and followed with my eye the direction of the scampering huntsman and there, on some high ledges, well above the sheep line, I saw the hounds, tearing up and down, very excited, while miles below, other hunt followers with some stray hounds were marooned in the valley.

The season begins around mid-September and ends in April, with May and June being kept free for specific calls from local farmers if their lambs are being worried. The official meets are listed in the local papers and start at nine in the morning, usually four times a week, meeting at a local pub, farm or crossroads.

The fell-hunting hound is smaller and lighter coloured than the foxhounds of the Shires, and it has a hare-foot, as opposed to a cat-foot grip, which helps it up steep rocks. It is kept light in weight so it does less damage to itself when jumping from high crags. It can catch a fox over level ground, but Mr Tod has the advantage on the rough ground. (Tod is an old word for fox, and it's interesting to notice how common the name Todhunter is in the Caldbeck area.)

The fox understands the scent it leaves and will deliberately cross water or run along walls to throw off the hounds. It uses its brush as an extra leg, balancing on it when descending steeply.

THE END OF THE HUNT?

HOW THE FUR FLIES—when the fox flees its pursuers, when the hounds tear it to pieces, when hunt saboteurs confront huntsmen, and when pro- and anti-hunt lobbies engage in debate.

The factual questions include these: is the fox a pest, ravaging lambs and poultry? Or does it, in preying on rats and rabbits, actually reduce pest-infestation? As an economic and ecological nuisance, isn't the hunt itself more guilty, damaging farmland and disrupting traffic? Are foxes overabundant, and in need of culling? What of the jobs and traditional, rural way of life that might disappear with the end of the hunt?

As for the moral arguments, the anti-hunt lobby cites 'animal rights'. Cruel sports, from bear-baiting to dogfighting, have long been banned, and fox-hunting should, it is argued, follow suit. That some citizens should actually relish such savagery is an affront to a 'decent society'.

The pro-hunt lobby counters by citing 'civil rights': hunting may be a minority hobby, but a 'tolerant society' should protect, not suppress, minority interests. As for cruelty, nature is cruel. Anyway, foxes roam free, and most escape the hounds. Save your sympathy for battery hens or crated pigs and veal calves.

An opinion poll in 1997 showed that 74 per cent of the British public opposed fox-hunting. In that year too, a Private Members' Bill in Parliament received similar backing, only to lapse through lack of time. Many hunt enthusiasts concede, though, that time is no longer on their side.

BELOW *Animated debate persists between the anti-hunt lobby and huntsmen.*

In the close season, the hounds are boarded out in local farms. The stars in each pack have names that go back for centuries, with certain farms always being allowed to walk the same-named hound, often a descendant of the original. The names are always two syllables, to make shouting easier, and John Peel's hounds' names—Ruby, Ranter, Royal and Bellman—still appear at Lakeland shows.

CAIRNS AND CASTLES

I set off from Caldbeck, heading south for Lowther country, and came first to Hesket Newmarket, a one-street village. On closer observation, you realise that the street is actually a village green and that lined up on either side are some attractive cottages.

Charles Dickens stayed here with Wilkie Collins in 1857, and wrote up his tour in *Household Words* in an article called 'The Lazy Tour of Two Idle Apprentices'. They couldn't have been all that idle because they climbed Carrock Fell. I decided to do the same. As High Pike dominates the top end of the northern fells so Carrock Fell, just seventeen feet higher at 2,174, stands guard on the eastern slopes, looking over to Penrith and Eden Vale.

It was a very hot day and I decided to climb it the easy way, if the longest. The eastern slopes are surprisingly rocky, but then Carrock Fell is an anomaly in the northern fells, having outcrops of volcanic rock, like the Langdales to the south. High Pike is beautifully smooth by comparison. I headed inland from Mosedale, following the Caldew River, aiming to attack Carrock Fell from the rear slopes. The valley entrance is half hidden, and I expected the little road to peter out and to have the valley to myself, even though it was the school holidays. But I was passed on the road by several cars full of people, all going nowhere, as the valley is a dead end. I eventually discovered them all parked at the end of the road, swimming in a pool made by the Caldew.

The Caldew is just a little river, but it makes a big impact, carving its way arrogantly through the high fells, a trickle that pushes all the big bullies aside. It provides an easy path along its banks almost all the way to Skiddaw itself. I headed the other way, up the slopes of Carrock Fell, making sure I didn't put my feet in any nasty holes. This was mining country at one time. Carrock mine, the main one, had been closed for decades, according to Wainwright's guide, so I was prepared to miss it, till I almost stumbled into one of its gushing water pits. It was back in full production. The market price of tungsten must have risen again.

I passed a very nice sheep pen on the way up, a three-room stone arrangement with walls about five feet high. As I neared the top, I came to large outcrops of rocks, slabs of it lying in large piles, easy to bound over, and even easier for foxes to hide under. No wonder the Blencathra often call it off when old Tod goes to ground up here.

The cairn on top of Carrock Fell came to a fine point, a perfect pyramid, which proved what good weather we'd been having. In normal conditions, the small pieces on top must all get blown away. At the base is a large mound of stone slabs which is supposed to be the remains of an ancient British hill-fort.

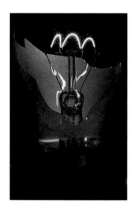

ABOVE *Tungsten is mined in the Lake District. The element and its alloys are used in high-temperature applications such as lamp filaments.*

I came straight down, not following any path, and immediately tore my bare legs to shreds in some thick bracken. On the top slopes there had been acres of beautiful, verdant bilberry shoots, so gentle to walk through, but on the scree sides it turned into heavy, wiry bracken.

My next stop was Greystoke Castle, home of the Howards, a family long famous in English history. Howards seem to have stately homes and castles all over England, and most of them are related to the little family of pig farmers—hog wards, as they were called, hence howard—who lived in Norfolk about one thousand years ago, and went on to produce three earls and, of course, the Duke of Norfolk. Howards came to the borderlands about five hundred years ago, when the king needed someone to sort out the Scots, and acquired land by judicious

LEFT *Greystoke Castle, painted in 1897. The castle is the seat of a family whose ancestors were simple pig farmers.*

marrying. There's a branch of the Howard family at Naworth Castle (the Earl of Carlisle), some twenty-five miles to the north, and another branch in Yorkshire at Castle Howard.

Two Dukes of Norfolk have lived in Greystoke Castle, and in the 19th century one of them was responsible for tarting up the basic peel tower (which dates back to 1126) with an ornate early 18th-century front. Stafford Howard (a third cousin of the present duke) inherited the castle and some six thousand acres in 1950, after Eton, Oxford and the Guards ('I'm an absolute stereotype, I'm afraid'), to find the castle in a very bad state, with the army in residence and Nissen huts in the courtyards. 'They did more damage than Cromwell.' Since then, he'd devoted his life to restoring the castle and grounds. Before the war, there were twenty-five live-in servants. He and his wife had none, managing with a couple of dailies.

Mr Howard's main claim to Cumbrian fame was as chairman of the National Trust in the Northwest (which means Cumbria and Lancashire). The National Trust is the biggest single landowner in the Lakes. The National Park has legal powers, being a planning authority, but it doesn't actually own very much. There are many other bodies, like the Friends of the Lake District, the Forestry Commission, Cumbria Tourist Board, the local councils and countless conservation groups, but, of them all, the National Trust is probably the most important single organisation.

The National Trust is not a government body, despite its name, but an independent charity. It's the biggest conservation society in Britain, set up at a time when only a few rather eccentric souls cared anything for preservation and the countryside. The Lake District has strong connections with its foundation, as Canon Rawnsley was one of its three founders, the others being Octavia Hill and Sir Robert Hunter.

There had been cries for conserving the countryside throughout the 19th century. Wordsworth on several occasions talked and wrote about the need for somebody to protect the Lakes—as later did John Ruskin. It was left to Canon Rawnsley, the ultimate agitator for nature, to get things moving.

ABOVE *Dedicated to conservation, the National Trust owns vast tracts of land in the Lake District, and has strong historical connections with the area.*

RIGHT *A marker at Brandelhow on the western side of Derwent Water commemorates the National Trust's first purchase of Lakeland property.*

In 1893 he and Hunter and Miss Hill met at the Duke of Westminster's London house, and it was from this meeting that the National Trust was formed, with Canon Rawnsley as its first secretary, a position he held till his death. The first property it bought in the Lakes was on the shores of Derwent Water in 1902.

The National Trust owns over ninety thousand acres in the Lakes, plus the care of a further 16,000. It owns 280 cottages, seventy-one hill farms, eleven lowland farms and 17,500 sheep. It owns Buttermere, Crummock Water, Loweswater and large sections of Derwent Water, Ullswater and Rydal Water; mountains such as Scafell Pike and Great Gable; famous houses such as Hill Top, Sizergh Castle and Wordsworth's Cockermouth home.

Mr Howard, being only a voluntary official, didn't take part in the day-to-day business enterprises, but he was particularly pleased about all the efforts to help the hill farmers on National Trust property. 'In the old days, the Trust was simply concerned with preservation, which was rather negative. If all you're doing is preserving, you could end up with dead villages and dead communities. We're now concerned with people as much as buildings.'

I went on a little tour of his own Greystoke estate before leaving, including a visit to his stables, scene of great excitement just a few months previously. He rented the stables to Gordon Richards, trainer

of Lucius, winner of the 1978 Grand National. The whole village of Greystoke naturally had money on its local horse. Mr Richards had fifty horses training at Greystoke and had built up a mini Newmarket. 'We now have an Irish community living in the village. Thanks to the National Health, English boys are too big to be jockeys.'

LOWTHER LAND

Lowther land begins just a few miles south of Greystoke and, in Cumbrian terms, the Lowthers have always been top of the bill. They have been based at Lowther, near Penrith, for almost a thousand years, probably from the time of the Norse settlements.

The Lowther who put the family into the millionaire class was Sir James Lowther, who became the first Earl of Lonsdale in 1784—the one who employed Wordsworth's father yet never paid him the money. He might have been rotten to the Wordsworth family but he transformed the area, bringing the Industrial Revolution to west Cumberland.

The Lowthers continued to increase their great wealth after Wordsworth's day, and when the fifth Earl of Lonsdale took over in 1882 he was regarded as one of the richest men in England. Nobody in Cumbria can be unaware of the family's influence. As a boy in Carlisle, I walked to school every day down Lowther Street and on Saturday morning went to the children's matinée

at Carlisle's smartest cinema, the Lonsdale. Almost every town and village in Cumbria has similar connections, showing where the family has been and bought and conquered.

The fifth earl had a long run, holding the title from 1882 to 1944—and what fun he had ruining the family. The Yellow Earl, as he was called, is still talked of in Cumbria today. He loved yellow, the family colour, and painted his carriages yellow, later his motor cars, and had all his servants in yellow livery. He had an enormous number of servants. When the Kaiser came to stay with him, one of many royal visitors, he had on duty in Lowther Castle over sixty indoor staff.

He was a great car man and the first President of the Automobile Association. (Their colour today is yellow, thanks to the Yellow Earl.) In Cumbria, the Tory party's colour is still yellow, despite the fact that in the rest of the nation the Tories always sport blue. (This dates back to Wordsworth's day when the Lowthers controlled most of the Cumbrian constituencies.) He was a great sporting earl, and was always organising sports for his tenants and employees, such as on Burgh Marsh when the whole area had a feast day. His name today is probably known nationally only through boxing and the Lonsdale belts that he bequeathed.

By 1910 he was spending at the rate of £180,000 a year which, even for the Lowther coffers, couldn't go on. He lived on mineral royalties, but put none of it back, the worst sin in any landed family. When the 1930s depression came—and it hit west Cumberland so hard it has today hardly recovered—his income dried up overnight. Then, on his death in 1944, £1.7 million had to be paid in tax.

That was the end, it seemed, of Lowther power, of 1,000 years of almost continuous feudal control of a vast chunk of northwest England. The next earl was

LEFT *All that lies behind the grand façade of Lowther Castle is ruins. Financial troubles forced the family to neglect the upkeep of the property.*

BELOW *The fifth Earl of Lonsdale is pictured on the prized Lonsdale Belt, first awarded for excellence in boxing in 1909.*

an old man of seventy-six when he took over. Then onto the scene came his grandson, young James Lowther, who, in 1949, at the age of twenty-seven, was brought across from Newcastle, where he was working as a businessman, to manage the estates. His father had died suddenly and in 1953, on the death of his grandfather, he became the seventh earl.

There was yet another set of enormous death duties to be faced, and Lowther Castle, the family seat, had fallen into such disrepair that it was partially demolished and became the semi-ruin it is today. But in eight years, by massive rationalisation, judiciously selling outlying portions of the estates, the new earl had discharged liabilities of £2.1 million.

In 1953, when he became earl, the estate had been turning over about £100,000 a year and employed seventy people. In 1978, the turnover was £6 million, the employees numbered 307, and the Lowther Estates were now run as a corporate body with seven trusts and twenty shareholders owning different sections, just like a modern business organisation.

It was lucky for the family that the earl showed the business acumen and energy of the first James Lowther, the one who built up the family fortunes in the first place. He diversified into things like a wildlife park, a caravan site and property companies. Their own management business was now so successful that it managed thirty other big estates in and around Cumbria.

The Lowther revival not only assured the family fortunes but brought new money and jobs and opportunities to Cumbria as a whole. The most profitable single division was their sawmills. The Lowthers, over the centuries, had always planted oak, as a good landed family should, in fact as only landed families can do, being in a position to wait 120 years for any return. The oak went for ships in the Napoleonic Wars, then for railway wagons during Victorian days. Those markets had obviously gone by the time the seventh earl took over, but by careful research he found a new one—oak for fencing the new motorways. He produced £750,000 from motorway contracts, and the sawmills that he opened to process the wood went on to become a thriving business in their own right.

The Lowthers were still the biggest private landowners in the Lakes (coming third in the overall league table after the National Trust and the Forestry Commission) and they owned the freehold of 40,000 acres in Cumbria and manorial rights over a further 35,000 acres of common land. Lord Lonsdale himself lived near the famous castle, just a couple of miles away at Askham Hall. He had several bits of Wordsworth memorabilia, such as three poems in the poet's hand, written in the visitors' book. He had let the National Trust have 16,000 acres of Lake District fells for his lifetime, and 1,500 acres along the Solway for five pence a year until the year 2000. 'My successors can then decide what to do with it.'

I had a last look at Lowther Castle before I headed for Ullswater. It really is a most remarkable sight, especially from a distance, all rounded turrets and fairy-tale battlements, the sort so loved by romantic Victorians. I've seen old photographs of it with rows of carriages lined up outside, and the ladies and gentlemen in all their finery. The north face of the building is 420 feet long, so you can see why all those indoor servants were needed.

Now it is just a shell. 'What pain must it be to the owners to live so near this memorial of past glories,' observes Nikolaus Pevsner in his series on the buildings of England.

The castle is bolted and barricaded, and the public aren't allowed inside for fear of falling masonry, but I went round the back and discovered a strong smell of hens. The back gardens had been taken over by the ever-enterprising Lowther Estates and were covered with huts for broiler chickens. Such is progress.

A WALK ALONG THE HIGH STREET

I cruised down Ullswater on the good ship *Raven*. I had got on at Pooley Bridge.

Ullswater is my favourite lake, and my favourite walk—one I've done so many times—is from Howtown, up Martindale, round Place Fell, coming back along Ullswater to Howtown. It's the perfect round walk, with so many different types of scenery, wild and lush, hard and easy, cosy and bleak, empty and busy yet never overcrowded for all its popularity. On the last stretch, the lake unfolds in front of you, peeling itself away in layers, a new perspective round every corner. This time, however, I was aiming to walk to Kendal, the last long, overland stretch of my journey.

At Howtown pier, I headed away from the lake. Hidden behind the Howtown Hotel is a little valley called Fusedale. In under fifteen minutes since leaving Howtown pier, I was halfway up the valley, walking in complete isolation. I followed the beck through several little gorges, each with a couple of rowan trees. Rowan is my favourite tree.

Once I'd climbed out of the valley and reached the high ground, the landscape went blank. Miles of empty, treeless, rough grass stretched into the distance, the only break in the grey-green monotone being some patches of peat hags, which looked from afar like giant brown earthworms crawling over the hillside.

I rested at a ruined cottage, where I heard some heavy breathing. A couple in blue anoraks, sitting behind the wall, jumped up when they saw me and walked with me for a while. The man had been doing the heavy breathing, a gentleman of about fifty, rather overweight, who said it was his first-ever visit to the Lakes and this was his first walk. They had booked in the day before into a farmhouse in Martindale and had planned themselves a six-hour walk up and round High Street. By the look and sound of him, he was never going to make it. He said he was from Hertfordshire and spent most of his working life driving a motor car.

BELOW *Ullswater, the author's favourite lake, is the second largest in the Lake District and is popular with sailing enthusiasts.*

The mountain-rescue people are forever giving out lists of common-sense instructions, because even normally sensible people do silly things. I consider myself fit but I wouldn't attempt a six-hour climb on the first day of my hols, especially if I wasn't used to fell walking. No wonder exhaustion is such a prime cause of accidents.

I'd chosen this route as it looked a quick way up to High Street. High Street is the name both of the highest point on the ridge, some 2,719 feet high, and of the ridge itself. It's a high-altitude path that cuts a swath right across the eastern flanks of the Lake District. Once you're on the top, it soars for over ten miles, up and down, taking everything in its stride. The Romans walked this way, using it as part of their main route from Penrith across to Windermere.

On the very top, a strongly built stone wall follows the path for several miles. It reminded me of Hadrian's Wall in the way it followed the slopes of the dominant ridge, commanding the heights. In ancient days, the valleys and fell sides were forested. This path was not just the best but almost the only way into the Lakes. Over the centuries, it's been trodden by marching soldiers, raiding Vikings, government

ADVENTURE-LOVING ALTRUISTS

A CLIMBER IS REPORTED missing. The police notify the local mountain-rescue team, whose duty officer alerts his task-force by means of electronic pagers. The team members assemble— dentists, carpenters, youth-hostel managers—and begin sweeping the fellside in worsening weather. Their dog eventually traces the hapless victim, trapped on a rock ledge with a broken ankle. Night and a rainstorm are fast approaching. Word is swiftly relayed to the SAR (Search and Rescue) at RAF Valley, near Holyhead, who quickly despatch a Wessex helicopter to the area.

Two heavily laden rescuers, meanwhile, are descending by rope to reach the injured man. They give him emergency medical treatment, and secure him in a casualty bag to a lightweight stretcher. With the helicopter, guided by a flare, hovering above, the casualty is winched on board and flown to hospital.

An extreme case, of course, but one that mountain-rescue volunteers are trained for. There are thirteen teams

of volunteers in the Lake District, each containing about forty members. Training is rigorous, honing such skills as rock climbing, radio communications and first aid. Thank goodness that most call-outs are far less dramatic. There are about 500 a year, with perhaps only a quarter of them involving injuries. The man-hours spent on rescue missions total about 20,000. Add the training time and the

ABOVE *Rescue workers carry a casualty out of a gully in Langdale. These hard-working heroes are all volunteers.*

danger, and one can only marvel at these courageous altruists. And all without pay. The service's income—a mere £20,000 per team per year, derived entirely from voluntary contributions—goes solely on operating and equipment costs.

inspectors, celebrating shepherds. It was once used, not so many decades ago, as a sports arena where shepherds wrestled and ran fell races. I can imagine it as a good meeting point, and a good playing ground, as the ridge is smooth and level.

The Romans have left few traces in the Lakes. They concentrated their energies some thirty miles to the north, on Hadrian's Wall, and down the Cumbrian coast, where it now looks as if they had a complete string of forts guarding themselves from seaborne attack. In central Lakeland, they had only a few little forts, as at Ambleside, Hard Knott and Ravenglass.

However, there's a surprising amount of evidence of the Celtic people who were here when the Romans arrived. The Celtic people in Lakeland were related to those in Wales, both calling themselves Cymry, which is where Cumbria comes from. The prefixes Pen, Glyn, Caer and Blaen as in Penrith, Glenridding, Carlisle and Blencathra are all part of the Celtic–Welsh connection. Yan, meaning one, is common usage throughout Cumbria, and many Cumbrian shepherds still use the old Celtic form when counting their sheep—yan, tan, tether.

The people who had the biggest influence on the Lake District were the Norsemen. They didn't come direct from Scandinavia but raided the Cumbrian coast from Ireland and the Isle of Man. They settled here, unlike the Romans who saw us as a colony, not their home. They cleared space in the forests and left their mark on countless place names. Thwaite, meaning clearing, appears in many place names, and in surnames. Then there's beck, fell, pike, dale, force (meaning waterfall), gill (ravine), hause (pass), holme (island in a lake), how (hill), rigg (ridge), scale (hut), ness (promontory) and wath (ford)—all of which have Norse origins.

I left High Street, and the paths of history, at the top of High Street itself, where I turned left for Haweswater. I was heading for Long Stile and I was glad I didn't miss it. It's a narrow route down a razor's edge of jagged rocks and steep scree. I wouldn't dare have tried to descend that way in mist.

ABOVE *Roman soldiers often marched along the nine-mile plateau of High Street in order to avoid the more difficult terrain and dangerous tribes that inhabited the lower-lying valleys. In later centuries the flat, wide expanse was sometimes used as a horse-racing course.*

MARDALE—THE LOST VILLAGE

I could see a glimpse of Haweswater as I came down the valley, and what a strange sight it is. Around the entire lake is an enormous white kerb about fifty feet wide, a strip of bleached stones and rocks. Something's gone wrong, but you can't at first work out what has happened. It's as if the Ice Age has just left, scouring the valley and leaving strange formations. I could see a little island with its own bleached tidemarks all round it. It is caused purely by the rise and fall of the water level.

I walked down to the water's edge. The water level was very low, and out in the lake I could clearly see lines of stone walls marking old fields and buildings. It was as if there had been a flood quite recently and the farmers had abandoned the land and their buildings, but would be back soon. They won't, of course. A whole village has gone, including a church and a pub, never to return.

Haweswater is a reservoir. Manchester Corporation flooded the valley and the village of Mardale just before the last war. The huge dam at the far end, which is 1,550 feet long and ninety-four feet high, was completed in 1940. There was originally a little lake called Hawes Water, but they flooded the valley right up to the dale end and increased its size by roughly threefold.

There are two lakes in the Lake District that are wholly reservoirs, Thirlmere and Haweswater, with others like Ennerdale, Windermere and Ullswater being part used. Up to 140 million gallons a day is taken from Thirlmere and Haweswater reservoirs and flows by gravity underground some ninety miles to Manchester. Thirlmere was lost first, after a struggle. Manchester had its eye on Thirlmere from the 1870s, when it sent men up on horseback to look for water, and there was a national outcry when their plans were made public.

ABOVE *In times of drought the water levels at Haweswater reservoir drop so low that remnants of the drowned village of Mardale are visible.*

Thirlmere isn't ugly unless you object to the conifers that now dominate almost every side. They've even got nature trails. It's just south of Keswick and so ruined by the main road that runs right along it, down to Windermere, that even if it had never become a reservoir, the traffic would have killed most of its natural beauty.

The trouble with a reservoir is not just the loss of a valley and perhaps a village, but that you lose a lake. You can't use it any more for swimming or anything very much. They even stop you throwing stones in.

The nicest part of Haweswater is the dale end. It comes as a surprise, if you've been following the road and the concrete-looking sides of the lake, when the road comes to a dead end and there in front of you are the magnificent crags and soaring heights of the High Street range. There are no buildings in sight and not that many walkers, considering the richness of the views. Perhaps the Water Board have done the valley a good turn, keeping down the crowds. This is the area, so they say, where the eagles have returned. I didn't see any as I worked my way over to the head of Longsleddale.

I practised trying to say Longsleddale as I came down over the rough, wild fell tops. Could it be Longs-le-Dale, or perhaps Long-Sled-dale or possibly they shorten it altogether and pronounce it Longs'dale, almost like Lonsdale as in Lord.

When I reached the valley, the stone walls were bold and strong, soaring up impossible heights, disappearing over the tops, marking one chunk of apparent wildness from another, demarcation lines that only eccentric millionaires would now build. The dry-stone walls are a great feature of the Lakes, but they're not really all that old, mostly having been built in the early 19th century, at the time of the enclosure movement. Since 1850, they've hardly been touched. Nobody could afford to build them now, even if they could find anyone skilled enough to do it. I've tried it myself, and it's far harder than it looks.

The secret is to have a wide base to give stability, two layers with rubble in between, and regular through stones binding the wall together. Well, I was told those were the secrets, but my walls still fell down. The cam stones on top are supposed to point downhill, to let the water drain off, and individual wallers left their own mark by the way they laid the cam stones. Good wallers also built hogg holes, to let young sheep pass through.

On the high fells many walls have been allowed to crumble these days, but in the valleys they are kept in good repair, often topped with a wire fence. Sheep are incredible at jumping and scrambling. Dry-stone walls also have an extra quality I had never imagined till a farmer in Caldbeck told me how he'd lost six sheep in a snowstorm once for four weeks. He fell through a drift one day in a corner of a field and found them beneath the snow, huddled against the wall. They were still alive, though they'd eaten most of their wool. Thanks to it being a dry-stone wall, they'd been able to breathe *through* the wall.

I scrambled down into Longsleddale and soon hit the road beside the little Sprint River. There was an old shepherd standing with his dog beside a bridge so I stopped and chatted to him, hoping he would pronounce Longsleddale the correct way, so I could hide my ignorance. Further up the valley I'd seen a cottage for sale, so I asked if he knew the price.

'I might do,' he said, pausing. 'What do you think?'

I suggested £20,000. 'Add another 10,000, then you might be near it.'

He said it was the planning people's fault that house prices were so high. They won't allow any new buildings, so the old ones cost a fortune and no locals can buy them.

'Them planning folk don't live here, but they tell us what to do. They tell us we don't want new people and new houses. Who says we don't? You need permission for everything. I could tell you some stories about caravans nobody knows about. The money they take in. They never declare it, you know. But good luck to them.'

It was a rather elliptical conversation, but in passing he had mentioned the name of the valley, pronouncing it Long-sledle. So now I know.

ABOVE *Conveniently placed 'hogg' holes—apertures in dry-stone walls—are big enough to allow only young sheep to pass through to better grazing.*

CHAPTER SIX

THE GRAND OLD MEN OF LAKELAND

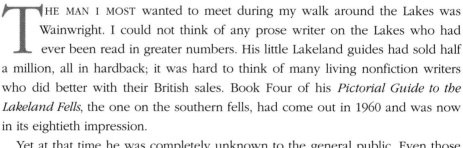

ABOVE *A man who preferred the company of mountains to that of men, A. Wainwright spent a good deal of his life rambling around Lakeland.*

THE MAN I MOST wanted to meet during my walk around the Lakes was Wainwright. I could not think of any prose writer on the Lakes who had ever been read in greater numbers. His little Lakeland guides had sold half a million, all in hardback; it was hard to think of many living nonfiction writers who did better with their British sales. Book Four of his *Pictorial Guide to the Lakeland Fells*, the one on the southern fells, had come out in 1960 and was now in its eightieth impression.

Yet at that time he was completely unknown to the general public. Even those half a million or so who had bought his books had little idea who he was. I had consulted his fell guides all year, yet I had learned no details about the writer himself. You saw them everywhere, a status symbol for all Lakers who spread them out in the back of their cars or clutched them on cairns. Many people I spoke to thought he must have lived about a hundred years ago.

His books will doubtless last for ever, partly because it's unlikely that anyone else will ever have the energy to climb and describe every fell in the Lake District; partly because they are already collectors' items; and, most of all, because they are a joy to read. It's not just the contents but his individual style of presentation that is unique and such a delight. Each book contains no line of printer's type. It's all in his own handwriting, from the covers and headlines and numbers to the words, which is why it looks at first sight like the facsimile of some 19th-century gentleman's commonplace book. In many ways it is. He did it for himself—and to everyone's amazement, the public flocked to buy them. The books are full of his quirky personality. He admits in them that his drawings are often just 'to fill up awkward spaces' and that 'the hills don't really look as good as this.'

I had rather tricked him into seeing me. I got his wife on the phone and she was kind enough to say she was sure he would see me. I said I just wanted to talk to him about his own experiences in the Lakes and hear any advice he might give me. He agreed, on condition that nothing ended up in any newspaper.

A very tall, well-built man of seventy-one, with thick white hair and a soft Lancashire accent, he lived in a modern house in Kendal. He told me he was born in Blackburn and christened Alfred, a name he obviously disliked. He always put 'A. Wainwright' or simply 'AW' when signing off at the end of another book.

His father was a stonemason. Alfred went to the local elementary school and left at thirteen to be an office boy in the council offices. He moved to accounts as a clerk, where he was persuaded to take the professional exams to become a municipal accountant. 'The boss forced me to do it and it took me eight years of study at nights. I think those years of killing study killed any reading instinct I ever had. I've hardly picked up a book since. I hate any sort of research. But it did turn me into a hard worker. If I'm not working, I think I'm wasting time. I still do ten hours a day, seven days a week. I have no social life, by choice.'

His youth was spent in Blackburn, in an environment of dingy houses and shabby streets, gaunt mill chimneys, huge factory walls that shut out the sun, flickering gas lamps, hot potato carts, fish-and-chip shops, public houses. 'I was twenty-three before I could afford a holiday away from home. The Lake District was only sixty miles away but it was another world, distant, unattainable. I went there for a week's walking. Well, I was utterly enslaved by it. I gazed in disbelief at the loveliness around me. I never knew there could be so much colour and charm in landscape. That was the first time I'd looked upon beauty, or even imagined the idea of beauty.'

After that, he took his holidays in the Lakes, when he could afford it, and in 1941 came to Kendal to work in the treasurer's office. In 1948 he was made Borough Treasurer of Kendal. He now spent all his spare time on the fells, and in the winter, when it was too dark to climb, he sat by his fireside doing pen-and-ink drawings of Great Gable and other places he'd climbed, reclimbing them in his mind.

A MAMMOTH UNDERTAKING

In 1950 Wainwright moved into his present house, which was then new, and drew up a five-year plan to knock the untouched garden into shape. He worked day and night, even digging with the aid of electric light, and had finished it in two years. He felt desolate without a plan of campaign to occupy himself. In November 1952 he decided to set himself a new task. He would climb all the fells and mountains in the Lake District and keep a notebook and drawings of all the routes, just for his own enjoyment. He was by then

ABOVE *The unique style of Wainwright's pocket-sized walking guides has ensured their enduring popularity.*

forty-five, with a full-time job, and he calculated that doing the two hundred or so climbs in his spare time would take him thirteen years, nearly up to his sixtieth birthday.

It was the publication of the Ordnance Survey's new two-and-a-half-inch maps of the Lakes that triggered off the idea. 'With the larger-scale map, you have the illusion of covering more ground more quickly. You can move from the top of the map to the bottom in a day's trek. I wanted to check out the new, bigger-scale maps and fill in details like fields and walks.'

He didn't start off with the idea of publishing a book. He did it simply for the pleasure of doing it, something for when his fell-walking days were over and he could relive the memories. 'I thought they would be nice to read when I was an old man. Now I am an old man I never read them. I'm too busy.'

On the fells, as he went around making notes for himself, he was continually being asked by other walkers where paths led to, what was this and what was over there. He began to realise that other people might like some advice, but he never thought of submitting his notes to a publisher. 'I knew they wouldn't

THE ORDNANCE SURVEY: PUTTING BRITAIN ON THE MAP

OUTDOOR ENTHUSIASTS in Britain are fortunate enough to have at their disposal a series of wonderfully detailed maps. Covering the country north to south and east to west, these indispensable travel guides show everything from windmills and waterfalls to pubs and public toilets. They are the work of the Ordnance Survey, or OS, Britain's national mapping agency.

Back in the Middle Ages, the Board of Ordnance was a war department mainly responsible for artillery, with cartography being a minor sideline. Only when the British army marched to the Scottish Highlands after the Jacobite Rebellion of 1745–6 did it realise there was a dearth of maps of the local terrain. Surveyor and engineer General William Roy was duly commissioned to conduct an extensive survey of Scotland. Roy proposed going one step further and undertaking a nationwide mapping programme, but it wasn't until 1791 that his brainchild was born.

The Ordnance Survey took on a more commercial role only in the early 20th century. Tourism in Britain was burgeoning, with motoring, rambling and cycling surging in popularity. These pastimes were the focus of a ground-breaking meeting on changing the face of the OS in 1914. But within the year the outbreak of the First World War channelled all the Ordnance Survey's skills onto the Western front. Over the next four years it produced a staggering 30 million maps.

The OS has always been at the cutting edge of mapping technology, whether exploiting the most up-to-date theodolites in the 18th century or taking today's computers to their limits with digital mapping. Today the OS updates its map database hour by hour, and new series are forever hitting bookshop shelves.

ABOVE This detail of Derwent Water is taken from the first OS map of the Lake District, produced in 1866.

LEFT OS staff who died in the First World War were commemorated in a stained-glass window at the OS's Southampton headquarters, which itself was bombed in the Second War.

be interested in something handwritten.' So he went to a local printer in Kendal, and asked him if he could do him a few copies. The printer, Sandy Hewitson, said that he would have to print 2,000 copies to make it economic—and that would cost £900. Wainwright didn't have that sort of money.

But Hewitson was so interested in the guide that he said he would print it at his own expense, and then wait for the books to be sold before being paid. 'Over the next two years, I sent him nine cheques for £100 each as the books began to sell.'

He was helped with the selling of the first book by the local librarian in Kendal, Henry Marshall. He advised Wainwright not to have his name on the book as both author and publisher. Booksellers might think it smacked of amateurism. 'So I borrowed his name and put it on as the publisher.' Together they spent a day going round bookshops in the Lakes. They got orders of 250 and then waited for repeats, which at first came in very slowly. By the time they did, Wainwright was well on with the next book.

By being his own publisher, he was able to produce the books exactly as he wanted them. He wrote and drew every page by hand, using a steel nib and pen, laying out every word and drawing as he wanted it. He had a phobia about never breaking words, which regularly happens at the end of lines of printed type, so if you look carefully at his very neat, symmetrical handwriting you'll see him fiddling the spaces so that he can squeeze all the words on each line. It took him a long time to perfect his style—he scrapped the first 100 pages after eight months and started again. He wanted it to look as neat as printer's type—with straight alignments at both the right- and left-hand side. Each page, exactly as he had drawn it, was then photographed so that the end result was like an engraving.

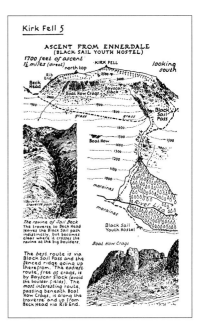

ABOVE *Wainwright's painstakingly neat handwriting and detailed pen-and-ink drawings make his books works of art and set them apart from all other walking guides.*

'I did it all in pen and ink because I've always been a pen-and-ink man. I was trained to believe that accountancy was an art, and it seemed to my juvenile reasoning in those far-off days that accountants must therefore be artists. I remember being told that every page of my ledgers should be fit for framing. I never saw anything that came out of a machine that was.'

But he did use one machine—a camera. He admitted that the drawings were a bit of a cheat because he never did them on the spot. 'A quick halt and a clear photograph were enough for me. I then drew the mountains later, based on my photographs.'

He finished his self-imposed task in exactly thirteen years as planned, in 1965, with the completion of Book Seven in the series, the *Western Fells*. These fells were the furthest away from his home in Kendal and he saved them till the end, being the only ones he couldn't get at in a day. To finish them off he had to stay in digs for a week in Whitehaven.

After printing the first four books in the series, the Kendal newspaper, the *Westmorland Gazette*, became his publisher. Then, when his final book in the fell guides series was finished in 1965, he was straight into more books, producing guides and drawings on other parts of the Lakes, such as the coast, the limestone region and the lower fells (suitable for OAPs). He had also moved to other fell regions, such as the Yorkshire Dales and Scotland. He had so far produced twenty-nine books.

He did a book of drawings in 1975 of local villages, called *Westmorland Heritage*, brought out to commemorate the end of Westmorland, which was then disappearing to become part of Cumbria. He thought the market would be very limited, as there weren't all that many Westmerians around, and decided to do only 1,000 copies. The price had to be £11 for such a small print, but he decided to sign each one and make it a limited edition, never to be reprinted. Two years later, copies of the book were changing hands at £85 each.

The day I was with him he'd just brought out another book, drawings of 19th-century Kendal. He'd based them on old photographs that had recently been discovered, glass negatives that were too worn to reproduce as photographs. That afternoon his wife was busy hanging his hundred or so originals in Abbot Hall Art Gallery, getting ready for an exhibition the next day. I went along later and bought three of them—and found I had to sign the cheque to 'Animal Rescue Cumbria'.

In Book One of his fell guides he had explained in his personal note at the end that he wasn't doing the book for material gain—just for his own pleasure. By Book Seven he had had to admit in his final personal note that things had changed. 'Unexpectedly, it has been a profitable venture, bringing me a small fortune through the continued support of the many kind readers who have both bought and recommended the books. It is money I have not spent and do not want. These books have been a labour of love. I have had full reward in a thousand happy days on the fells. One surely does not wish to be paid in cash for love-letters.'

Instead, he had devoted himself to an animal charity. His biggest project now was to acquire a farm in the Lakes somewhere which would have land and staff and be a sanctuary for stray or unwanted animals.

It was fitting, as he pointed out in one of his books, that the proceeds from his fell guides should go back on to the fells. 'Every true fell walker develops a liking and compassion for birds and animals, the solitary walker especially for they are his only companions, and it seemed appropriate that the windfall should be used to provide a refuge in Lakeland where ailing and distressed creatures can be brought for care and attention.'

On the official writing paper of Animal Rescue Cumbria was his name as chairman—A. Wainwright, MBE.

BELOW *Wainwright's wish to establish an animal sanctuary was granted in 1984, when Animal Rescue Cumbria— the charity he helped to set up and fund— purchased suitable premises near Kendal.*

LEFT *Kendal has been an important town since the days of the Romans. Its vibrant heritage of famous people and diverse industries, including wool, shoe-making and mint cake, is well documented in a wealth of local museums and galleries.*

KENDAL, GATEWAY TO THE LAKES

Kendal is well off for galleries and museums, especially in the visual arts, a tradition that dates back to George Romney's days. He was born in south Lakeland, at Dalton-in-Furness, but received some training in Kendal, eventually returning there, where he died in 1802. In his early days, the local quality in Cumberland and Westmorland commissioned him, before he moved to London and painted the stars of the day, such as Lady Hamilton. There are still several families in Cumbria who have Romney portraits on their walls.

Kendal used to be an important wool town, a trade that flourished for six centuries. Shakespeare refers to 'Kendal Green' in *Henry IV, Part I*. It's a busy, grey-stoned, independent little market town with a population of 25,000. It likes to call itself the Gateway to the Lakes, which it is, if you come from the South as most people do, but though it has its share of tourist shops selling Kendal Mint Cake, they're almost incidental to the town's well-being. One feels that Keswick, Windermere and Ambleside would collapse if the tourists decided one year not to come, but Kendal would shrug its shoulders and carry on.

The town stands by the Kent River, a dark, tough-looking river which always seems to be swollen by flood streams from Kentmere and Longsleddale. The second dominant feature is a one-way system that takes you round and round the river for ever, without actually dropping you where you want to be. At least the local taxi drivers are honest, advising you to walk across the town as it will be quicker. There's the remains of Kendal Castle, once the seat of the Parr family, whose daughter Catherine was one of the wives of Henry VIII. The Parrs, the Bellinghams and the Stricklands were for centuries the three ruling families.

I went to visit Sizergh Castle, just south of Kendal, which has been the home of the Stricklands for over 700 years. Like other castles in Cumbria, it started as a peel tower to repel the Scots, but its best features are the Tudor Great Hall and Tudor wings, decorated with some very fine Elizabethan woodwork. The gardens

CATHERINE PARR, QUEEN OF DIPLOMACY

THE SIXTH, last and luckiest of Henry VIII's wives, Catherine Parr was the only one not to be divorced or beheaded, or to die as a result of bearing his child.

Tradition has it that Catherine Parr was born at Kendal Castle, but this is unlikely to be true: although the castle was her family's ancestral home, she was more likely to have been born in the South of England, where her ambitious father was spending more and more time at court. Equally, Catherine's mother had high aspirations for her family, and made great efforts to arrange good matches for her children. Catherine was married and widowed twice before reaching the top of the matrimonial ladder in 1543. Aged thirty-one and about to wed her true love, Sir Thomas Seymour, she caught the eye of Henry VIII who instead took her for his own.

Catherine was, from the start, more of a nurse than a lover to Henry, who was by now old, bloated and incapacitated through ill health. She also acted as an able regent while the King

ABOVE *Catherine Parr's book of devotion is housed in the town hall in Kendal, her ancestral home.*

LEFT *Catherine Parr sat for this portrait c.1545 while she was Queen of England; it is attributed to Guillim Scrotts.*

was abroad. Deeply religious, she was an enthusiastic Protestant reformer—indeed, she almost lost her life when pro-Romans implicated her in a Protestant plot. But Catherine was a diplomatic woman, and, despite the dangers inherent in Henry's court, she managed to survive not only those bent

on bringing about her downfall but also her notoriously capricious husband, who died in 1547. Sadly, the following year she succumbed to that all-too-common affliction of 16th-century women, death in childbirth, less than a year after fulfilling her long-cherished wish of marrying Sir Thomas Seymour.

and castle had a lived-in feeling, and many rooms had bits of personal tat, such as old coronation tickets, locks of people's hair, as well as valuable antiques. In one bedroom there were photographs of the present Stricklands and their children. There were flowers in the vases and clocks ticking. The castle is owned by the National Trust but, judging by that bedroom, was still used by some of the family.

RETREAT TO RYDAL

Rydal Water is just a little lake, a twin sister for Grasmere next door, nothing like big brother Windermere further along which can more than stand up for itself, despite the hordes. Wordsworth wrote a lot of verse about Rydal Water, about it being soft as a cloud, tender green, dazzling sheen, staid simplicity, that sort of stuff. He even wrote one to the laurels on Rydal called 'Adieu, Rydalian Laurels!'.

I had a marvellous day in hot sun walking on White Moss Common, my copy of Dorothy's journal in hand, looking for her favourite spots. Then I booked in for the night at Nab Cottage, a little guesthouse I had always thought an attractive place. It's halfway along the bank of Rydal Water, a fantastic setting with beautiful views from all around. From the back of the cottage your eyes rise steeply up to Nab Scar. Viewed from the other side of the lake, from Loughrigg Fell, it looks like a child's painting of the perfect cottage. It's long and low, with church-like pointed windows and a plaque above the porch dated 1702.

De Quincey himself lived here for a while, and Hartley Coleridge lodged here during the last years of his life, dying in an upper room.

Hartley, the child prodigy, had become a fellow at Oxford, but lost the fellowship for intemperance. Then he tried journalism and schoolmastering without success, returning to the Lakes to live in a series of rented rooms, drinking too much, talking too much, borrowing money from the Wordsworths and other old friends of his father's, yet he was loved by everyone for his cheerful nature, his charm and his good conversation.

Next morning, before breakfast, I walked round Rydal Water, a mystical walk in a dreamy dawn with mayflies wakening, cuckoos calling and little black slugs glistening on the paths. It was bluebell time and on Loughrigg Terrace they looked like an ethereal blanket that had dropped in the night, an unreal colour, more purple than blue.

My main object in visiting Rydal was to see Rydal Mount, Wordsworth's last home in the Lake District.

When he moved into Rydal Mount, in the spring of 1813, he was moving into yet another rented property. It was no more than two miles down the road from Grasmere, but it was a move into another life, another setting.

They had been thirteen years at Grasmere, the last two of them at the Parsonage, and the women of the household were fed up. The Parsonage was damp and the fires smoked. Most of all, they were reminded each day by the graves opposite, in Grasmere churchyard, of the deaths of two of the children,

BELOW *The author was lucky enough to visit Rydal Water when its shores were emblazoned with bluebells. Glimpsed between the trees, on the opposite shore, is Nab Cottage.*

Thomas and Catherine. Thomas had died just a few months previously and they were all very glad to get away. 'The house only reminded me of desolation, gloom, emptiness and cheerless silence,' wrote Dorothy.

Rydal Mount was a posh house with posh neighbours and the Wordsworths got very excited at the thought of furnishing it accordingly. They knew that the gentry in Ambleside of the 'calling' type would soon be popping in and they wanted to look the part. Ambleside, socially, was more elevated than Grasmere. 'We are going to have Turkey!!! carpet in the dining room and a Brussels in William's study,' wrote Dorothy to a friend. 'You stare, and the simplicity of the dear Town End cottage comes before your eyes and you are tempted to say "Are they changed, are they setting up for Fine Folks? For making parties, giving Dinners, etc etc?"'

Wordsworth himself didn't change his normal appearance, never being a one for smart clothes, and most days, wandering the countryside, he looked rather like a seedy country schoolmaster or poor curate, but their domestic life from now on was much more genteel and he made an effort if he was visiting the local nobs. They entertained much more and often gave smart parties in their drawing room. During most of their long years in Rydal, they employed two maids and a gardener.

The local nob Wordsworth was most keen to impress was Lord Lonsdale. It's strange that Wordsworth should have wanted to get mixed up with the Lowthers again, as his father's connection with them had proved so disastrous, but the present earl had long since paid off all the old debts. Wordsworth attended dinners in Kendal, at which Lord Lonsdale was in the chair. Eventually, he got onto visiting terms, spending a few days every autumn as a guest at Lowther Castle, where he met 'heaps of fine folk'. In a letter he wrote to a Cockermouth friend, apologising for not having called on him, he added 'but as you would learn I was in the carriage of the Earl of Lonsdale when I passed through Cockermouth'.

Wordsworth had now become an ardent Tory, and he supported the Lowther family's Tory nominees at election times. He had good reason to be grateful to Lord Lonsdale, because it was thanks to him that he had become financially secure in 1813, just two months before he moved into Rydal Mount. It was partly due to this bit of luck that he was able to afford a rather grander lifestyle when he did move.

He had been writing begging letters to Lord Lonsdale, going on about how he'd been unable to provide properly for his family, how the sort of literature he'd devoted his life to didn't sell. The earl said he had no jobs for Wordsworth

ABOVE Rydal Mount was Wordsworth's last and grandest home in the Lakes. He spent 37 years there, designing gardens that are little changed to this day.

at the moment, but offered him £100 a year. Wordsworth decided to wait till a proper job came up, which it did in 1813. He was made Distributor of Stamps for Westmorland.

A Distributor of Stamps was a sort of local taxman. All legal documents in those days had to bear stamp duty, and you bought the stamps locally from sub-distributors, usually local shopkeepers.

The Distributor had to tour the outlets, take in the proceeds and give out new stamps. Wordsworth thought he would make £400 a year from the job when he took over, but in the event he rarely cleared more than £200 a year. His friends were pleased, knowing it would relieve the women of a lot of domestic hardship, but it was looked upon as a sellout by many of the younger writers and poets who had earlier admired him.

Keats was very disappointed that Wordsworth had become a government man. When he met Wordsworth in London, calling on him one day, he was shocked to discover him all dressed up in knee breeches and silk stockings, just because he was to meet his government superior, the Comptroller of Stamps. Keats thought this was really creepy.

Wordsworth had become more a Lowther man than a government man.

ABOVE *This sketch of Ambleside shows the Stamp Office (centre right) where Wordsworth worked as Distributor of Stamps from 1813 to 1842.*

It's hard to realise today what enormous power one family could have over such a large area as Cumberland and Westmorland.

Life for almost everyone in Cumbria throughout the 19th century was in some way influenced by the Lowthers. No wonder Wordsworth thought he'd made it when he started weekending at Lowther Castle. He used to work in references to the Lowthers in his poetry, and even wrote poems to them. The worst is a sonnet to Lowther Castle which begins:

> *Lowther! In the majestic Pile are seen*
> *Cathedral pomp and grave, in apt accord*
> *With the baronial castle's sterner mien.*

Well, if you have a patron you've got to perform for him now and again. With a big house and a large household to support, and a smarter living style, Wordsworth needed Lonsdale, if only to secure him his stamp job.

The household, when he moved into Rydal, consisted of his wife Mary, his sister Dorothy, sister-in-law Sarah and his three surviving children, John, Dora and William. None of them was very strong and Wordsworth was always fretting about their health, which was understandable, having lost two children already.

Dora was Wordsworth's favourite. He fussed most of all over her, and she was indeed always ill—it now looks that from as early as the age of eighteen she was showing signs of tuberculosis. 'She is a complete air gauge,' wrote her mother in 1827. 'As soon as damp is felt the trouble in her throat returns.'

WORD GAMES

As for Wordsworth's poetry, today's experts, the literary critics and academics, consider that he had written all his best stuff by the time he came to Rydal, but not many were aware of it at the time, least of all William, who was turning it out in enormous quantities.

The initial excitement among the young poets and reviewers, caused by the publication of *Lyrical Ballads*, had begun to fade, but his work was reaching a wider public. The critics were extremely tough in those days, much more savage, and at much greater length, than today, and most writers took a hammering at one time.

They had it in for Wordsworth, partly because of his reactionary views and his support of High Tories like the Lowthers, and of course for some bad poetry, which had always been an essential part of Wordsworth's output. He himself never knew what was good or bad. He felt the muse coming on, and out it all came, regardless of the quality.

Keats and his friends played a rotten trick on Wordsworth in 1819. They saw advertised a forthcoming poem by Wordsworth, *Peter Bell, A Tale in Verse*, and before reading it they produced a skit on it, using the same title. Keats's publisher even got it out on the streets *before* the original. In the fake *Peter Bell, A Tale in Verse*, which is in the style of a previous Wordsworth poem, *The Idiot Boy*, they dragged in all Wordsworth's well-known rustic obsessions and language, having Peter as a leech gatherer who goes around 'poring and prosing' over the graves of other *Lyrical Ballads* characters. He ends up over a very strange grave—which turns out to be the grave of Wordsworth himself.

It was a clever bit of teasing, and it led to other wits of the day producing a spate of skits, all at the expense of Wordsworth. The first published work of Thackeray, then a student, in a Cambridge magazine, was in fact a Wordsworth parody. But Wordsworth had the last laugh. Thanks to all the publicity, the real *Peter Bell, A Tale in Verse* went into a second edition after only two weeks and became one of his better-selling poems.

Shelley did his own skit on *Peter Bell, A Tale in Verse*, but a much more savage one, writing it after he'd actually read the real one. He wasn't just upset by what Wordsworth was now writing—Mary Shelley said that some of the lines used to send him into fits of laughter—but by what he thought Wordsworth now stood for, the English Tory Establishment who were keeping the poor in their place, allowing terrible social conditions in the new towns and factories and depriving people of their rights.

De Quincey felt that Wordsworth was probably unaware of the irritation and disgust that the younger writers now had for him. After all, the great of the day, the other established figures, were rushing up to the Lakes to see him.

Eminent visitors included William Wilberforce, who arrived at Rydal with a huge party of family and servants, taking over two houses at the foot of Wordsworth's lane.

Wordsworth also made regular tours abroad. In 1820, during a four-month tour of the Continent, he visited Annette, their first meeting since their separation on Calais sands some eighteen years previously. By this time, his daughter Caroline had got married. Dorothy had planned to go to the wedding, but Napoleon escaped from Elba and mucked up her plans. Caroline now had two young girls of her own, Wordsworth's first grandchildren. Wordsworth gave them two volumes of his poetry, despite the fact that none of them could speak English. (There are direct descendants of Wordsworth living in France today, and one of the families still has one of these volumes.)

Ever since Caroline's marriage, Wordsworth had been sending her £30 a year, a generous sum, considering his English family commitments, but of course being a Distributor of Stamps had eased his burdens. In 1835 he brought the arrangement to a conclusion by settling a lump sum on her of £400.

Wordsworth was never ashamed of his French family. His close friends all knew, and it's a wonder the story never became public. Several magazines and papers of the day specialised in such gossip, and had already carried nasty tales about Wordsworth, usually about his creeping to the Lowthers or being mean with hospitality, unless he was entertaining the quality. They would have gone to town on any real scandal, or even just a hint of it, especially now that Wordsworth had become such an Establishment, moralistic figure, attracting hordes of pilgrims to worship at his Rydal home.

As early as 1816, Sarah Hutchinson in a letter talks about a party of fourteen Cambridge students who were on a walking and reading tour of the Lakes. 'I suppose most of them will find means to get a sight of the Poet before the summer is past.'

After that, it became a regular, almost round-the-year event to see handfuls of admirers arriving at Rydal, hanging around hoping for a glimpse of the great man. In July 1840 Wordsworth at last received a royal visitor at Rydal—not Victoria herself but Queen Adelaide, widow of William IV.

In 1843 he became poet laureate. Two years later he made a special trip to London for the Queen's Fancy Ball and was presented to the Queen, putting on the full court dress, with sword and cocked hat. He was a rather grand figure by now, certainly among the poets. Southey had of course died, and so had Coleridge and Scott, three of his eminent contemporaries. By one of those tragic coincidences of history, so too had all the young poets, the generation poised to take over— Keats, Shelley and Byron. Wordsworth was virtually left on his own.

In his letters Wordsworth records long fell walks until late into his seventies, and he describes how one day when he was seventy-five he helped with the hay

ABOVE *Wordsworth reached the pinnacle of his career in 1843 when he was appointed poet laureate.*

LEFT *Wordsworth
attended the colourful
Queen's Fancy Ball in
1845, depicted here in
a painting by Louis
Haghe. As poet laureate,
he was introduced to
his patron, the young
Queen Victoria.*

in his field. This field, just beside his garden, was bought by him in 1826 when it looked as though the owners of Rydal Mount were going to evict him, wanting the house for their own family. Wordsworth threatened to build a brand-new house in the field, right beside the house, and they relented. He later gave the field to Dora, and they knew it as Dora's Field, which is its name to this day.

On his seventy-fourth birthday there was a party given in the garden at Rydal Mount to which all the children in the neighbourhood were invited, some three hundred of them, and they each got an orange, a piece of gingerbread and a hard-boiled pace (Easter) egg. (Cumbrian children still get similar eggs at Easter time.) Wordsworth to the end was a great lover of children, and all his contemporaries noted it, but was he still in touch with the ordinary people in his old age? Had he perhaps moved away from the rustic characters, the rural workers, he had written about so often in his early poetry?

One of the most interesting bits of journalism that the great Canon Rawnsley did was to go round, some thirty years after Wordsworth's death, and interview all the people he could find who ever knew or worked with the Wordsworths. This was his famous 'Reminiscences of Wordsworth among the Peasantry of Westmoreland', with which he delighted the members of Keswick Lecture Society and which he later published.

One of the people Canon Rawnsley went to see was a publican who in his youth had been the gardener's boy at Rydal.

'He was ter'ble thrang with visitors and folks, but if he could git awa fra them for a spell, he was out upon his gres walk; and then he would set his head a bit forrad and put his hands behint his back. And then he would start a bumming and it was bum, bum, bum, bum, stop; then bum, bum, bum, reet down till t'other end; and then he'd set down and git a bit o' paper out and write a bit; and then he

ABOVE *Brightly painted
hard-boiled eggs, known
as pace eggs (from the
Hebrew Pesach meaning
'Passover'), are a
traditional Easter gift
in Cumbria despite
today's mass marketing
of chocolate eggs.*

git up, and goa on bumming. I suppose, ya kna, the bumming helped him out a bit. His lips was always goain' whoale time he was upon the gres walk.'

Although Canon Rawnsley had gone to talk to them about Wordsworth, almost everyone brought the subject round to Hartley Coleridge, or Li'le Hartley as he was known. They all liked him much better. 'Wudsworth was quite different fra Li'le Hartley. Hartley allus hed a bit of a smile or a twinkle in his face, but Wudsworth was not lovable i't face by nea means. He niver exed fowk aboot their wark, nor noticed t' flocks or nowt.'

Cumbrians pride themselves on not dissembling. Professor Geoffrey Tillotson thinks the memories give a good account of Wordsworth in his middle and later years, living in a region but not fully of it, withdrawn from the sort of people who'd inspired poems like 'The Idiot Boy' and 'Goody Blake'.

From the evidence of his own letters, Wordsworth always gave to beggars, sometimes the same ones twice a day, but it was obvious that he preferred the world as it had been, in its old class divisions. He was completely against things like the Reform Bill or campaigns to give the working classes more power and freedom.

REFORM, NOT REVOLUTION

THE SYSTEM OF 'one person, one vote' is fairly recent in Britain, and in the early 19th century such democracy was almost inconceivable. At that time the right to vote was not only haphazard, differing vastly between counties and boroughs, but it was also restricted to male property owners. In so-called 'Potwalloper' boroughs, only householders with a fireplace on which to boil a pot were enfranchised. Just as arbitrary was the distribution of Members of Parliament. For instance, the rotten borough of Old Sarum, with its seven voters, was represented by the same number of MPs (two) as were the 5,000 voters of Liverpool.

Despite such glaring inequalities, many members of the upper and middle classes continued to oppose even moderate reform, fearing it would open the floodgates to further changes. But the ruling party, the Whigs, believed that immediate reform was necessary to stave off insurrection: the working classes, encouraged by a succession

of European revolutions and agitated by a domestic economic slump, looked ready to revolt.

Reform finally arrived in a Bill in 1832, and although the public were initially pacified, many were disappointed with its minimal changes: the working class and large sections of the lower middle class were not enfranchised; many constituencies were still unfairly represented; open (as

LEFT *A contemporary cartoon entitled* Four Weighty Authorities on Reform *by C. J. Grant satirises the various political positions that prevailed in advance of the first Reform Bill of 1832.*

opposed to secret) voting ensured that bribery and corruption remained rife; and wealthy landowners continued to hold the reins of power. But in the long term the 1832 Reform Bill proved to be of the utmost importance, catalysing as it did further reform: over the rest of the century the franchise gradually widened, and the secret ballot was introduced in 1872. The British public would have to wait until 1928, though, before everyone, including women, had the vote.

The first death in his household was Sarah Hutchinson's in 1835. The whole house had been struck down with flu, and Dora and Dorothy had looked the most seriously ill; then Sarah suddenly weakened and died very quickly of what looks like rheumatic fever.

Dorothy recovered physically from the worst of her illness, but not mentally. For the next twenty years of her life, her mind and her memory had gone. She had long spells of crouching over the fire, both winter and summer, in unbearable heat, and eventually became confined to a wheelchair.

In 1835 Wordsworth's daughter Dora was proposed to by Edward Quillinan, a retired army captain. He was a person of charm but with no settled home, no visible means of support, no profession apart from a bit of poetry and some translations from the Portuguese.

Dora was by now thirty-one. She had devoted her life so far to her father and the family and she very much wanted to marry Quillinan. For four years Wordsworth refused his consent to the engagement. She'd always been delicate and marrying Quillinan would be giving his daughter up to 'a rough chance'. Then Wordsworth was talked into it by the family, and Dora was eventually married in 1841 in Bath.

Dora's health was not improved by the wandering life Quillinan led her, though she did feel better during a spell in Portugal. They returned in 1846 to live in the Lakes, renting a house near Rydal. But in 1847 Dora caught a bad cold. She never recovered, and died several months later. Wordsworth was distraught, overwhelmed with grief for many months.

In March 1850, Wordsworth developed pleurisy. Mary came to his bedside to tell him he was dying.

Wordsworth died on April 23, 1850, Shakespeare's and England's day. He had celebrated his eightieth birthday just a couple of weeks previously. Dorothy lasted another five years, dying in 1855 at eighty-three; Mary lived until 1859, dying at eighty-eight.

Mary's last literary task, on William's death, was to take his autobiographical poem from its resting place, where it had lain untouched for eleven years, and prepare it for the publisher. The dedication was to S. T. Coleridge, as it had been when he'd begun it some fifty years previously, but it had never been given a title. It was Mary who named it *The Prelude*.

Rydal Mount is a lovely surprise. You can understand how pleased the Wordsworths were to move into it, after all the problems with their Grasmere houses, and why they stayed there for over thirty-seven years. The rooms are light and airy, gracious and spacious.

In the doorway are some tiles on the floor given to Wordsworth by his great friend Henry Crabb Robinson. They spell the word *Salve*—a smart greeting for all classically trained visitors. There's some fine furniture in the house and portraits of Wordsworth, Dorothy, Coleridge, Christopher Wordsworth (brother), Queen Victoria and the Prince of Wales (presented to William by the Queen when he became poet laureate) and Robert Burns (presented to William by Burns's sons). The four-and-a-half-acre garden is kept very much as the Wordsworths had it.

ABOVE *Wordsworth and Mary Hutchinson had been friends since childhood, but it was not until 1802 that they married. She was to outlive him and three of their children.*

There's not much else to see in the way of buildings as there's not really a village, just a church and a few houses, but the church is worth a visit as Wordsworth helped to choose the site for it. Behind the church is Dora's Field, which was left to the National Trust in 1935 by Gordon Wordsworth, the poet's grandson. In the spring, it's a mass of flowers, especially daffodils.

A WALK AROUND THE GRAVES

I went to visit the Grasmere parish church, St Oswald's. At the gates there's a little cottage announcing 'Sarah Nelson, Original Celebrated Gingerbread'. Gingerbread has a long history in Grasmere. The floor of the church was earthen until 1841 and every year for centuries, so the earliest records of the church show, there was a rushbearing ceremony in which rushes were brought from the lakeside and laid on the floors. Every year in August the ceremony is repeated, this time by children, and, as in the old days, they are rewarded with a piece of gingerbread.

The church from the outside is rather blank and boring, being roughcast and featureless, and the gravestones of Wordsworth and company are equally blank. They lie in a corner of the churchyard, just beside the little River Rothay, in the spot Wordsworth himself chose, near where he planted eight yew trees. The very simplicity of his stone and inscription, 'William Wordsworth 1850, Mary Wordsworth 1859' is rather striking. Beside them is a veritable army of

ABOVE *A visit to Grasmere would not be complete without sampling the sweet wares of its famous gingerbread shop.*

BELOW *The rushbearing ceremony in Grasmere is such an important event that special gingerbread is baked for the occasion.*

Wordsworths, almost the whole cast list of his life, and it provides good sport for anyone with a bit of Wordsworthian lore, working out who Edward Quillinan was, or Catherine Wordsworth and Thomas Wordsworth. William Wordsworth junior and his family are also there.

Inside, the church is much more attractive. It has beautifully whitewashed arches and a most unusual roof of open wooden rafters, the upper timbers being supported by the lower timbers. They date back to 1562.

Wordsworth described the interior faithfully, very much as it is today, in Book Five of 'The Excursion':

> Not raised in nice proportions was the pile,
> But large and massy; for duration built;
> With pillars crowded, and the roof upheld
> By naked rafters intricately crossed,
> Like leafless underboughs in some thick wood,
> All withered by the depth of shade above.

Wordsworth wasn't a great churchgoer in his young days, but in later years, now a solid local Establishment worthy, he and his family walked to church most Sundays at Grasmere. The church is much as it was in Wordsworth's day,

LEFT *Each year on the Saturday nearest to August 5, local children dressed in traditional costume carry rushes through the village to St Oswald's Church.*

LEFT *The floor of St Oswald's is now paved, but before 1841 it was bare earth, laid annually with rushes.*

RIGHT *The simple, unadorned graves of the Wordsworth family can be found in Grasmere churchyard.*

with the same bells, though stone slabs have now been laid on the bare earth. In his day, rushes were more than necessary on the bare floors as aisle burials were still allowed.

Wordsworth and his family spent two years living in Grasmere rectory, from 1811 to 1813, before moving to Rydal, though at the time it was known as the Parsonage, the rector living elsewhere. Wordsworth did not retain happy memories of the Grasmere Parsonage. He thought it was the damp that helped cause Thomas's death. Luckily for the present inhabitants, the rectory is now a lot better to live in, having been completely renovated and raised five feet to avoid flooding.

I knocked at the rectory door. Dr Richard Bevan, the rector, sat throughout our chat with his coat on—despite the fact that he was in front of an electric fire with all its bars on. Even raising the floor and putting in a new drainage system hadn't made the five-bedroom rectory much easier to heat than in Wordsworth's day. 'This part of the valley still gets totally flooded. One night last November we had six and a half inches of rain—just in one night!' They all seemed obsessed by the weather in Grasmere, as in Wordsworth's day. The normal greeting, when two locals met, was, 'Managing to keep warm?'

RIGHT *Thanks to the fervent campaigns of local residents and celebrities against development plans, the original character of the Rothay Hotel in Grasmere, now known as The Wordsworth Hotel, is set to remain intact for the next few years at least.*

Dr Bevan was active in all aspects of Grasmere life. As president of the Grasmere Village Society, he was playing a leading part in trying to save the Rothay Hotel, the large, eccentric-looking hotel next door to the churchyard. A Newcastle builder had bought the hotel and eleven-acre site in order to redevelop it, planning to put up holiday flatlets. He'd got planning permission, much to the horror of the inhabitants, who'd organised a national appeal to buy and preserve it—roping in such figures as Chris Bonington, Joss Naylor and Melvyn Bragg. 'We have to stop such new building. This is a Wordsworth shrine. Wordsworth himself was against the encroachment of man on nature.' A week later a large anonymous donation arrived and they secured the hotel at last.

Dr Bevan went almost every day to look at Wordsworth's grave and thought he could feel his presence everywhere around him. 'I've looked at his picture so many times that I feel I know his features. His face is so vivid to me, as if I really have met him. I would love to have done. Like him, I see spiritual reality from natural objects and I know I would gain insights from talking to him.'

One of the highlights of the year is a Wordsworth summer school which is held in the Tithe Barn, part of the rectory. 'They talk and eat Wordsworth and it's the most incredible resurrection of the Wordsworth spirit that you can imagine. You see that Wordsworth is a real force in the world, a spiritual power.'

ABOVE *Jonathan Wordsworth, a descendant of the poet, conducts an auction at the annual Wordsworth summer conference.*

On the other hand, Wordsworth has been parodied and criticised and ridiculed almost from the moment he was published. 'Why don't you hire somebody to abuse you?' Wordsworth remarked to a friend. 'For myself, I begin to fear that I should soon be forgotten if it were not for my enemies.' Yet implicit in most of the parodies has been knowledge of his work and even affection. Hartley Coleridge did one of the earliest unkind versions of the 'Lucy' poems:

> *He lived amidst th'untrodden ways,*
> *To Rydal Lake that lead;*
> *A bard whom there were none to praise*
> *And very few to read.*

It was Hartley, too, who first put his finger on the two-sided Wordsworth. 'What a mighty genius is the Poet Wordsworth! What a dull proser is W. W. Esqre of Rydal Mount, Distributor of Stamps.' The most famous version of this thought is, of course, the one by J. K. Stephen, which first appeared in *Granta* in 1891:

> *There are two Voices; one is of the deep*
> *And one is an old half-witted sheep*
> *And, Wordsworth, both are thine…*

The very idea of a Jekyll and Hyde poet is probably a reason why he is still being studied to this day. How could a person of such genius write such bad verse? Meanwhile, research continues, pilgrims gather, passers-by come in out of the rain.

GAMES AND THE GOURMET

GRASMERE IS more than just Wordsworth. The biggest single event in Grasmere's year—in fact the biggest single event of its kind in Lakeland's year—is the Grasmere Sports. Over ten thousand people turn up to watch the fun and games, which must make it the most popular old English sports day in the whole country. It's very much a rural occasion, like an overgrown village fête, with races for boys and girls as well as traditional sports that are peculiar to the Lake District. It's always held on the third Thursday after the first Monday in August.

I'd waited all year for it, like most of Cumbria, and Grasmere as usual was completely taken over. It's hard to believe that one small village, with a population of only 800, can grow so huge in a single day. You realise then why the bowl shape of Grasmere Vale, which can seem claustrophobic on a dull day, is so perfect for open-air sports. It's one of nature's amphitheatres.

There are sports all over Lakeland, from June to September, and some people, having once been to Grasmere, prefer the little, out-of-the-way sports, where you can park and wander and actually see everything that's going on. Each one is always on the same day each year—such as the Thursday before the first Monday in August for Ambleside Sports, the third Saturday in September for Egremont Crab Fair, and the last Wednesday in August for the Ennerdale Show.

It's the Norse blood that is supposed to have had such a big influence on the Cumbrians' passion for outdoor sports. Ever since local records have been kept, some sort of annual running and jumping, hunting and chasing, pushing and shoving, with or without the use of animals, has been a great feature of the Cumbrian year.

Over the years, several sports have died out. I used to hear tales as a boy that they were still practising cockfighting in secret meetings out at Dalston. Cockfighting was legally outlawed in 1835, and it was a savage, though ancient, sport. Silver spurs used to be tied on the cocks, and they would fight each other to the death. Bull baiting, prohibited by law in the same year, was also very popular.

A bull would be tied by a chain and a pack of hungry dogs was then set to attack it. The bull would chase round and round, tossing and killing a few dogs, till it eventually dropped dead from exhaustion.

Gurning is a speciality of Egremont Crab Fair, a fair that dates back to 1267, and consists of trying to pull the most awful or the funniest face. You put your head through a horse collar and grin, or gurn.

The thing about Grasmere Sports, which has been held since 1852, is that they have the best of the truly Cumbrian sports. It's been greatly commercialised by the bookies who are there by the score, shouting the odds. The competitors are professional as well, in that there are money prizes, though you could never get rich on them and they all have other jobs. But it means that true amateurs, like Joss Naylor, the best fell runner of all, have never taken part in Grasmere's fell

ABOVE Serene Grasmere Vale resounds each August to the roars and cheers of Grasmere Sports. Locals and tourists alike flock to the vale to see the cream of the North's sportsmen tackle such tests of strength as fell racing and wrestling.

race, or the Guides' Race, as they call it. This merits the best prize of the day, usually about £75 for the winner and, as with the flat races, the competitors come from all over the North of England and Scotland. It's a grand sight, as they all surge out of the field and up the hill opposite. You can see how steep it is, yet the best ones dash up and down in under fifteen minutes.

The other two big events, hound trailing and wrestling—both even more Cumbrian—are a bit harder for the outsider to really appreciate, at least to understand the finer points, but they are nonetheless very exciting.

Tony Bragg had come to Grasmere for the hound trailing. He was a driver from Skelwith Bridge and I had met him earlier in the year, exercising his dog while I was walking in the Langdales. The year before he had won third prize at Grasmere with his hound Screamer. The prize was only £12.50, not much when he could spend £6 a week on food for Screamer. His wife felt like screaming herself, he said, whenever she found out that he'd sneaked yet another bottle of sherry into the house, just to feed his hound.

RIGHT *Hounds eager to follow the scent of a purpose-laid trail lurch forward at the starting line.*

In the days of cockfighting they used to feed the fighting cocks on what was called cock loaf. When the cocks killed each other, their carcasses were then thrown to the trail hounds, who therefore got double grub, cocks and the loaves inside them. All hound-trail enthusiasts in Cumbria have their own secret cock-loaf mix which they give to their dogs.

'I usually bake mine when the wife's out. It weighs only 2lb, but it costs me £1.40. It's a sort of fruit loaf, made with wholemeal flour, plus sherry or port. I've used up three bottles of sherry in the last seven weeks. You bake it till it's really hard.'

The hounds follow a scent over a circular course, starting and finishing in the same place. The scent, or trail, is laid with a mixture of aniseed and paraffin, which the dogs appear to love. Two men, called trailers, who know the local area and conditions, lay the trail with a rag soaked in the mixture, dragging it round the course, over fences and walls and up hillsides. The trails for dogs over two years are about six to eight miles in length (shorter than they were in the old days) and about half that for puppies.

It's been a popular sport in Cumbria for well over a century and is presumed to have started when huntsmen laid down trails, dragging fox skins, in order to teach young hounds how to follow a scent. Local associations of hound trailers joined themselves together in 1906 to form the Hound Trailing Association, which governs the sport today. There are trails all over Cumbria, from March to October, many of them associated with the big sports meetings, like Grasmere, but mostly they take place on their own. They draw good crowds—not least because it's a betting sport. You often see little huddles of rather furtive-looking farmers standing by the roadsides in out-of-the-way dales, heads together, their hounds at their feet, haggling away, comparing notes, working out strategies.

It takes specialist knowledge to train a good hound, but it takes no knowledge to get pleasure out of watching a trail. The hounds strain at the leash, whining and yelping, till they're released, race towards the distant hills, and then disappear completely from sight over the fell tops. Other sports continue, down in the arena, till there's a great shout when the first hounds can be seen returning. The owners yell and whistle and often wave rattles, trying to will their particular dog to be first over the line and win the trail.

There was a bit of fiddling in the old days, with favourites being drugged by rival owners or lured off the course, but naturally, everyone says that's all stopped today. One ploy, in the bad old days, which took a bit of bribery, was to get the trailer to lay the trail wearing your boots. Halfway round the trail, he'd pick up the aniseed rag for two hundred yards or so, leaving a stretch with no scent. When the hounds came rushing round, they would grind to a halt, unable to find the trail—while your dog went racing on, following the smell of your old boots. Very cunning.

ABOVE *Binoculars are an essential accessory for anxious dog owners and punters at a hound trail.*

Something certainly went wrong when I watched the senior hound trail at Grasmere, a most unusual occurrence. Nearly half the hounds went off on the wrong scent. Some officials blamed sightseers, tramping over the trail and splitting the scent. The Earl of Lonsdale, who was the starter and judge, thought it was the hounds' own fault, some of them trying to be too crafty. 'It looks as if one hound led half a dozen off the scent, thinking he knew the trail better than the trailers. These dogs are known as "guessers". In these circumstances we declared the trail void.'

'It was a real mess-up,' said Tony Bragg. 'I think Screamer would have won. He's had a good season—second at Keswick, third at Patterdale. It was a great shame.'

ABOVE *Prize-winning Cumberland and Westmorland wrestler Tom Harrington (right) battles it out with an opponent at the Grasmere Sports.*

WRESTLING WITH THE LOCALS

Perhaps the most important event at Grasmere every year is the Cumberland and Westmorland wrestling, at least it always *sounds* very important. Fell runners and hound trailers are quite modest in their claims. Only the wrestlers (and gurners) proclaim their champions as *world* champions.

That year Tom Harrington was the best-known name in Cumberland and Westmorland wrestling. He held three world titles, each at a different weight. Nobody in the history of the sport has held more than that at one time, though there have been champions in the past who have won more matches in one season. The previous season he had had forty-six wins, including three world titles. Ted Dunglinson, now retired, had won fifty-two matches in his best season. So Tom still had some way to go.

He was eleven stone, which is why his record as a heavyweight was not quite as brilliant as he would have liked. He very often competed out of his weight class, trying to win even more titles, wrestling against blokes almost twice his weight.

Tom was employed as a farm worker about four miles south of Carlisle. He was thirty-three, with sticking-out flaxen hair and a country-lad complexion. He wore spectacles and didn't look at all strong or aggressive, more like a rural David Hockney. He looked like a walkover for any complete stranger mad enough to challenge him.

When Cumberland and Westmorland people talk about having world championships, they really mean it. It is indeed open to the big wide world. The rules are utterly simple. You start by clasping hands behind the neck and shoulder of your opponent. The first one to unclasp his hands, or touch the ground with any part of his body, is the loser. There are no more rules. You can kick if you like, although they tend not to. The skill is in twisting your opponent so that he touches the ground. Using the buttock as a lever is one of the best-known moves—or chips, as the movements are called. You see headlines in the *Cumberland News* like 'Tom's Winning Buttock'.

Judo experts often have a go, or big strong men who've done well in other sports, like boxing or freestyle wrestling, but in all Tom's years he'd never seen anyone come out of the crowd and do well. 'He might be lucky and get one fall, but they never win. You have to practise. I'm very nimble on my feet and I've got these long arms. It's not strength in Cumberland and Westmorland that matters most, it's speed.'

He was born in Loweswater, where his father was a tenant farmer; then they moved near Bootle in west Cumberland. Tom was one of eleven children, which he thought was lucky. 'Being a lot of us, we wrustled amongst oursells.' He remembered his father challenging boxers at country fairs. Tom had enrolled at Bootle Academy at fourteen. This is not some fancy seat of learning but what the wrestlers call their winter indoor meeting place. The outdoor season, wrestling on grass at village shows, is from May to October. In the winter, they practise inside in local halls.

Cumberland and Westmorland-style wrestling goes back at least two hundred years. It's confined to the northern counties—Cumbria, Lancashire, Northumber-

land, bits of Yorkshire, and the southern Scottish counties. In a season, Tom goes as far north as Luss on Loch Lomond for their Highland Games, which has a Cumberland and Westmorland section; east to Ponteland near Newcastle; and south to Blackburn in Lancashire. But the greatest number of matches are in Cumbria, especially to the west.

You can wrestle at some shows in jeans and a jumper, but most Cumbrian shows demand the proper costume. Tom would always wear it anyway, as he was proud of it. The proper costume is long-john white underpants worn with a velvet centrepiece (this can be a swimming costume, if you're hard up), plus a white vest and socks. Fancy costumes, by which they mean embroidery all over your codpiece, is left to you, but at the big sports, like Grasmere, this is actively encouraged, as the public like to see it. At many sports, such as Grasmere, there are extra prizes for the best costume.

There are seven weights in all—10½, 11, 12, 12½, 13, 14 stone and heavy-weight—plus four categories for boys. Each year the ruling body of the sport decides, among all the different places holding C. and W. matches, which one will have the honour of staging one of the world champion events. This way, by spreading it out, even little villages can stage a world meeting. The really big glamour shows, like Grasmere, don't need to stage world champion events to bring in the crowds. Just winning any championship at Grasmere is considered the big time.

Tom Harrington was technically a professional wrestler as he got money for it, but he'd never made enough in one season to cover his petrol, what with having to trail round the North of England all summer. But he had got sixty cups he'd won outright and could keep for ever.

On that day he had mixed success. He only reached the third round in the heavyweight championship, which it was his major aim to win, being thrown by the eventual winner. In the twelve-stone class he was again thrown by the eventual winner, this time in the semifinal, when he was thrown by his own brother, Joseph. He did, however, win the eleven-stone Grasmere championship. So that was something.

A TALE OF TWO HOTELS

One of the most amazing changes in the Lake District in recent years has been the food. The hotel that started the transformation is called Sharrow Bay, and it's on the banks of Ullswater.

Today, there are two hotels in the Lakes that regularly win the top awards from the experts and are always being described as the best place to stay in England, Western Europe, the World. There can't be a current eating guide to the United Kingdom that doesn't have Sharrow Bay and Miller Howe in their all-time greats.

There are now about five or six other hotels in the Lakes with similar pretensions, who also feature in the best food guides, but the Sharrow Bay–Miller Howe methods are very hard, and very expensive, to follow.

Their style positively drips good taste. You get nothing so vulgar as a reception desk, a bar or any hotel-like notices. You're meant to think you're in an exquisite country house. It's such a performance that at times they can be parodies of themselves. At Sharrow Bay they can garland a simple dish of vegetables with so many flowers you think you're in Kew Gardens. At Miller Howe they dim lights, turn on the effects and present the meal like a five-act play at the National Theatre. But whether you approve or not, they've set themselves enormously high standards in food, surroundings and service. The excitement in each of them, among the staff and guests, before dinner every evening is unbelievable.

BELOW *The author treated himself to the luxuries and gourmet food of Miller Howe.*

Francis Coulson opened Sharrow Bay in 1948, having travelled up from Euston with his cooking pans hanging from the haversack on his back. His partner, Brian Sack, who later joined him, was formerly a surveyor. Coulson had been in the theatre. They were both very much amateurs, starting with little money and experience, building it all up painfully slowly.

Sharrow Bay is an isolated country house on the shores of Ullswater, a sensational situation as far as views are concerned, with the dining room looking straight up the lake; it's on the remote side of Ullswater, the Howtown side, away from civilisation.

Miller Howe has equally good views, this time over Windermere, though it's on the busy side which is not so quiet for guests. Like Sharrow Bay, the building itself is basically rather ordinary, just one of the many Edwardian summer houses that litter the lakesides. It's the internal transformation that has made them seem so rich and gilded, bursting with antiques, precious knick-knacks, and the heaviest of soft furnishings.

The bedrooms have individual names, not numbers. At Sharrow Bay they're named after family and friends. Miller Howe has the names of local lakes.

I've stayed at Sharrow Bay many times, always with enormous pleasure, so this time, as I completed my circuit back to Windermere, I booked into Miller Howe, never having spent a night there before. There was no glass of sherry in the bedroom, as there always is at Sharrow Bay, but I found binoculars, Scrabble, dictionary, puzzle, and the collected *Punch* for 1905 (original volume).

There was a terrific view when I opened the French windows and stepped onto my private balcony, which was why someone had provided binoculars. I won't bother listing the items of furniture. I gave up after counting twenty-nine pieces of decorated china or glassware. Nothing gets stolen, so I was told, though it would be so easy. In the early days, when they had far less clutter—sorry, I mean objets d'art—an occasional item did disappear. Now, with so much, people must become overawed by it all.

Downstairs I found myself in a huge leather chair in a large, rather formal, lounge, wondering if I'd wandered into the Harvard Club in New York. I was surrounded by Americans, the sort who are more tweedy and more gentlemanly and more English than the English. That evening, by my estimate, 90 per cent of the guests were Americans.

In the dining room I had a seat next to the main window, giving me a panoramic view of the lake. The waiters hovered, charming for England, their smiles as well pressed as the creases in their fawn slacks. Their lovely green blazers, on close inspection, had the name Miller Howe and a pestle-and-mortar symbol embroidered on them.

The man of the match, star of the show, creator of the words and the music, was John Tovey. I arranged to speak to Mr Tovey after dinner, and I went with him for coffee at his own home, about a mile away along the lakeside. He was a bachelor and was living alone.

He told me that he was a local lad and came from Barrow, an industrial town in south Cumbria. He had a job as secretary to the boss of a hotel on Windermere, moved on to waiting and cooking, and then to becoming a manager. In 1970 he worked for six weeks at Sharrow Bay.

Miller Howe began in 1971 when he bought the house for £26,500. He put up half the money, and a sleeping partner put up the rest. He expected to be 100 per cent full from June until the end of October. April and May had been only 99.9 per cent full. You needed to book at least six days ahead to get a meal and six weeks ahead to get a bed.

There were twelve bedrooms, seating for seventy, and he had a staff of fourteen, eight of whom had been with him for six years. He kept them on all year, and when the hotel was closed, from January to April, he still had to pay them. He would get them painting and decorating and then he would be off round the world, taking his staff with him. He was a great lad for publicity and promotion, and during the last close season he had taken them on a tour of the States, demonstrating the art of English Country House Cooking.

BELOW *John Tovey worked hard to make Miller Howe a success. He has retired since the author's stay, but the hotel remains hugely popular.*

Before breakfast the next morning, as the guests came down the stairs, he was standing in the hall, bouncy as ever, handing out glasses of Buck's Fizz. Just the thing to perk you up for another hard day's eating.

PICTURE PERFECT

I got a taxi to Windermere station, back to where I began. The taxi driver said that ten years before, when he was thirty-three, he had been an engineer working for General Motors in Liverpool. He'd been to the Lakes on holidays, thought it was magical, and decided that was where he wanted to spend his life, not in a Liverpool factory.

The Lake District is full of such newcomers, people who've fallen in love with the Lakes and decided to live there, and a surprising number of them come when they're still relatively young, dropouts from the rat race who are willing to take any old job. Like Coleridge, Southey, De Quincey, Ruskin, Beatrix Potter, Walpole, Arthur Ransome and thousands more, they feel they will get spiritual uplift from the lakes and fells. Most of the newcomers are, of course, artists at heart, even though they may be driving Co-op vans or taxis.

Until the middle of the 18th century, however, outsiders never visited the Lakes, and the population at large, if they ever thought about the Lakes, had curiously medieval notions of a land of monsters and falling rocks, wild beasts and frightening legends. Adventurous gentlemen went instead to the Alps for their scenery, but around 1770 (when Wordsworth was born) guidebooks and writings about the Lakes started to appear, and it soon became fashionable to explore one's own native wild areas, such as Scotland, Wales and the Lakes.

The first visitors to the Lakes looked upon themselves as explorers, writing in their books about the terrifying sights, the valleys that simply couldn't be entered, the mountains that were impossible to pass, but very soon the explorers gave way to tourists.

One big-selling and highly influential early guidebook was by a cleric, the Reverend William Gilpin. His book was called *Observations, relative chiefly to Picturesque Beauty, made in the year 1772, on several parts of England; particularly the Mountains and Lakes of Cumberland and Westmoreland.*

They're exceedingly handsome volumes, with hand-coloured aquatints of idealised Lakes' settings. The whole object of Gilpin, and his followers, was to find the Picturesque, the sort of beauty that would be effective in a picture. Everything is described in strictly visual terms, deciding whether views should be painted or done in pencil, laying down rules of what was and was not a picturesque view. He divided mountains according to their shape, their light and shade, saying whether they would make a good background to a painting or not.

This passion for the Picturesque was a tremendous fashion at the turn of the century. Visitors would come to the Lakes, armed with guidebooks like Gilpin's, and head for the 'stations'—the places he had decreed were the best viewing spots—to admire the view, then perhaps get out their painting materials, or pencils if Gilpin had decreed it was a better pencil view.

Gilpin was himself a Cumbrian, born at Scaleby Castle, near Carlisle, and educated at Cumberland's public school, St Bees, before going to Oxford. He took over a school at Cheam—and did so well out of it that he retired at fifty-three, and took a living in the New Forest. Every summer he did a long tour, to places like the Lakes or Scotland, which he turned into his books, giving the public the benefit of his judgments, marking Loch Lomond or Buttermere so many out of ten, criticising mountaintops for not being smooth or lakes for not having enough bends, or islands for not being formal enough.

These and other early guidebooks brought in the first visitors, and Wordsworth, when he returned to live in the Lakes in 1799, was often moaning about the number of tourists that were now arriving, longing for the good old quiet days before the Lakes had been discovered.

The closing of most of Europe from the turn of the century, due to the Napoleonic Wars, meant that even more tourists came north for their holidays and excitement, and to experience the Picturesque. The turnpike roads were being improved, hotels were growing up, and the rush to the Lakes was soon

THE PICTURESQUE

NATURE, to the medieval mind, was a hostile and uncontrollable force: forests were inhabited by wolves and bandits, the seas harboured horrifying creatures, and mountains marked the end of the known world. But by the 18th century, man was learning to tame nature. Towns began to creep across formerly rural areas. Urban folk could now look at the countryside with more detachment; no longer a part of it, they could enjoy the rural landscape as if it were a picture. This new way of seeing was termed the Picturesque.

It was a Cumbrian, William Gilpin, who established the fashion for the Picturesque in England. On summer tours around the country, he compiled a series of journals famous for judging the landscape on its visual merits, ignoring any emotions the scene might arouse. Accompanying the text were aquatints, in which figures were used to show the scale of a scene and to depict rural life.

Wordsworth shared the Picturesque movement's interest in rural life and

ABOVE *J. M. W. Turner's Picturesque view of Keswick Lake (now Derwent Water).*

grandeur, despite being out of sympathy with its detached view of nature. His rustic figures—shepherds, beggars, labourers—provide a poetic counterpoint to the Picturesque artists. Wordsworth's great artistic contemporary, J. M. W. Turner, was commissioned in 1825 to paint a series of watercolours for engravings that were published as 'Picturesque Views in England and Wales'.

The watercolours—slightly more carefully arranged, perhaps, than his more familiar scenes, in keeping with the Picturesque tendency—feature human figures fairly prominently, and dazzle with golden sunrises, summer sunlight, shimmering haze and luminous mist.

being satirised in London magazines and on the stage. In 1798 there was a comic opera in London called *The Lakers*, which was what the new breed of tourists were being called, and it contained the following song:

Each season there delighted myriads throng,
To pass their times these charming scenes among
For pleasure, knowledge, many thither hie,
For fashion some, and some… they know not why.

After the Picturesque, the next craze was for the Gothic Horror, when ruins were the big thing to go and see. Scott's novels and poems helped fire people's imagination to look for old castles and haunted abbeys, and to visit the scenes of ancient legends. If you didn't have an old ruin for visitors to gape at, you built a new ruin. In the Lake District there was a gentleman called Colonel Braddyll, who built his own hermitage in his garden near Ulverston and employed a full-time hermit who lived in it for twenty years and never cut his hair. The same colonel turned one

GOTHIC EXTRAVAGANZA

LEFT *Lanercost Priory in Cumbria, built 1169–1220, epitomises the ruins that thrilled 18th-century tourists with their sinister beauty.*

RIGHT *The first illustrated version of Mary Shelley's* Frankenstein, *published in 1831, shows the awful moment when life stirs in the creature.*

A S THE TREND STARTED in the 18th century for visiting ruins, and people began to see a thrilling new beauty in the dilapidated and the desolate, so a new literary genre was born: the Gothic novel.

The word 'gothic' originally meant anything destructive of classical style. Classicism in art and architecture was at its height in the early 1700s, but towards the end of the century an anti-Classicist movement began to take hold, and simplicity, proportion and restraint were abandoned in favour of the wild and savage.

The first Gothic novel is acknowledged to be Horace Walpole's *The Castle of Otranto* (1764). Another early author was Mrs Radcliffe, whose book *The Mysteries of Udolpho* (1794) can also claim to be the first proper thriller. Both of these authors were highly influential on Sir Walter Scott, whose novels and poems echo the creaks and whispers of ghostly ruins and medieval castles with their hidden passageways and dark dungeons. In 1818, Mary Shelley produced the classic Gothic horror story *Frankenstein, or the Modern Prometheus*, a dire warning to man not to try to emulate the work of his Creator.

Although many Gothic novels are literary works of art, the craze produced many sensationalist stories designed merely to thrill the reader and freeze the blood with supernatural happenings, ghostly manifestations and crimes of unspeakable horror. But crude as these effects might be, the horrors of the Gothic can be seen as an early attempt to explore the primitive fears of the subconscious mind, at a time when advances in science meant that people were no longer taking for granted the existence of God.

of Derwent Water's islands into an 18th-century version of Disneyland, combining the fashion for the Picturesque and the Gothic by building a mock church and fort as well as his own Druids' circle, based on the Castlerigg stones.

Wordsworth, for all that he moaned about the tourists, in the end did more than anyone else to pull them in. His poems never sold all that well, compared with Scott's, but his *Description of the Scenery of the Lakes* was a best seller.

Its origins go back to 1810 when Wordsworth wrote an anonymous introduction to a collection of drawings of the Lakes made by a Norfolk vicar. Dorothy later suggested that he should write his own guide to the Lakes, using the introduction. That's precisely what happened, the anonymous preface being expanded and emerging under his own name in 1820, firstly as part of some other writings, and then as a book on its own in 1822. At regular intervals he added to it, bringing out revised editions in 1835 and 1842.

In the very first version, back in 1810, he used a simile that has been used about the Lakes by many people since. He asked the reader to imagine himself on a cloud, hanging between Great Gable and Scafell, and seeing 'stretched at our feet a number of valleys, not fewer than eight, diverging from the point at which we are supposed to stand, like spokes from the nave of a wheel'. Thousands of people since have looked at the Lakes—on maps and in the flesh—and likened their shape to a wheel.

ABOVE *A satellite image of the Lake District reveals its wheel-like shape, with the lakes forming rickety spokes.*

DRAWING THE CROWDS

The early tourists, as the guidebooks hoped, were the educated classes, but the railways changed all that.

Britain in the 1840s was in the grip of railway mania, with lines being planned everywhere. Wordsworth enjoyed travelling to London on a train, and had nothing against them as such, but when they planned a line almost to his doorstep, he was up in arms, writing to Prime Minister Gladstone, writing to the local papers, doing anything to stop the Kendal and Windermere Railway. He claimed that the poor would not benefit from the Lakes and that they would ruin it for people of taste. No reactionary today would use such emotive, class-ridden language, and indeed Wordsworth was criticised by the press and some of his friends for his outburst.

Of course, many residents were tourists themselves once—and today they are the worst when it comes to considering tourism in the future. They don't want it any more than Wordsworth did. They want the roads closed and trains halted and every outsider turned back. I did see one letter in a local paper that wanted all cars stopped at the National Park boundary and only those with proper climbing gear allowed in. I looked at the figures for what the millions of visitors a year put as their favourite activities. These were, in order of preference: driving round the area, sightseeing in towns and villages, shopping for presents, visiting pubs, climbing

WILDLIFE OF THE LAKES

LEFT *As a habitat for plant and animal life, lakes vary greatly in their hospitality. The more silted a lake is, the more life it will contain.*

ABOVE *The great crested grebe's startling black head plumes are present only during courtship, and disappear in the winter.*

CURIOUSLY, PERHAPS, the purer a lake is, the poorer it is in plant and animal life. So the clear and remote lakes such as Wast Water have less to interest the amateur naturalist than shallow and murky but mineral-rich lakes such as Esthwaite Water. In the poorest lakes, for instance, plant life consists mainly of algae and primitive quillwort, whereas the more silty lakes will add bulrushes, various pondweeds, and sometimes water lilies in sheltered bays. One popular highlight is the water lobelia, flowering in fine lilac profusion in midsummer.

In the animal food chain, lowly links include the freshwater shrimp, tiny

BELOW *Away from the most crowded areas, otters may be glimpsed at a lake's edge.*

leeches and flatworms, and mayfly larvae. Of the lake fish, minnows and stickleback are widespread, and three related game fish too— salmon and sea trout (migrating to or from the sea), and the char. The richer lakes support eels, perch and pike as well. Two other coarse fish, roach and rudd, were probably introduced by anglers. And there are two famous rarities, now protected species—the schelly, found in Ullswater and Haweswater, and the vendace, formerly unique to Derwent Water and Bassenthwaite Lake, though now reintroduced into Scotland.

Lakeland's aquatic mammals, such as the water vole and water shrew, generally prefer becks (stony brooks) to lakes, though the lucky visitor may occasionally spot an otter cavorting in a quiet tarn or lake bay. Far more conspicuous is the Lakes' bird life. Three great avian fishermen have enjoyed varying fortunes in recent times—the patient heron seems immune to the passing

LEFT *Although tiny, the freshwater shrimp plays a vital role in the food chain of the lake, and is a particular favourite of the trout.*

BELOW *The schelly occurs in only a handful of lakes in Britain, and is protected by the 1981 Wildlife and Countryside Act.*

of time; kingfishers have suffered from it, and are now very rare; and the cormorant has thrived on it and become a local breeding species rather than just a regular visitor. Other notable birds, whether full-time residents or seasonal visitors, include mute swans and whooper swans (Elter Water takes its name from a Viking term meaning 'swan'); grebes and gulls; sandpipers on the lake edges and diverse ducks in the shallows; and Canada and greylag geese. Most celebrated of all, perhaps, are the unruly coots, wintering in vast communes on reed beds in the bays of Windermere.

and fell walking, visiting historic buildings, visiting exhibitions and museums, going to the beach, and, finally, going on a lake steamer. So if you only let in those equipped for climbing, the Lake District economy would collapse overnight.

One of the things the Tourist Board always proudly point to is the fact that tourism revives local crafts and industries that would otherwise die. A lot of the stuff in the local gifte shoppes is locally made. They also maintain that tourism helps farming, which might seem a contradiction, when you hear farmers moan about walkers leaving gates open, or about farm workers leaving the land to work in the tourist towns. But they have figures to show that the hill farmers are directly subsidised by their bed and breakfasts in the season. Joss Naylor is an example.

Wordsworth was, of course, right about the numbers of tourists. Over the last 200 years, tourism has grown well beyond his worst fears, but the Lakes can't really be said to have been ruined. Indeed, in theory nothing can alter them, now that they're a National Park.

The National Park is neither nationalised, despite the word national, nor is it a park, in the sense of a public park. The owners of the land inside the Park are private people, like anywhere else, though large slices are owned by bodies like the National Trust or the Forestry Commission, also like anywhere else.

The National Park Authority is a ruling body, first of all, with legal powers to give or refuse planning permission. It's also a protection agency, with staff and amenities to look after that area designated as a National Park. Thirdly, it's a propaganda machine, churning out information to help visitors enjoy the amenities, without hindering, so it is hoped, the residents.

The Lake District National Park was created in 1951, and it's the biggest National Park in the country, covering some 885 square miles. Roughly, most of the hill region to the west of the M6 is National Park. It's quite smart to be in the National Park, to feel part of an ancient monument, a listed property, but, on the other hand, it leads to endless palaver when putting on a new kitchen, altering the titles, or in any way changing your house or garden.

The population is small—just over 42,000. It doesn't include Cumbria's biggest town, Carlisle, and it narrowly misses Penrith and Kendal, the two gateways to the Lakes from the M6, nor does it take in the coastal towns like Maryport, Workington, Whitehaven or Barrow. It even makes a little loop to omit Cockermouth. The main centres inside the National Park are Windermere and Bowness, with a population of around 8,000; Keswick, 4,600; and Ambleside and Grasmere, 4,800.

The National Park information centre is at Brockhole, on the shores of Windermere. The building was formerly a private house, yet another of those grand mansions with lavish lakeside grounds, built by a Lancashire merchant as his holiday home.

I feared it would be yet another little information bureau, like the local ones the National Park (and the National Trust) open in the season all over the Lake District. But Brockhole is a fun palace, an exhibition centre, a modern museum using all the latest audiovisual equipment, designed to tell you about the Lake District flora and fauna, complete with sounds and movement. They also get

RIGHT *From the highest peaks to the deepest valleys, the Lake District is a diverse and ever-changing landscape, constant only in its beauty.*

experts coming in to give talks and do day-long courses. Brockhole is now the biggest single attraction in the Lake District, attracting more people than any other fee-paying place.

Here I met John Wyatt. He was the only warden in the Lake District when he joined in 1960. Now he was Head Warden, with ten full-time wardens under his command, thirty part-timers and 250 volunteers. Their aim, he said, was to help the public enjoy the Lakes, which means things like policing Ullswater in motorboats (Windermere is done by real police), teaching map reading, protecting lambs in lambing time, helping to run mountain-rescue teams, patrolling popular walks and picnic places, picking up litter, picking up bodies.

Their police work, which only took up about 3 per cent of their time, was the part they liked least. They had no legal powers, and could only use heavy persuasion, but they were responsible for about two dozen people a year ending up in court for some offence, such as breaking the speed limit on Ullswater or vandalism.

'All the dire warnings about the huge increase in crowds has not happened,' said Mr Wyatt. 'Walkers can still get peace and solitude in ten minutes. It's only the valley floors that get many people. Talking of overcrowding in the Lakes is rubbish. The Lakes can't be all that ruined by people if the eagles have returned. Three pairs have tried to nest here this year, and one has succeeded. And there's the peregrine falcons. We're now the most important breeding ground for them in Europe.

'Rock climbers used to be unhelpful people in the old days. Some of my best friends are mountaineers, but you used to get some disreputable ones. If you tried to ask them not to go a certain way in order to protect a certain part, they'd soon tell you where to go. Now you'll get a mountaineer ringing up a warden to say he's seen a peregrine on a climbing crag and shouldn't its nest be protected. That's a great change. What's happened in the last eighteen years is that the general public realise that the countryside is being protected for *their* good.'

He was right. The Lakes are not being ruined, but they are changing. I often thought, during the year, when I was on high with not a trace of man in sight, that this must be the view the Romans had, or the Vikings saw, or this was the path Wordsworth must have taken, but nothing in nature is ever exactly the same from year to year. The natural forests have long since gone. Becks continue to eat into the fellsides. The weather still works away at the landscape. The new forests have different shapes and different content and attract different flora and fauna.

The Lakes will always change, so long as they are alive. We want living lakes, not museum pieces. Most of all, we want the Lakes loved and appreciated. That's the best protection.

I could do the whole walk again and see it all differently. The sun might be out on the Old Man of Coniston. The mist will have cleared from Skiddaw. I do plan to do it all again, and again. My wellies are all clean. Wordsworth awaits. ∎

HIGHLIGHTS

The best that the Lake District has to offer

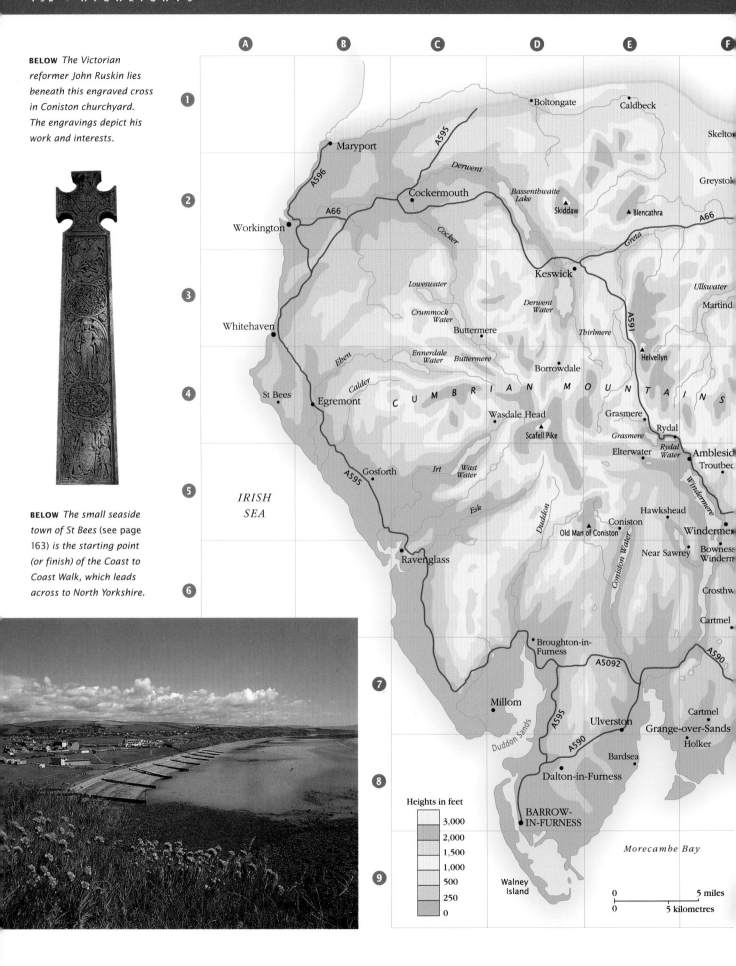

BELOW *The Victorian reformer John Ruskin lies beneath this engraved cross in Coniston churchyard. The engravings depict his work and interests.*

BELOW *The small seaside town of St Bees (see page 163) is the starting point (or finish) of the Coast to Coast Walk, which leads across to North Yorkshire.*

A B C D E F

1 2 3 4 5 6 7 8 9

Boltongate
Caldbeck
Skelton
Maryport
Derwent
Greystoke
A596
A595
Bassenthwaite Lake
Skiddaw
Blencathra
Cockermouth
A66
Workington
A66
Cocker
Greta
Keswick
Ullswater
Loweswater
Derwent Water
Martindale
Crummock Water
Thirlmere
A591
Whitehaven
Buttermere
Eben
Ennerdale Water
Buttermere
Borrowdale
Helvellyn
Calder
CUMBRIAN MOUNTAINS
St Bees
Grasmere
Rydal
Egremont
Wasdale Head
Grasmere
Scafell Pike
Elterwater
Rydal Water
Ambleside
Troutbeck
Gosforth
Irt
Wast Water
A595
Esk
Hawkshead
Windermere
Duddon
Coniston
Old Man of Coniston
Near Sawrey
Bowness-on-Windermere
IRISH SEA
Coniston Water
Windermere
Ravenglass
Crosthwaite
Cartmel
Broughton-in-Furness
A590
A5092
Millom
A595
Cartmel
Ulverston
Grange-over-Sands
Duddon Sands
A590
Holker
Bardsea
Dalton-in-Furness
BARROW-IN-FURNESS
Morecambe Bay
Walney Island

Heights in feet
3,000
2,000
1,500
1,000
500
250
0

0 — 5 miles
0 — 5 kilometres

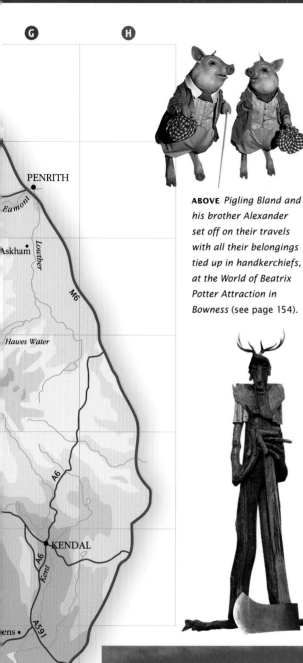

G   H

PENRITH

Eamont

Askham

Lowther

M6

Hawes Water

A6

KENDAL

A6

Kent

A591

ens •

nside

ABOVE *Pigling Bland and his brother Alexander set off on their travels with all their belongings tied up in handkerchiefs, at the World of Beatrix Potter Attraction in Bowness (see page 154).*

ABOVE *Stock Ghyll waterfall crashes down a wooded ravine after autumn rains. In the past the water was used to power several mills.*

RIGHT *The logo of the Lake District National Park, depicting mountains and a lake, was inspired by the view up Wast Water to Great Gable.*

LEFT *David Kemp's characterful oak-wood sculpture* The Ancient Forester *stands in Grizedale Forest (see* **Hawkshead** *page 155).*

ABOVE *The grand stately home Holker Hall (see page 158) is surrounded by 25 acres of gardens, some formally set out, as here, and others left wild.*

CONTENTS

LAKE DISTRICT NATIONAL PARK

ABOUT THIS SECTION

DON'T LET STATISTICS put you off: even though the Lake District receives some 14 million visits a year, it is surprisingly easy to get off the beaten track and find tranquillity and beauty, to fall under that special spell that Lakeland casts. Go out of season and you could have even the most popular beauty spots practically to yourself.

In this next section, the editors have selected some of the most rewarding sites to visit on a trip to the Lakes. They have chosen, in 'Great Journeys' on pages 160–63, three excursions that take in the full range of Lakeland landscapes. In 'The Fame of the Lakes' (pages 164–7), you will learn about local personalities, past and present; and, using the calendar on page 169, you can plan your visit to coincide with local festivals and events. On the same page are the details of Lake District tourist offices, where you can obtain further information about specific sites, such as opening times and entry fees.

To help you find your way round, entries are followed, where appropriate, by grid references for the map opposite.

TOWNS AND VILLAGES

Ambleside F5
This busy Victorian resort at the head of Lake Windermere grew after the Waterhead ferry terminus opened in 1845. Above tiny Bridge House, a 17th-century summer house built over Stockghyll stream and now a National Trust information centre, lies Above Stock, the old centre of Ambleside. Farther up, Stockghyll Force is a romantic waterfall. By the lake are the scant remains of Galava Roman Fort, which guarded the approaches from High Street to the north and the Wrynose Pass to the west.

Askham G3
Tree-shaded grass verges line the long, broad street of this unspoilt village sited amid gentle limestone country. At the eastern end is the

bridge *(above)* over the River Lowther, on the far side of which the ruin of Lowther Castle, built in 1806–11, occupies spacious parkland.

Barrow-in-Furness D8
In their 19th-century heyday, Barrow's steelworks were the world's largest, and the town prospered as a port and shipbuilding centre; now Trident submarines are made here. The Dock Museum documents the town's changing role. Statues of Victorian magnates stand in the broad main street, with its Gothic town hall of 1887. To the west of the town, the 12-mile-long Isle of Walney shelters the harbour and has miles of sands ending in nature reserves, inhabited by sea-bird colonies. Piel Castle, reached by ferry from Roa Island, was built in the 16th century by monks from nearby Furness Abbey to guard the harbour entrance.

Bowness F5 and Windermere F6
These two Victorian resorts merge into one. Windermere developed after the opening of Windermere railway station in 1847: local

ABOVE *Cockermouth stands on the edge of the Lake District National Park, at the spot where the Rivers Derwent and Cocker meet. Wordsworth's childhood home overlooked the River Derwent.*

landowners campaigned against the railway coming any nearer the lake, for fear of losing the views from their gardens. Bowness, a departure point for steamers, is thronged with visitors in high season. Highlights include the World of Beatrix Potter Attraction, where characters and scenes from her books are re-created, and the Windermere Steamboat Museum, which has a display of antique vessels and offers steamboat trips. Superb views of the lake are gained by walking up Orrest Head and by strolling along the shore from Bowness to Biskey Howe.

Broughton-in-Furness D7
Colour-washed 18th-century houses face the unspoilt central square of this former market town, which now has a village-like calm. At the centre an obelisk, commemorating the golden jubilee of George III in 1810, stands beside the town's stocks. To the west, Duddon Furnace, a partly restored ruin dating from 1736, is an impressive relic of the iron industry; iron ore was smelted here using charcoal and harnessing water power to blast the furnace. It was eclipsed by the introduction of coke for smelting, and closed in 1867.

Caldbeck E1
The rolling Caldbeck Fells harbour relics of the copper, barytes and lead-mining industries that made Caldbeck a busy industrial community. A walk from the church, where John Peel is buried, and past

terraces of former miners' cottages, leads to the ruins of Bobbin Mill, one of the village's eight former mills. It stands beside the Howk, a waterfall tumbling into a limestone basin. Southeast of Caldbeck, Hesket Newmarket was renamed from plain Hesket in the 18th century when a roofed market cross was erected in the centre of the village green.

Cockermouth C2
William and Dorothy Wordsworth spent part of their childhoods in what is now known as Wordsworth House, in Main Street. Attractive 18th- and 19th-century houses are found in Kirkgate and around Market Place. Jennings' Brewery, open for tours, still takes its water from the well that supplied 13th-century Cockermouth Castle. Visitor attractions include the Printing House, a working print museum with historic presses; the Lakeland Sheep and Wool Centre, which gives sheepdog and shearing demonstrations; and the Cockermouth Motor Museum.

Coniston E5
Its position as the major settlement close to Coniston Water, and at the base of the Old Man of Coniston, has made this village a popular resort. In the 19th century, mining in the nearby 'Coppermines Valley', on the lower slopes of the Old Man, was at its peak, and a walk along Church Beck reveals many reminders of this industry, including shafts and ruined engine houses. A museum honours the life and works of John Ruskin, who is buried in the churchyard.

Dalton-in-Furness D8

The squat 14th-century castle by the triangular marketplace once defended the northern approaches to Furness Abbey from Scottish raiders, and was used as a prison until 1774. Wallabies, porcupines and other exotic fauna can be seen at the South Lakes Wild Animal Park. Three miles northwest, rare natterjack toads breed at Sandscale Haws Nature Reserve.

Elterwater E5

Walkers frequent the ancient Britannia Inn at this tiny village in the heart of Langdale, from where paths lead along Great Langdale Beck to the lake of Elter Water itself in one direction, and towards the rugged profiles of the Langdale Pikes—Pike of Stickle and Harrison Stickle—which loom over the valley in the other. The village of Elterwater used to produce gunpowder for the area's many quarries and mines; a slate quarry still functions just outside the village.

Grange-over-Sands F7

Ornamental gardens, bowling and putting greens, and a promenade line the waterfront of this Morecambe Bay resort. A footpath climbs from the town up to Hampsfield Fell, crossing natural limestone pavements and reaching a 727-foot summit capped by a refuge for travellers erected in the 19th century.

Grasmere E4

Wordsworth's associations with Grasmere and nearby Rydal—he lived at Dove Cottage, Allan Bank, the Parsonage and Rydal Mount, and is buried in Grasmere churchyard—have made the village a place of literary pilgrimage as well as a popular base for hikers. Paths explore the southern shores of the dale's two lakes, Rydal Water and Grasmere, and there are rewarding walks into Easdale.

Greystoke F2

Sandstone cottages cluster round a green with an ancient stone cross in the middle. Northwards and westwards spreads the Greystoke Estate (*see feature on page 157*), which includes three estate farms built in the late 18th century as eye-catching follies: Fort Putnam resembles a medieval castle, while Bunkers Hill is a curious polygonal shape and Spire House incorporates a tower with a churchlike spire.

Hawkshead E5

In medieval times Hawkshead became the market town for a number of scattered farming

MADE IN KENDAL

"Remarkably fine Boots, sir"

"yes, they're 'K' BOOTS
SOLD BY

LEFT *K shoes have had a fine reputation since the late 1800s. This poster dates from the first decade of the 20th century.*

THE TOWN OF KENDAL owed its early prosperity to the wool trade (*see feature on page 36*) but is more famous today for two products—'K' shoes, and Kendal Mint Cake, a 'cake', or slab, of hard sugar confectionery flavoured with mint oil, popular with climbers, hikers and other outdoor adventurers.

Kendal Mint Cake was first made in 1869 by Joseph Wiper, who had married into a confectionery-making family, the Thompsons, and worked in their shop. But he soon moved on to developing new lines, one of which was the famous Mint Cake. Business boomed. In 1914, Wipers supplied Mint Cake to Ernest Shackleton's Trans-Antarctic Expedition, and in 1922, on the first-ever Mount Everest expedition, sherpas made their way up the mountain

carrying a forty-pound load of the energy-giving bars. Wipers was bought by Romney's in 1987, but the sweet remains popular, and few expeditions set off without some Mint Cake tucked into their rucksacks, whether they are scaling Mount Everest or braving the elements on the fells.

Another prerequisite for hiking is a good pair of shoes—and Kendal can supply those, too. The K shoes company was founded in Kendal in 1842 by Robert Miller Somervell, initially to supply leather to the thirty-odd shoemakers working in the town, but within twenty years, K were manufacturing shoes themselves. The first style did not prove popular, and the unsold stock was sent to America to be given to freed slaves. With improvements in manufacturing, however, the reputation of K shoes grew and they remain today a byword for quality and comfort.

BELOW *Every bar of Romney's Kendal Mint Cake carries a personal endorsement from Everest mountaineer Sir Edmund Hillary.*

Romneys Extra Strong Kendal Mint Cake

Manufactured by GEORGE ROMNEY, L.^{TD} IN KENDAL.

communities, and it has grown little since. Through traffic is excluded from its centre, its tiny lanes and cobbled yards. William Wordsworth attended the grammar school—now a museum, which proudly exhibits the desk in which he carved his name. William Heelis, the husband of Beatrix Potter, had his solicitor's practice here, and his former office is re-created within the Beatrix Potter Gallery. Close by is Tarn Hows, with its two tarns joined together in a wooded setting. South of Hawkshead lies Grizedale Forest, with

waymarked walks, cycling routes and picnic sites. A gallery is open all year round, and some 90 sculptures also line a long-distance trail through the forest.

Kendal G6

The 'auld grey town' prospered in medieval times as a woollen centre and has many reminders of its manufacturing and trading heyday. Numerous old weavers' yards survive, while the narrow alleys of Old Shambles and New Shambles once ran

TOWNS AND VILLAGES (CONTINUED)

red with blood from butchers' shops. Abbot Hall, an 18th-century house in Kirkland, the original centre of Kendal, is now an art gallery with works by Kendal artist George Romney (1734–1802) as well as paintings by 20th-century British painters. The Museum of Lakeland Life and Industry recalls how local people lived and worked, with reconstructions of period rooms and workshops as well as displays on Arthur Ransome and A. Wainwright. In the Quaker Meeting House hangs a tapestry of more than 70 panels, begun in 1981 and created by more than 4,000 people in 15 countries, illustrating the history of the Quaker movement, which started in the Lake District in 1652. Catherine Parr lived in the 12th-century castle, now a ruin giving views of the Pennines. (*See also feature on page 155.*)

Keswick D3
The churchlike Moot Hall of 1813 forms the focus of the town, most of which developed in the late 19th century after the arrival of the Keswick and Penrith Railway. Victorian tourists flocked to Keswick, many drawn by the long climb up Skiddaw and the beauty of Derwent Water. Cumberland pencils are still made here (*see feature on page 86*), and a museum attached to the factory contains such items as the world's largest pencil. Other visitor attractions include the old-fashioned Keswick Museum and Art Gallery, with its literary manuscripts and 1834 scale model of the Lake District. To the east, Castlerigg stone circle dates from the late Neolithic or early Bronze Age and is memorably set against a backdrop that includes Grisedale Pike and Cat Bells.

Maryport B1
Laid out on a grid plan like its neighbour Whitehaven, Maryport takes its name from Mary Senhouse, the wife of an entrepreneur who built the harbour to serve the Cumbrian coal trade. It is now home to a marina and a Maritime Museum, which has a 1951 Clyde tug and a Second World War navy supply vessel berthed in the harbour. The Senhouse Roman Museum, beside the site of a Roman fort, has a fine collection of Roman inscriptions.

Millom D7
The closure of Britain's largest ironstone mines at nearby Hodbarrow in 1968 ended a way of life for Millom that had lasted a century. Millom Folk Museum displays

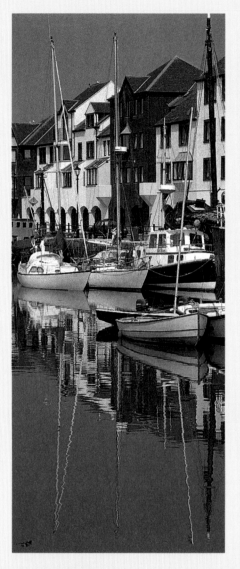

a reconstruction of part of the Hodbarrow Mine, and also honours the town's most famous son, the poet Norman Nicholson (*see page 165*). The sea wall encloses a lagoon that is now an RSPB reserve.

Penrith G2
Vulnerable for many centuries to Scottish raiders, the ancient market town has seen many skirmishes. Livestock used to be herded into its squares in times of trouble, and its castle, now in ruins, was often attacked. William and Dorothy Wordsworth attended Dame Birkett's school here. Southeast of Penrith, Brougham Castle was another defence erected to counter Scottish incursions and was restored by Lady Anne Clifford, the last of the Clifford family, in 1651; the castle contains an exhibition of Roman tombstones from a nearby fort.

LEFT *The harbour at Maryport has been redeveloped and is now an attractive marina.*

Ravenglass C6
The Lake District National Park's only coastal settlement is now a sleepy village with a silted-up harbour, and is best known as the terminus of the narrow-gauge Ravenglass and Eskdale Railway. Until the 17th century, however, Ravenglass flourished as a port for ships trading with Ireland. The Romans established a naval base here called Glannoventa; the 12-foot-high walls of its bathhouse still stand beside a footpath.

Ulverston E7
Towering over the market town and former port is a 100-foot lighthouse-shaped structure erected in 1850 in memory of the locally born explorer Sir John Barrow. A museum pays tribute to another distinguished son of Ulverston, Arthur Stanley Jefferson—better known as Stan Laurel, of Laurel and Hardy fame (*see page 165*).

Wasdale Head D4
Wasdale's lone hamlet is little more than an inn and a few farmsteads, but its magnificent position beneath Scafell Pike—England's highest mountain—and at the end of Wast Water—England's deepest lake—draws many visitors. The view up Styhead Pass to the pyramidal form of Great Gable features as the logo of the Lake District National Park.

Whitehaven A3
Laid out in a regular grid pattern in the 17th century, Whitehaven was Britain's first planned town and developed as a coal port. During the 18th and 19th centuries the docks and harbour were constructed and many strikingly uniform terraced houses survive from that time. Tales of the port are told at the Beacon, a lively local heritage museum with an interactive Met Office gallery. (*See feature on page 38.*)

Workington A2
Vast collieries once extended far out beneath the seabed, and today steel rails are shipped out from the busy port. Its historic core includes Portland Square, a tree-shaded cobbled expanse flanked by terraced cottages, and the ruins of Workington Hall, where Mary, Queen of Scots spent her last days of freedom after escaping from Scotland in May 1568. An 18th-century house contains the Helena Thompson Museum, with a collection of local history, furniture and costumes.

HOUSES AND GARDENS

Brantwood near Coniston E5

John Ruskin converted this building into an idiosyncratic haven, living here from 1872 until his death in 1900. Many of the pictures, books and geological specimens that still fill the house were bought at auction by John Howard Whitehouse, an ardent follower; Whitehouse also purchased Brantwood itself as a memorial to one of the most remarkable men of the era. Ruskin made the most of the westerly views across Coniston Water, adding a turret which contained his bedroom, and creating landscaped grounds with paths threading between azaleas, alpines and Cumbrian ferns.

Conishead Priory near Ulverston E7

This spectacular early 19th-century stuccoed Gothic fantasy takes its name from a 12th-century Augustinian priory that once stood on the site. The present structure was built as a private house and later functioned as a hydropathic hotel, a miners' convalescent home and then a holiday camp. Now undergoing a massive restoration and run as a Buddhist institute for followers of the Dalai Lama, it contains many features

alluding to its monastic origins, including arched windows, vaulted corridors and stained-glass illuminating a vast cantilevered staircase. The former billiard room now houses a Buddhist shrine.

Dove Cottage Grasmere E4

From 1799 to 1808 William Wordsworth spent his happiest and most creative literary period at this humble cottage, built in the 17th century as a pub, the Dove and Olive, and known only after the Wordsworths' departure as Dove Cottage. After they moved out, Thomas De Quincey (author of *Confessions of an English Opium-eater*) rented it; his opium scales are on display. The world of the Wordsworths and their circle is brought compellingly to life in the adjacent Wordsworth Museum.

Greystoke Castle Greystoke F2

(see feature below)

Hill Top Near Sawrey F6

Using the royalties from her book *The Tale of Peter Rabbit*, Beatrix Potter bought this farmhouse and made it her sanctuary, away

ABOVE *The cottage garden of Beatrix Potter's former home, Hill Top, overflows with a riotous array of plants in all shapes and colours.*

from the stifling atmosphere of her parents' home in London. Many of the local scenes are recognisable from illustrations in her books; Hill Top itself appears as Jemima Puddle-Duck's farm and as Tom Kitten's house. Because of the huge numbers who

TARZAN: LEGEND OF GREYSTOKE

FANS OF THE screen legend Tarzan, long-lost heir to Greystoke Castle, might be surprised to learn that the Lord of the Apes' connection with the famous castle is a matter of pure coincidence. While travelling across Europe in 1923, Stafford Howard, owner of the castle in Cumbria, came across the novel *Tarzan of the Apes* by American author Edgar Rice Burroughs. Howard was amazed to read that Tarzan was an English nobleman, born in 1888, with the title Lord Greystoke, the very name of Howard's home. Burroughs had chosen this name for his character by chance, after crossing out the title Bloomstoke in his original manuscript. The first edition of this work, published in hardback in 1914, was an immediate success in the USA and later in Britain.

In 1988 the Edgar Rice Burroughs Society in England planned a convention to commemorate the 100th birthday of Burroughs's character. Stafford Howard

was approached for permission to hold the Tarzan centennial at Greystoke Castle, and, permission granted, a banquet was subsequently held in the Great Hall.

Tarzan also appeared in comic-strip form in the *American Sunday Newspaper* comic section between 1936 and 1950. The illustrations were drawn by Burne Hogarth,

ABOVE *A Burne Hogarth cartoon from 1950 shows the all-powerful Tarzan locked in combat with a lion.*

LEFT *Originally medieval, Greystoke Castle was rebuilt in 1868. It is not open to the public.*

the Michaelangelo of the graphic novel, whose work has become highly prized and collectible. After Hogarth's death on January 28, 1996, the Society, with the blessing of Neville Howard, now owner of Greystoke Castle Estates, planted trees in the castle grounds in Hogarth's memory and erected a plaque in his honour alongside them.

HOUSES AND GARDENS (CONTINUED)

walk through the house's tiny, low-ceilinged rooms, a timed entry system operates; visitors are asked to avoid peak times such as mornings during school holidays.

Holker Hall near Holker F8
The atmosphere of aristocratic living in Victorian times is strongly evoked here. Fire destroyed the main part of the house in 1871, and the Jacobean and Elizabethan-style rebuilding was executed by Paley and Austin, one of the leading country-house architectural firms of the day. Beyond the entrance hall, lit by Venetian chandeliers, are the high-ceilinged ground-floor rooms furnished with 18th-century French pieces and boasting such contrivances as radiators disguised as oak panelling and light switches hidden behind dummy books; a Van Dyck self-portrait hangs over the dining-room fireplace. Each of a hundred-plus balusters of the cantilevered oak staircase bears a different carving. A limestone cascade is a highlight of the grounds, which have formal beds as well as woodland gardens, and where the blooms and scents provide interest throughout the seasons. Also within the grounds is the Lakeland Motor Museum, with its display of vintage cars and motoring memorabilia.

Hutton-in-the-Forest near Skelton F1
Set on the tranquil northeastern fringes of the Lake District amid grounds that include a 1730s walled garden, Victorian topiary and wooded walks, the house has been an ancestral home for centuries, first of the Hutton family, then from the 17th century of the Fletchers of Cockermouth, and later of their heirs, the Vanes. A 14th-century peel tower tells of the house's medieval origins as one of three main manors of the Royal Forest of Inglewood, since when it has acquired a white-stone baroque façade and 19th-century crenellations. Its interior was adapted for comfortable living, and has a notable 17th-century staircase and gallery, and tapestries of the same period. The drawing room is hung with wallpaper personally designed for the Vanes by William Morris, who was a family friend.

Levens Hall near Levens G7
Alan Bellingham, deputy warden of the North Marches, and his son James were responsible for remodelling the medieval peel tower in Elizabethan times, giving the house its mullioned windows, carved overmantels and ornate plaster ceilings. After James Bellingham gambled away the family fortune, one Colonel

ABOVE *The topiary at Levens Hall was designed by landscape gardener Guillaume Beaumont in 1694, and is the oldest in Britain.*

James Grahme acquired the house. Grahme added much of the splendid furniture that is seen today, as well as the famous topiary of clipped yews and box hedges designed by the King's gardener, Guillaume Beaumont, in 1694. Grahme also hung some of the walls with 17th-century Spanish leather.

Muncaster Castle near Ravenglass C6
Like many other houses in the region, this began as a fortified peel tower and was later adapted, albeit in a rather heavy manner. In 1862 the fourth Lord Muncaster engaged the architect Anthony Salvin, who remodelled the octagonal galleried library and created the barrel-vaulted drawing room. A full-length portrait of about 1600 depicts the family jester and agent, and there are portraits by Reynolds and a copy of a Titian painting that Gainsborough drew with crayons for a bet (which he won) to see if he could reproduce the original colours successfully. Ruskin described the outlook of Eskdale and the fells from the terrace as 'Heaven's Gate'. The grounds include specimen trees, magnolias and one of Britain's finest collections of rhododendrons, many gathered from plant-hunting expeditions to Nepal in the 1920s. Muncaster Castle is also home to a centre for the rehabilitation of owls, and flying displays and talks take place.

Rydal Mount Rydal E4
Hordes of sightseers used to come to the gate of Rydal Mount in the hope of catching a glimpse of William Wordsworth, who rented the house from 1813 until his death in 1850. Much of this time he devoted to his garden. Family portraits and possessions, including Wordsworth's collection of first editions, fill the interior.

Sizergh Castle near Kendal G6
For some 700 years the Strickland family have lived here, although since 1950 they have been tenants of the National Trust. The house originated as a medieval peel tower and has a predominantly Elizabethan character; the interior reveals superb carved overmantels. The Inlaid Chamber has recently been refitted with its original 16th-century wood panelling, sold to the Victoria and Albert Museum 100 years ago. Family portraits include one of Thomas Strickland and his wife by local artist George Romney; this hangs in the Upper Hall. The gardens are rich in colour from spring to autumn, and the diverse features include a terrace, lake, limestone rock garden and wild garden.

Townend Troutbeck F5
In 1626 the Browne family, who belonged to a class of wealthy farmers known as 'statesmen', built this farmhouse. It is an outstanding example of Cumbrian vernacular architecture, with its thick, whitewashed walls and slate roofs, and it falls into two sections: the 'downhouse' (*below*) for washing, cooking, brewing and pickling, and the 'firehouse', where the family lived. All the furniture is handmade by the Brownes, and

there is a fascinating array of domestic implements. After the death in 1943 of Clara Browne, the last surviving member of the family, the house passed to the National Trust.

Wordsworth House Cockermouth C2
The birthplace of William and Dorothy Wordsworth is a handsome, classical town house set back from Cockermouth's Main Street. The children loved the house, its walled garden and the adjacent River Derwent, which became their playground. There are Wordsworth memorabilia, period furnishings and pictures of Lake District scenes; the interior panelling and staircase are original features.

PLACES OF WORSHIP

All Saints' Boltongate D1

Conventional from the outside, the church reveals an extraordinary, steeply pointed stone-vaulted roof within—a feature associated with Scottish church architecture. Legend tells of it being built in a single night by Michael Scott, a 13th-century Scottish wizard. In the 19th century, a visiting bishop pronounced: 'mathematically it ought to have fallen down, because the weight of the massive stone roof should have forced the walls out.'

Cartmel Priory Cartmel F7

Lakeland's finest medieval church has a cathedral-like scale, with its soaring proportions, fine 17th-century screen and great east window of 18 main lights and 80 tracery lights. The 14th-century Harrington tomb displays a wealth of stone carving, featuring a frieze of mourning figures round its base, and the misericords depict an array of figures and scenes—among them a mermaid, a dragon, an elephant and castle, and Alexander being carried up by eagles. Bullet holes in a door are a legacy of a Cromwellian attack, while a glass case contains a rare 18th-century umbrella used by vicars at inclement funerals.

Furness Abbey near Barrow-in-Furness D8

Until the dissolution of the monasteries in the mid-16th century, the abbey was the second-richest Cistercian house in England (after Fountains Abbey in Yorkshire), and owned large estates in northwest England. The imposing sandstone ruins include a 12th-century transept, with walls rising almost to their original height. The canopy over the sedilia in the presbytery has weathered little with the passing of time. Nearby Bow Bridge, a triple-arched 15th-century packhorse bridge, once served the abbey grange.

Holy Trinity Kendal G6

Its extreme breadth is this Victorianised 13th-century building's most striking feature: it is the second-widest church in Britain at 103 feet—just narrower than York Minster. A helmet and sword on display are said to have been lost at the time of the Commonwealth by Robin, the 'Devil of Belle Isle', who was struck down here as he rode into church to avenge a Colonel Bridge, whose men had besieged his house. There is a memorial to the painter George Romney, who died in Kendal in 1802.

St Andrew's Dacre F2

Four stone bears stand in the church-yard of St Andrew's. They are of unknown date and purpose, but are

ABOVE *Furness Abbey was once the second-richest monastery in England. It took over 20 years to build and covered some 22 acres: the elaborate ruins still give the impression of greatness.*

probably medieval and may originate from the gatehouse of the adjacent 14th-century castle. One theory is that they depict one bear in a series of tableaux: first it is asleep, then it is attacked by a wild cat; the bear then captures the cat and finally devours it. Also of interest are two pre-Norman cross-shafts: one is intricately carved with a representation of a mythical beast, while the other shows Adam and Eve and two men—perhaps King Athelstan of England and King Constantine of Scotland, who met in Dacre in 926.

St Anthony's Cartmel Fell F6

Remotely sited in the limestone landscape of the Winster Valley, this charmingly rustic building dates from about 1504 when it was built as a chapel of ease for the parish of Cartmel. It was not licensed for burial until 1712, and in the intervening years corpses were taken to Cartmel, some seven miles away. Grooves etched into the porch are said to have been made by people sharpening arrows prior to archery practice in the churchyard. The interior features a triple-decker pulpit of 1698 and a box pew made from the former chancel screen: for many years the church doubled as a school, and inside the pew, one bench is carved with the old children's game of 'fox and geese'.

St Kentigern's Crosthwaite F6

The poet Robert Southey used to attend services here, and is buried in the churchyard; his memorial inside the church, in the form of a marble figure with one hand on his heart and the other clutching a book, was, according to his son Cuthbert, the best likeness made of him. Wordsworth supplied the inscription, but changed the ending after it had been carved; the erasure is still visible. One aisle is dedicated to Canon Rawnsley,

co-founder of the National Trust, who was once vicar here.

St Martin's Martindale F3

Martindale's solitary 'old church' has changed little since the late 16th century, when it was built. The floor is flagstoned, the walls whitewashed and pierced by rectangular windows; the pews and pulpit are original, and the timeless-looking font—much scratched by dalesmen who have sharpened tools on it over the centuries—may have its origins as a Roman shrine. The building fell into disuse, and in the 19th century the new church of St Peter was erected to the north.

St Mary's Gosforth B5

Resplendent with enigmatic carvings, the remarkably slender 10th-century Gosforth Cross stands 15 feet high in the churchyard. Precisely what the carvings depict will probably never be known: one explanation is that they relate Nordic sagas—including a hornblower guarding a rainbow 'bridge'. One face displays Christ with outstretched arms above two men, one holding a lance. There is more pre-Norman masonry inside the church, including 10th-century memorial stones, one shaped to resemble a cottage and another representing a battle scene. Another fine cross, dating from the 9th century, can be seen at St Paul's in the nearby village of Irton.

St Oswald's Grasmere E4

The Wordsworths' family grave has become a focus for literary pilgrims: here lie buried the poet William, his sister Dorothy and wife Mary. William's prayer book is preserved inside, where there is also a memorial to him. The church is thought to be the third on the site: St Oswald preached here in the 7th century.

IT WOULD BE IMPOSSIBLE *to list all the great journeys one could make in the Lakes. Each one of the millions of people who visit the region each year probably has their own personal favourite. But here are three journeys that stand out for the variety and beauty of the scenery they pass through.*

FROM AMBLESIDE TO RAVENGLASS BY ROAD AND RAIL

ONE OF THE GREAT scenic mountain roads of Britain, this route closely follows that taken by the Romans between their forts of Galava, beside modern-day Ambleside, and Glannoventa, on the coast at Ravenglass. The drive follows the A593 to Skelwith Bridge, just downstream from Skelwith Force, which carries the greatest volume of water of any of the Lakeland waterfalls in its broad 15-foot plunge.

The B5343 leads into Langdale, dominated by the brooding crags of the Langdale Pikes— seen to perfection from the shores of Elter Water, lying just off the road. During Neolithic times some 5,000 years ago, volcanic rock was cut here with granite hammers prior to being taken to the coast for polishing with sandstone and then exported; evidence of this axe 'factory' still litters the slopes.

Beyond the Old Dungeon Ghyll Hotel and Blea Tarn—magnificently set below Pike of Blisco and flanked by a clump of pines—Fell Foot Farm stands at the foot of the Wrynose Pass. The farm is backed by a steep hillock which is believed to have been a 'thing mound', where Viking leaders held meetings. The pass itself climbs 1:3 gradients to the Three Shire Stone, where, until 1974, the counties of Lancashire, Cumberland and Westmorland met at the 1,281-foot summit. As the road drops steeply into Wrynose Bottom, the course of the Roman road can be seen as a faint grassy track just to the north, on the far bank of the River Duddon.

Beyond the junction with the Duddon Valley road, the route hairpins up the formidably steep Hardknott Pass, giving a view from the top of the coast and, on a clear day, the Isle of Man. Just before the steepest part of the descent, the well-preserved remains of the Roman fort of Mediobogdum—usually known as Hardknott Castle—are seen to the right, perched dramatically above Eskdale.

Eskdale provides a verdant contrast, with farmsteads scattered among its green hills. On the south side, Stanley Ghyll waterfall rushes down a spectacular ravine hidden in the woods, and joins the River Esk. Another tributary, Whillan Beck, powers a restored watermill—now a museum—at the end of Boot's tiny main street.

The final seven miles to the coast can be completed by riding a quaintly undersized steam- or diesel-hauled carriage on the narrow-gauge Ravenglass and Eskdale Railway from Dalegarth station. The line opened in 1875 to serve ironstone mines, but later brought tourists into the valley; seven years after closure in 1953, it was bought by a band of enthusiasts. A station serves visitors to Muncaster Mill, another restored watermill. Ravenglass station has a museum explaining the line's history, and a path leads past Walls Castle, the bathhouse of Glannoventa Roman fort, whose 12-foot walls make it the tallest Roman building in northern Britain.

ABOVE *The occupying Roman army built the fort of Mediobogdum in the 1st century AD to protect the road between Ravenglass and Ambleside. The remains of the fort testify to its size and importance.*

FROM KESWICK TO BUTTERMERE BY ROAD

THE B5289 PROVIDES a succinct cross-section of the northwestern Lake District. Southwards from Keswick it glimpses Derwent Water, with the double-humped form of Cat Bells as a backdrop. Friar's Crag, a miniature promontory by the shore, presents what John Ruskin rated as one of the four finest views in Europe; a loftier viewpoint is Walla Crag, approached through Great Wood, where red squirrels may be spotted. Near the lake's southern end, the dead-end road to the remote hamlet of Watendlath crosses Ashness Bridge, with its much-admired panorama of Derwent Water and Skiddaw. The main road continues past Lodore Falls—immortalised in Robert Southey's 200-line onomatopoeic poem *The Cataract of Lodore*—and enters Borrowdale, characterised by its rugged crags, unspoilt hamlets and broad-leaved woodlands. The double-arched stone bridge over the Derwent at Grange provides a starting point for strolls along the river to Castle Crag, an excellent vantage point over the dale.

Borrowdale's woodlands were largely replanted in the 19th century after timber had been felled to provide charcoal for smelting. Trees now partly obscure the outlook from the Bowder Stone, a 2,000-ton boulder that was transported by a glacier and is balanced on its corner; it is less precarious than it appears—steps lead up to its top.

BELOW *The Ravenglass and Eskdale Railway uses steam- and diesel-powered engines to ferry passengers between the two towns.*

At Rosthwaite, the dale broadens and the road veers westwards through Seatoller and climbs the Honister Pass. At the working green-slate quarry at the top, the road reaches 1,176 feet above sea level, giving something of a head start for walkers making the ascent of Great Gable to the south, which rises to 2,949 feet.

The road roughly marks a divide between two rock types: to the south rise the gnarled, craggy fells of the Borrowdale Volcanics, while the north side of the dale is bounded by the smooth, grassy slopes of Skiddaw Slates, which constitute much of the northern Lake District. Buttermere lies below; the gentle stroll around its shores provides a breathtaking succession of mountain vistas, and includes a short section through a tunnel.

From the hamlet of Buttermere, the road heads up over Newlands Pass and on towards Keswick, threading through the tranquil Newlands Valley, once the scene of intensive mining activity. A boat trip on Derwent Water makes for a pleasant diversion: launches circle the lake or rowing boats can be hired.

FROM ARNSIDE TO ST BEES BY RAIL

THIS TRAIN JOURNEY, skirting the southern and western fringes of the Lake District, encounters an eye-opening sequence of coastal and industrial landscapes. Home to some 200,000 waders, Morecambe Bay— a vast expanse of water, or sand, depending on the rapidly changing tide—is the prelude. Before the advent of the railway in 1857, stagecoaches used to make the treacherous short cut across the bay; because of the danger of being trapped by tide changes or in quicksand, the walk can only be undertaken with a guide, from Arnside to Grange-over-Sands and Kents Bank.

Arnside Knott, above the fishing village-turned-resort of Arnside, is one of a series of limestone hills flanking the bay and looking far beyond to the southern Lake District fells. The railway crosses the low Kent Viaduct, its piers embedded deep into the sands, and then edges round the coast past the sedate resort of Grange-over-Sands. Flookburgh, once, but no longer, beside the water, is still a fishing village: 'flukes' (flounders) and

shrimps are sold locally after fishermen bring in the catch across the sands by tractor.

Passing to the south of Holker Hall estate, the railway crosses Leven Viaduct across another of the bay's great inlets, and enters Ulverston, which is presided over by a lighthouse-shaped monument on Hoad Hill to Sir John Barrow; the public can climb its interior staircase when a flag is flown. Barrow-in-Furness is Cumbria's southernmost industrial town; between it and the former iron-mining centre of Millom, sands stretch two miles across the mouth of the Duddon estuary; lapwings, oystercatchers and great numbers of other waders frequent the mud flats. North of Millom, the sprawling mass of Black Combe shelves down to within a mile of the sea from its 1,970-foot summit— from which, in exceptional conditions, Scotland, Wales, Ireland and the Isle of Man can be seen.

Beyond the dune-flanked estuary of the Esk at Ravenglass, the line hugs the coast from Seascale; ahead looms the huge Windscale, or Sellafield, complex, incorporating Calder Hall nuclear power station and the Thermal Oxide Reprocessing Plant (THORP), as well as a

UNDOING THE DAMAGE: CONSERVATION IN LAKELAND

THE LAKELAND LANDSCAPE of today is hardly pristine. Over recent centuries, forests have been felled, lakes redesigned, and filigrees of dry-stone walls created. But the modern mood is a conserving one, and diverse organisations have taken up the challenge—the Lake District National Park Authority, the Friends of the Lake District, the National Trust, and others besides.

Their work is fairly straightforward when their adversaries are easy to identify, whether poachers, polluters or property-developers. But what if the vandals are well-disguised or even well-meaning? For example, reforesting planners, whose well-intended projects formerly involved planting unpopular alien conifers in unnaturally straight rows. Rock climbers, whose innocent 'gill-scrambling' (scaling

LEFT *Well-trodden paths appear as scars on the landscape. Signs (right) encourage walkers to minimise the damage.*

the sides of narrow ravines) damaged the fragile mosses and ferns, and had to be curtailed. Farmers, too, whose over-eager stocking of sheep or cattle on lower slopes can cause pollution or erosion.

The most destructive of the unwitting vandals are the fell walkers. By tramping grooved and muddy footpaths (or by detouring and so creating new ones), they intensify the erosion of the fellsides and the loss of plant life. Huge resources go into repairing the most vulnerable stretches of footpath each year. The only real solution to this problem, however—short of imposing limits on the number of tourists—is to encourage some of the 7 million visitors a year to try less well-trodden routes, and to visit less-frequented sections of the region. Although arguably erosion will become more widespread as a result, at least its impact will be less severe on a local level.

The National Trust
EROSION CONTROL
Please keep to the footpaths provided
Avoid eroded or newly seeded areas

GREAT JOURNEYS (CONTINUED)

LIFE ON THE MOUNTAINSIDE

TREES ARE SPARSE on the fells nowadays, after centuries of clearing, though some junipers survive in clumps, with stragglers even in crevices in the crags. With the loss of the ancient forest that used to swath the Lake District, the mountainsides are ill-equipped for varied vegetation or wildlife. Poor soil, loose rocks and eccentric weather do not add up to a promising habitat.

Yet even the seemingly arid Wast Water screes manage to sustain a couple of species among the shale, notably the fragile parsley fern and the rare, shrubby cinquefoil. The high summits, exposed to extreme cold and parching winds, have a subarctic character, offering mainly lichens, grasses and mosses. Here and there, decaying mosses allow a foothold for bilberry, cowberry and crowberry. Elsewhere two arctic species, dwarf willow and stiff sedge, defy the elements, and on gentler slopes, varied alpine plants such as the red alpine catchfly find sanctuary. At lower and milder elevations, the star saxifrage is prominent, though it has its own adversary to contend with—sheep.

The highest peaks are uncongenial to bird life, too, apart from snow buntings and dotterels visiting in winter. The raven and peregrine falcon prefer mid-altitude crags, and have recently been joined by

ABOVE The stark, volcanic rock of the Wast Water screes presents an inhospitable landscape, yet a few plant species manage to survive on the arid slopes.

LEFT The raven is a characteristic bird of mountain country, nesting in inaccessible crags. It is found in the crags even during the depths of winter, and breeds in the snows of March.

BELOW The dwarf willow (Salix herbacea) is an alpine plant that thrives in exposed conditions. It appears on many mountaintops on the fells north of Ennerdale and in the Coniston area.

the golden eagle, triumphantly restored in small numbers to the region after two centuries of banishment. Merlins nest at slightly lower levels, and several versatile species haunt both higher and lower fellsides—buzzards and kestrels, meadow pipits, wheatears and skylarks.

Among the fells' most conspicuous insects are the mountain ringlet butterfly, in the Langdales especially, and—around the heather of the lower fells—two larger and showier moths, the northern eggar and the emperor.

As for mammals, only two species seem to

have the lofty ambition of venturing onto really high summits—the bank vole and the human mountaineer! On lower slopes, two other unexpected mammals thrive. Many foxes have established a presence here, as if cunningly to elude the hunt. And numbers of native red deer, likewise better suited to lower or flatter habitats, have adapted well to fell conditions, and the stag's rutting roar resounds above Ullswater in the autumn.

LEFT The mountain ringlet is the only alpine butterfly found in Britain. It is confined solely to the Lake District and the west Grampians of Scotland.

futuristic visitor centre that has become one of Cumbria's prime tourist attractions. The village of St Bees, with its fine Norman priory church and school founded in 1583, marks the western end of the popular Coast to Coast Walk, which crosses the neck of northern England to Robin Hood's Bay in North Yorkshire. A path along the top of breezy sandstone cliffs leads to Cumbria's most westerly point, St Bees Head, an RSPB reserve that is home to a huge sea-bird colony, including guillemots, razorbills and puffins.

LAKE CRUISES

CONISTON WATER is inevitably associated with the high-speed exploits of Donald Campbell *(see feature on page 49)*, but visitors can enjoy the lake by a distinctly sedate means of travel: the National Trust's steam yacht *Gondola*. She was one of two such vessels, both built in 1859, which made near-silent tours of the lake. By the Second World War, both had ended their days of service; *Gondola* escaped the breaker's yard and served as a houseboat before the Trust acquired her and meticulously restored her to working order. The hour-long trip makes a stop at Brantwood to allow a visit to Ruskin's house, and there are piers at Coniston and

Park-a-Moor (at the lake's southeastern end). Coniston Launch runs a cruise and ferry service on the lake.

Converted Victorian steamers travel the length of Ullswater from Pooley Bridge to Glenridding. The scenery unfolds dramatically as the boats sail southwards, with fine views of Place Fell, Helvellyn and Gowbarrow Park—where Dorothy Wordsworth first saw the immortal 'host of golden daffodils' later celebrated in her brother William's poem 'Daffodils'. Howtown Pier makes a useful stop for those wishing to take the lakeside path round the base of Hallin Fell and on to Glenridding.

Derwent Water has a launch service connecting seven landing stages and making a 50-minute tour, giving plentiful opportunities to walk parts of the shore and surrounding fells. The lake's islands include St Herbert's, where the saint established a hermitage in the 7th century, and Derwent Isle, home in the 16th century to a colony of German miners.

Windermere, ever-busy with boating activity, can be explored by steamer from Waterhead, near Ambleside, to Lakeside, at the lake's southern end. Its wooded shores, backed by views of tall fells to the west and north, are speckled with classical villas and imposing Victorian mansions, many built for nouveau-riche magnates bent on establishing

their own private Arcadias. On Belle Isle stands a unique circular house built in 1774 (and recently restored), while castellated Croft Lodge (1830) at the northern end of the lake exuberantly blends Renaissance and Strawberry Hill Gothic styles. Beatrix Potter spent her first Lake District summer holiday with her family at Wray Castle, a spectacular mock-medieval pile on the western shore.

Less than a mile from Lakeside stands Stott Park Bobbin Mill, a working museum illustrating the manufacture of cotton-reels, handles and similar bobbin products, which were made there from 1835 until closure in 1971; guides show how the lathes were operated and recall the dangerous working conditions that gave rise to numerous accidents. Lakeside itself still has a Victorian ferry pier; next to it is the Aquarium of the Lakes, which presents the journey of a Lakeland river from its source on the fells to Morecambe Bay. Although the railway that once brought in hordes of day-trippers no longer connects to the national network, a four-mile stretch has been preserved as the Lakeside and Haverthwaite Railway, giving a steam-hauled ride through Backbarrow Gorge, once busy with iron smelting.

BELOW *The steam yacht* Gondola *glides across Coniston's peaceful waters. The yacht takes an hour to sail round the five-mile-long lake.*

THE FAME OF THE LAKES

THE LAKE DISTRICT *makes up only a small corner of Britain, yet the halls of fame have never been short of Cumbrians. Many have waxed lyrical in verse or prose about the stupendous beauty of their surroundings. Others have applied their artistic skills on canvas. The Lakes have been home to those brave enough to put themselves on the stage or climb the highest mountains. But whether they have travelled the world through their professions or made their name in the local landscape, they remain, one and all, Lakelanders.*

Sir Chris Bonington
Mountaineer
(Born 1934 in London) A serious climber from his teens, Chris Bonington was the first Briton to complete many of the most difficult climbs in the world, including the North Wall of the Eiger in 1962. Most famously, he led a successful British expedition up the southwest face of Mount Everest in 1975. Bonington, now in his sixties, still undertakes challenging and little-climbed routes. He finances his passion for climbing by using the amazing sights and intriguing tales it provides in writing and photography. He lives in the Caldbeck Fells in the Lake District, and makes the most of the local mountains when he is at home.

Lord Bragg
Journalist and broadcaster
(Born 1939 in Wigton) With fingers in so many pies, Melvyn Bragg cannot help but be a household name. His face is familiar

thanks to the TV arts programme *The South Bank Show,* which he both edits and presents. He is a prolific writer, mostly of novels, many of which are based in the Lake District. In addition to these activities he also finds time to write a weekly newspaper column and act as Controller of Arts at London Weekend Television. His formidable CV makes him one of this century's most successful Lakelanders: in 1998 Bragg was made a life peer.

Donald Campbell
(see feature on page 49)

John Cunliffe
Writer
(Born 1933 in Lancashire) Cunliffe's first children's book was published in 1964 while he was an infant-school teacher in the Lakes. In 1978 the BBC commissioned him to write

the highly successful *Postman Pat* series, which is set in the valley of Longsleddale. Only in 1988, however, did Cunliffe take up writing full time. In the realm of television he also writes and presents another popular children's animation, *Rosie and Jim.*

John Dalton
(see feature on page 70)

Hunter Davies
Writer and journalist
(Born 1936 in Scotland) From Fleet Street journalist to writer of books, Hunter Davies has made a name for himself in the media and literary worlds, and is an authority on Lakeland. He divides his time between his homes in London and the Lake District, producing articles and reviews for national papers. He is married to the writer Margaret Forster (*see separate entry*).

Thomas De Quincey
Writer
(1785–1859, born in Manchester) De Quincey wrote prolifically from an early age, but he remained unpublished and relatively impoverished until he penned the enormously successful collection of essays *Confessions of an English Opium-eater* in 1822. A promising scholar in his youth, he nevertheless ran away from school and, despite going to Oxford, never took his degree, claiming to despise the university system. His use of opium began during his Oxford days to alleviate toothache; he controlled his intake during his marriage but became dependent again following his wife's death. Through his friendship with Coleridge he made Wordsworth's acquaintance, and for a time leased Dove

Cottage in Grasmere after the Wordsworths had moved to Allan Bank. His writings are still admired today for their variety and superlative use of language.

Margaret Forster
Writer
(Born 1938 in Carlisle) The author of 17 novels, Forster has also written nonfiction titles, including histories and biographies—notably the acclaimed authorised biography of Daphne du Maurier. She was educated in her home town of Carlisle and won a scholarship to Somerville College, Oxford. She chooses to avoid the social gatherings of the literary world, preferring instead to concentrate on her writing and her family; she is married to Hunter Davies.

Bernard Gilpin
Preacher
(1517–83, born in Kentmere) Known as the Apostle of the North, Gilpin was a man of the cloth in post-Reformation England. One of the early Protestants, he was accused of heresy during the reign of Queen Mary, but evaded arrest. In a time of great religious uncertainty he chose to support the English sovereign as the head of the Church, but continued to adhere to some Catholic doctrines, including celibacy. Gilpin was a respected preacher who did not crave promotion within the Church, devoting himself instead to pastoral work. He travelled widely in the North, preaching his own brand of broad-minded Protestantism. He died in Houghton-le-Spring, near Durham, where he had established a grammar school to help poor scholars.

Geoffrey Kendal
Actor–manager
(1909–98, born in Kendal) Geoffrey Bragg changed his name to the town of his birth when he entered the theatre. As the actor–manager of Shakespeareana, an English theatre company that travelled India from north to south from the 1940s to the 1960s, he and his family were responsible for bringing Shakespeare and a whole repertoire of classic plays to the subcontinent. In 1965 the Kendals starred in the Merchant-Ivory film *Shakespeare Wallah,* which was loosely based on their Asian experiences. It was this film that launched his daughter Felicity's successful acting career. Kendal was the original 'Shakespeare Wallah', and he continued to tour India well into his seventies.

Stan Laurel
Comedian
(1890–1965, born in Ulverston) As the skinny half of the comedy duo Laurel and Hardy, Stan Laurel made nearly 90 comedies in a film career that spanned a quarter of a century. Born Arthur Stanley Jefferson into a theatrical family, he worked for a while with Charlie Chaplin. By 1916 Laurel had moved to America, where he worked in theatre. He teamed up with Oliver Hardy in 1926, by which time he was well ensconced in the burgeoning film industry. Unlike his bumbling and incompetent on-screen character, he was skilled at all aspects of film-making, including writing and directing; Laurel led the life of a film star, with a flamboyant lifestyle and five turbulent marriages (twice to the same woman). Laurel and Hardy toured extensively in Britain in the 1940s and 50s. In 1961 Laurel was awarded an Oscar for his pioneering work in cinema comedy. He is buried in Hollywood.

Joss Naylor
Athlete and shepherd
(Born 1936 in Wasdale Head) A perennial achiever in the sport of fell running, Joss Naylor continues to astound spectators and fellow athletes alike with his excellent race times, despite being in his sixties. What is even more astonishing is that in his youth he suffered from acute back problems, undergoing one operation to remove two spinal discs, and another (bungled) one on his knee cartilage. He began fell running in his mid-twenties, and by the age of 30 was unbeatable. He has raced all over Europe and broken numerous records. He spends every day out on his local fells, not only running but also earning a living as a sheep farmer. It is this lifestyle and natural ability, rather than intensive training, that have brought him such success.

Norman Nicholson
Poet
(1914–87, born in Millom) This award-winning poet's love of Cumbria is demonstrated in his poems and in his less famous topographical writings on the area he never left. His works often pay homage to the mix of rural and industrial landscapes found in and around Millom; his committed Christian faith is also evident. When only in his mid-twenties, Nicholson was discovered by T. S. Eliot, and he soon joined the ranks of acclaimed poets published by Faber and Faber.

Catherine Parr
(see feature on page 120)

John Peel
Huntsman
(1776–1854, born in Caldbeck) Peel's love of, and skill at, hunting were so famous in his day that his friend and fellow-huntsman John Woodcock Graves penned a song about him, 'D'ye ken John Peel?', which is still sung today. He kept a pack of hounds all his adult life, and the memory of him as a dedicated huntsman is undiminished in the Lakes. Many locals pay homage to Peel today by using the same names for their hounds as he did.

Beatrix Potter
Writer and illustrator
(1866–1943, born in London) The talents of Beatrix Potter extended beyond imaginative children's stories and skilful watercolours. Following a lonely childhood and repressed youth she used the royalties from the sale of her tales to make herself independent of her

SWALLOWS AND AMAZONS FOR EVER!

WHILE HOLIDAYING in Lakeland in 1884, a professor of history from Leeds climbed to the top of the Old Man of Coniston, carrying his baby son. For the infant Arthur Ransome, this was the first of countless trips to a region he came to know and love—so much so that it became the setting for many of his evergreen children's novels, including *Swallows and Amazons*, published in 1930.

Children's novels were not Ransome's first literary venture, and he only turned his hand to them when he was in his mid-forties. His writing career began—once he had abandoned a university science degree—with modest commissions in London as a ghostwriter and book reviewer. Beyond writing, his interests included languages and folklore, and it was in pursuit of these interests that he visited

Russia in 1913. Here Ransome remained for the next five years, reporting for British newspapers on the First World War and the Russian Revolution. He soon became a highly regarded foreign correspondent, and spent the 1920s travelling to places as diverse as the Sudan and China.

But Ransome always craved the quiet life of the English countryside. Reflecting on his childhood visits to the Lake District he reinvented the surroundings in his children's tales. The mysterious Wild Cat Island, for example—setting for the antics in *Swallows and Amazons*—is probably based on Peel Island in Coniston Water. He relived the fun of those early holidays in the adventures of the Blackett and Walker children. Their motto was *Swallows and Amazons for ever!* and, with the books still in print, the motto continues to hold good.

RIGHT *The writings of Arthur Ransome have fired the imaginations of children since the 1930s.*

BELOW *Ransome's desk is now housed in the Museum of Lakeland Life and Industry, Kendal.*

THE FAME OF THE LAKES (CONTINUED)

parents. She moved to a farm in Near Sawrey in the Lake District and became immersed in the life of a farmer. Potter eventually replaced writing with sheep breeding, and was well-respected in these fields. She was a fervent campaigner for the National Trust, and on her death she bequeathed her estate to them.

Arthur Ransome
(see feature on page 165)

George Romney
Painter
(1734–1802, born in Dalton-in-Furness) Romney was one of the greatest portrait painters of the 18th century. His work is hung in galleries all over the world as well as in No. 10 Downing Street. His father, a cabinet-maker, recognised Romney's talent and apprenticed him to a local artist, Christopher Steele. Romney married locally but left his family behind when he went to make his name in London. He established himself

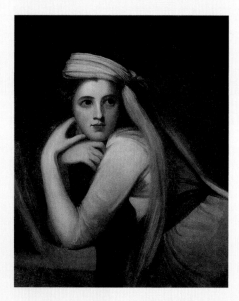

as a society portraitist, but remained aloof from the mainstream artistic world centred around the Royal Society of Arts, following an early snub from that institution in favour of his rival Sir Joshua Reynolds. His favourite sitter was Emma Hart (Lady Hamilton), whom he painted in numerous guises (*see painting above*) and mostly from memory. In his last years he returned to his wife in the Lakes, and is buried in Dalton.

Sir John Ruskin
Art critic, artist and social reformer
(1819–1900, born in London) Ruskin commented on so many elements of the

ANGELS OF THE LAKES

LEFT *Margaret Gillies's watercolour of Dora Wordsworth shows her, aged 37, at the time of her engagement to Edward Quillinan. Her father opposed the marriage.*

THERE WERE TWO great literary households in the Lake District in the 18th century: the Wordsworths at Grasmere, and the Coleridges and Southeys at Keswick. The relationship between the poets is legendary, but the bond between the female members was also strong.

The women were thrown into each others' company by marriage, friendship and relative geographical proximity. Although separated by a distance of twelve miles, the families thought nothing of walking to visit each other regularly, even daily. The womenfolk comprised two groups of sisters: the Frickers (Sarah and

Edith—the wives of Coleridge and Southey—and Mary Lovell) and the Hutchinsons (Mary—Wordsworth's wife—and Sarah), plus Dorothy Wordsworth (Wordsworth's sister).

But the Lake District in the 18th century was far from a rural idyll, and relations in the group were not always harmonious. Mary Wordsworth, for example, had to compete with Dorothy for Wordsworth's attentions throughout her married life. Sarah Coleridge was abandoned by her husband in favour of Sarah Hutchinson, and she and her three children became dependent on Southey. Intelligent and creative, the women found 18th-century married life stifling. Ill health, childbirth, the strain of running a household when there was often no money coming in, and—for Dorothy—addiction to the only painkiller available, opium, led to extreme stress, or, as it was then known, 'hysteria'.

The poets' daughters suffered equally. The talented Sara Coleridge also became an opium addict, and Dora Wordsworth gained her father's permission to marry only when she was 37 and already dying. Surrounded by women for most of his adult life, it seemed that Wordsworth could not bear to lose any of his coterie of ministering angels.

world around him that he is to be found in almost every text written on Victorian England. In particular, his views on art and architecture—he was a great proponent of the Gothic Revival Movement and the Pre-Raphaelite Brotherhood—influenced public opinion. Ruskin believed emphatically in the importance of nature, and opposed the forces of industrialism. Today he is recognised more in his role as social reformer. In his personal life Ruskin was less successful: an unhappy marriage was annulled on the grounds of non-consummation, and he later became infatuated

with a young girl, Rose la Touche, who eluded him. Rose's early death left him subject to depression and mental instability for the rest of his life. From 1872 Ruskin lived amid outstanding natural beauty—a luxury he believed should be available to all—at Brantwood on Coniston Water.

A(lfred) Wainwright
Writer
(1907–91, born in Blackburn) In 1930 Wainwright made his first visit to the Lakes on a fell-walking holiday, a break from his job as

HISTORIC HOTELS, INNS AND PUBS

a clerk at Blackburn town hall. It was the start of a lifelong love affair with the area to which he eventually moved. He became obsessed with fell walking and made records of his tramps across the Cumbrian landscape, which were published from 1955. His pictorial guides are immediately identifiable by his exactingly neat hand-lettering and skilful illustrations, as well as by his down-to-earth appreciation of the Lakes and often quirky opinions. Wainwright shunned fame until he was in his eighties, when he finally ventured into the media limelight. In death he remains at one with his beloved fells: his ashes are scattered beside Innominate Tarn on Hay Stacks.

Dorothy Wordsworth
(see feature on page 166)

William Wordsworth
Poet

(1770–1850, born in Cockermouth) Probably Britain's most famous 19th-century poet and a founding member of the English Romantic Movement. He began to write poetry seriously in his early twenties, often drawing on the natural beauty of his surroundings. He was born and bred in the Lake District, and returned there after university and his travels abroad. Many young gentlemen of the middle classes visited Europe in this period, but recent research suggests that Wordsworth's wanderings in France and Germany were not completely innocent—rather that he was employed by the British government to supply information on British revolutionaries abroad. Wordsworth's growing conservatism as he grew older makes it more credible that his early radical leanings were a sham. But it is doubtful that this covert career continued on his return to Britain, and the quiet family life he led in the Lakes until his death was probably no more than it seemed.

BELOW *Wordsworth was a true outdoors man, and loved to skate when the lakes froze over. His ice skates are on display in Dove Cottage, his one-time home.*

The Bitter End Cockermouth C2
For those interested in brewing, this is the perfect place to while away a few hours. The landlord's personal brewery is on view to the public through windows looking in from the bar. If you happen to be patronising the establishment when the landlord is brewing, then you are welcome to go and take a closer look at the process. Brewed on site are ales with bizarre names such as Cockersnoot and Cuddyluggs, and new beers are often being created.

The Fish Hotel Buttermere C3
At the beginning of the 19th century the landlord of this inn thought his daughter, Mary Robinson, had made a good match when she married the Hon. Augustus Hope. Mary's marriage was the talk of the town later in the year, but for all the wrong reasons. The scandalous news had come to light that her husband was a bigamist and a fraud, more commonly known as John Hatfield. Hatfield went to the gallows for his sins and Mary returned to Buttermere's local hostelry. The Fish Hotel is now more popular with climbers than con men, thanks to its close proximity to Honister Pass.

The Hole in't Wall
Bowness on Windermere F6
If you were to ask a local for directions to New Hall Inn, the proper name for this

ABOVE *A pint of beer rests in the hole through which ale was passed to the thirsty smithy. The pub came to be called The Hole in't Wall.*

pub, you might end up wandering the streets all evening. The pub is known to one and all as the Hole in't Wall after an opening was made between the pub and the next-door blacksmith's. Too lazy to keep walking round for his beer, the smithy negotiated a beer-passing hole between their two properties. The pub has now expanded to take in the whole of the blacksmith's, but the original opening has been retained.

Lancrigg Vegetarian Country House Hotel Grasmere E4
Overlooking the lush Easedale Valley, Lancrigg had long been a favourite spot of the Wordsworths, and it soon became a popular meeting place for the Lakeland poets. In 1839, Wordsworth encouraged his friend Elizabeth Fletcher to purchase the property, then a modest farmhouse, as a summer home. Later, through Elizabeth Fletcher's children, it also accommodated Charles Dickens and Robert Burns. Elizabeth's daughter, Mary, married Arctic explorer Sir John Booth-Richardson. As a friend of Charles Darwin, Sir John received many unusual specimens of trees and plants which were planted in the lovely woodland walks round the house. Lancrigg was transformed into a hotel in 1985.

The Mason's Arms
Strawberry Bank, Cartmel F7
Funny handshakes and rolled-up trouser legs were what a visitor might well have found had he stumbled upon this remote old pub in the past. But fashions have changed, and the Kendal Freemasons have new premises in which to practise their rituals, leaving this inn to be enjoyed by those who appreciate a cosy local with good homemade ales and a friendly atmosphere. Fans of Arthur Ransome, in particular, would enjoy a pint or two here, as they can choose from a range of ales dedicated to the writer, including 'Amazon' or 'Captain Flint'.

Miller Howe Windermere F5
Voted 1998 *Which? Good Food Guide* 'Restaurant of the Year', Miller Howe is admired not only for its good food but for its superb views across Windermere. From 1971 Miller Howe's then-proprietor, John Tovey, established a reputation for luxury which includes serving Buck's Fizz before breakfast and liqueurs in the lounge after a sumptuous and theatrical dinner. His successor continues to implement Tovey's recipe for success.

HISTORIC HOTELS, INNS AND PUBS (CONTINUED)

LEFT *Guests at Sharrow Bay can expect the finest cuisine combined with utter tranquillity.*

Sharrow Bay Ullswater F3

This was possibly the first 'country-house hotel' when it opened in 1948. Fifty years on it has an international reputation for fine cuisine, opulent atmosphere and unbeatable views. The remote lakeside location of Sharrow Bay makes it an attractive place whatever the season. The hotel is bursting at the seams with ornaments and antiques, and the proprietor's aim is to make paying guests feel that they are relaxing at the wonderful country home of friends.

The Tower Bank Arms Near Sawrey F6

This pub is famous for its appearance in one of the best-known children's stories, *The Tale of Jemima Puddle-Duck*. The author and illustrator of the story, Beatrix Potter, settled in the little hamlet of Near Sawrey when she bought Hill Top, the farmhouse next door to the Tower Bank Arms. Potter often incorporated her surroundings into her tales, and her illustration of the pub has made it forever familiar to generations of children.

White Moss House
Rydal Water, Grasmere E4

Built in 1730, this property was once owned by William Wordsworth, who purchased it for his son, William. A keen rambler, Wordsworth senior often walked from Grasmere to Rydal, and when it rained he would seek refuge from the weather in the porch of White Moss House. In typically spontaneous fashion he composed poetry on that very spot. From the hotel it is easy to research the Wordsworth connection further by taking short walks through beautiful scenery to his well-known homes, Dove Cottage and Rydal Mount. Wordsworth's descendants lived at White Moss House until the 1930s, and it was another 40 years until it became the hotel you find today.

ABOVE The Edwardian youth hostel in Ambleside is a former hotel. Its superb location on the shores of Windermere makes it the perfect hostel for water-sports enthusiasts.

THE YOUTH HOSTEL ASSOCIATION

DEFINING A TYPICAL youth hostel is nigh on impossible: they vary from historic town houses to remote mountain huts. The one thing that is certain is the low cost of a stay. The price is reflected in the basic facilities available: bunk beds in shared dormitories are the norm. But the popularity of youth hostels is evident through sheer numbers: with 237 properties across England and Wales, the Youth Hostel Association is one of the largest accommodation organisations in Britain.

The youth-hostelling movement first took off in Germany at the beginning of the 20th century. The founding principle of budget accommodation was intended to encourage young people to experience the 'great outdoors'. The idea later caught on in Britain, and by 1930 there was a Youth Hostel Association of England and Wales, known to all as the YHA. The trend spread across Europe, and in 1932 the International Youth Hostels Federation was established.

Since those early days the YHA has gone from strength to strength, modernising to cater for the changing needs of tourists. The organisation's name itself is now outdated, as—in Britain at least—youthfulness is no longer a membership requirement, and hostels are increasingly popular with families. More and more hostels are opening in cities, and large groups can now hire whole hostels through the Rent-A-Hostel scheme. New ideas such as these ensure that youth hostels can maintain an income through the quieter winter months.

The Lake District is one of Britain's top tourist centres. The YHA's presence there reflects this—there are 28 hostels in the Lakes, including the organisation's flagship hostel, Ambleside, which is located in the town centre and can sleep 226 people. At the other extreme is isolated Skiddaw House, which has only 20 beds, no motor vehicle access and can only be reached after an exhausting climb to 1,500 feet above sea level.

CALENDAR OF FESTIVALS AND EVENTS A SELECTION

Details of specific *dates and information on numerous other annual and one-off events may be obtained from local tourist offices. Please note that dates may vary from year to year.*

FEBRUARY
GRASMERE WORDSWORTH WINTER SCHOOL Grasmere Literary Week, based at Dove Cottage and Wordsworth Museum.

MARCH
KENDAL MARY WAKEFIELD MUSIC FESTIVAL Classical music competitions and concerts (held in alternate, odd-numbered years).

MAY
CARTMEL HORSE RACES Held at the country's smallest National Hunt course; fairground.
CONISTON WATER FESTIVAL
HOLKER HALL GARDEN AND COUNTRYSIDE FESTIVAL
KENDAL MEDIEVAL MARKET
KESWICK JAZZ FESTIVAL

JUNE
COCKERMOUTH CARNIVAL
GRANGE-OVER-SANDS EDWARDIAN FESTIVAL

JULY
AMBLESIDE RUSHBEARING CEREMONY One of several such ceremonies in Cumbria, dating from the days when churches had earthen floors which had to be strewn with rushes.
GRANGE-OVER-SANDS LAKELAND ROSE SHOW Flower show, parachute displays, military bands and crafts.
KESWICK CONVENTION Inter-denominational Bible Convention.

LAKE WINDERMERE FESTIVAL Street and boat parades, fireworks.
PENRITH AGRICULTURAL SHOW
ULVERSTON CARNIVAL AND PARADE

AUGUST
AMBLESIDE SPORTS
CARTMEL RACE MEETING
CARTMEL, COCKERMOUTH, ENNERDALE, GOSFORTH, HAWKSHEAD, KESWICK, LANGDALE AND SKELTON COUNTRY SHOWS
GRASMERE RUSHBEARING CEREMONY
GRASMERE SPORTS Major sports event with fell races (*below*), Cumberland and

Westmorland wrestling, hound trailing and athletics.
LOWTHER HORSE DRIVING TRIALS AND COUNTRY FAIR
KENTMERE, PATTERDALE, THRELKELD AND VALE OF RYDAL SHEEPDOG TRIALS

VARIOUS LOCATIONS, INCLUDING AMBLESIDE, KENDAL AND KESWICK LAKE DISTRICT SUMMER MUSIC FESTIVAL

SEPTEMBER
BORROWDALE SHEPHERDS' MEET AND SHOW
EGREMONT CRAB FAIR Dates from 1267, and starts with the Parade of the Apple Cart; features the World Gurning Championship, won by whoever pulls the ugliest face, and a contest to shin up a greasy pole, plus shows, and track and field events.
KENDAL GATHERING Sports, flower shows, exhibitions and a torchlit procession.
LOWESWATER AND BRACKENTHWAITE SHOW
ULVERSTON (MARKET) CHARTER FESTIVAL Two weeks of events, culminating in the Lantern Procession.
ULVERSTON URSWICK RUSHBEARING CEREMONY
KENDAL WESTMORLAND COUNTY SHOW Major agricultural show, with sports, dog shows and horse-drawn carriage driving.

OCTOBER
BUTTERMERE SHEPHERDS' MEET AND SHOW
WINDERMERE POWERBOAT RECORD ATTEMPTS
WASDALE HEAD SHOW AND SHEPHERDS' MEET A leading Herdwick sheep show, with shepherds' crook making, and traditional Cumbrian sports.

NOVEMBER
SANTON BRIDGE (BRIDGE INN) BIGGEST LIAR IN THE WORLD COMPETITION Contest to see who can spin the tallest story.

DECEMBER
KESWICK VICTORIAN FAYRE
KENDAL JAZZ FESTIVAL

USEFUL INFORMATION

Listed below are the details of Tourist Information Centres for a selection of the Lake District's popular holiday areas. Please note that these details may be subject to change.

AMBLESIDE
Central Buildings,
Market Cross,
Ambleside LA22 9BS
Tel. (015394) 32582

CONISTON
Ruskin Avenue,
Coniston LA21 8EH
Tel. (015394) 41533

KENDAL
Town Hall,
Highgate,
Kendal LA9 4DL
Tel. (01539) 725758

KESWICK
Moot Hall,
Market Square,
Keswick CA12 5JR
Tel. (017687) 72645

ULVERSTON
Coronation Hall,
County Square,
Ulverston LA12 7LZ
Tel. (01229) 587120

WHITEHAVEN
Market Hall,
Market Place,
Whitehaven CA28 7JG
(01946) 852939

WINDERMERE
Victoria Street,
Windermere LA23 1AD
Tel. (015394) 46499

For general information, contact:

CUMBRIA TOURIST BOARD at
Holly Road,
Windermere LA23 2AQ
Tel. (015394) 44444

The following websites may also be of interest (NB website addresses can change):

Cumbria and Lake District EDGE guide
http://www.cumbria1st.com

Cumbria Tourist Board
http://www.cumbria-the-lake-district.co.uk

Lake-district.com
http://www.lake-district.com

Lake District National Park Authority
http://www.lake-district.gov.uk

Lakesnet
http://www.lakesnet.co.uk

The Wordsworth Trust
http://www.wordsworth.org.uk

Lakes Online
http://www.lakes-online.co.uk

INDEX

and acknowledgments

Note: page numbers in **bold** refer to captions for illustrations

ACKNOWLEDGMENTS

The editors gratefully acknowledge the use of information
taken from the following publications during the preparation
of this volume:

*A Passionate Sisterhood: the Sisters, Wives and Daughters
of the Lake Poets* by Kathleen Jones, Constable 1997
Britain: A Lonely Planet Travel Survival Kit by Richard
Everist, Bryn Thomas and Tony Wheeler, Lonely Planet
Publications 1995
Cumbrian Rock by Trevor Jones, Pic Publications 1988
The Dictionary of National Biography, Oxford
University Press
The Encyclopaedia Britannica
England: the Rough Guide, Rough Guides 1996
Focus on the Lake District, The Automobile Association
1997
The Hidden Places of the Lake District and Cumbria,
M&M Publishing Ltd
A History of the Ordnance Survey edited by
W. A. Seymour, William Dawson and Sons Ltd 1980
K Shoes: the First 150 Years by Spencer
Crookenden, 1992

The Kendal Weaver by John Satchell, Kendal Civic Society
and Frank Peters Publishing 1986
Lake District: a Geographia Guide by Roland Taylor,
Geographia
Land of the Lakes by Melvyn Bragg, Secker and
Warburg 1983
*The New Pelican Guide to English Literature: From Blake
to Byron*, edited by Boris Ford, Pelican 1982
Ordnance Survey Leisure Guide: Lake District,
The Ordnance Survey and The Automobile Association
1992
The Poets Laureate in England by E. K. Broadus, Oxford
University Press 1921
The Six Wives of Henry VIII by Antonia Fraser, Weidenfeld
and Nicolson 1992
The Tale of Beatrix Potter by Margaret Lane, Frederick
Warne & Co Ltd 1946
Three Gothic Novels edited by Peter Fairclough and
Mario Praz, Penguin 1968
Touring Guide: Lake District, Collins
Wordsworth and his World by F. E. Halliday, Thames
and Hudson 1970

PICTURE ACKNOWLEDGMENTS

T = top; *C* = centre; *B* = bottom; *L* = left; *R* = right

Front Cover Robert Harding Picture Library/Roy Rainford **Back Cover** *T* Ashley Cooper *B* Vic Guy **2** John Drews **4** Andy Williams **6-7** David Tarn **10-11** Val Corbett **12** The Wordsworth Trust, Dove Cottage **13** Images Colour Library **14** The National Trust Photo Library/Patricio Goycoolea **16** Collections/Roger Scruton **17** Val Corbett **18** Ardea, London/Chris Knights **19** Val Corbett **20** *T* David Herrod *B* Reproduced by kind permission of the Museum of Lakeland Life and Industry, Abbot Hall, Kendal, Cumbria **21** David Herrod **22** Woodfall Wild Images/David Woodfall **23** Val Corbett **24-5** The National Trust Photo Library/Val Corbett **26** Courtesy *The Cumberland News* **27** Bill Birkett **28** *T* Val Corbett *B* Photograph by Jonathan Becker/courtesy of *Cumbria Life* **29** The National Trust Photo Library/Stephen Robson **30** Reproduced by kind permission of Frederick Warne & Co./Courtesy of the Beatrix Potter Society **30-31** Wray Castle Ltd **31** *TL* Reproduced by kind permission of Frederick Warne & Co./Courtesy of private collector *TR* Reproduced by kind permission of Frederick Warne & Co./© Frederick Warne & Co., 1901 *CL* Reproduced by kind permission of Frederick Warne & Co./Courtesy of private collector *CR* Reproduced by kind permission of Frederick Warne & Co./© Frederick Warne & Co. *B* National Trust **32** Reproduced by kind permission of Frederick Warne & Co./© Frederick Warne & Co., 1905, 1987 **33** *C* Reproduced by kind permission of Frederick Warne & Co./Courtesy of private collector *R* National Trust/Robert Thrift **34** The National Trust Photo Library/Peter Baistow **35** *T* Division of Rare and Manuscript Collections, Cornell University Library *B* The National Trust Photo Library/Magnus Rew **36** *TL* Reproduced by kind permission of the Museum of Lakeland Life and Industry, Abbot Hall, Kendal, Cumbria *TR* Reader's Digest *BL* Dr J. E. Satchell *BC* © Manchester City Art Galleries *BR* Reproduced by kind permission of the Museum of Lakeland Life and Industry, Abbot Hall, Kendal, Cumbria **38** *L* Bridgeman Art Library, London/Guildhall Library, Corporation of London *R* The Beacon, Whitehaven **39** Aerofilms **40** The Wordsworth Trust, Dove Cottage **41** *T* By courtesy of the National Portrait Gallery, London *B* Bridgeman Art Library, London/South African National Gallery, Cape Town, South Africa **42-3** Val Corbett **43** Val Corbett **44** Courtesy of the Brantwood Trust, Coniston **45** *T* Reproduced by permission of Perth and Kinross Council, Perth Museum and Art Gallery, Scotland *B* By courtesy of the National Portrait Gallery, London **46** *TL* Woodfall Wild Images/David Woodfall *TR* Ann Ronan/Image Select *BL* David W. Jones *BR* The Anthony Blake Photo Library/Gerrit Buntrock **48** Val Corbett **49** *L* North West Evening Mail *R* Motoring Memories at the Lakeland Motor Museum, Holker Hall **50** Aerofilms **52** *L* David W. Jones *R* The National Trust Photo Library/Joe Cornish **53** Val Corbett **54** Alpine Club Library **55** *L* Robert Harding Picture Library/Roy Rainford *R* Chris Bonington Picture Library/Chris Bonington **57** The Wordsworth Trust, Dove Cottage **58** The Wordsworth Trust, Dove Cottage **59** *L* Bridgeman Art Library, London/Russell-Cotes Art Gallery and Museum, Bournemouth *C* Wellcome Institute Library, London *R* By courtesy of the National Portrait Gallery, London **60** Tony Stone Images/David Woodfall **61** The Wordsworth Trust, Dove Cottage **62** Courtesy *Whitehaven News* **63** Images Colour Library **64** *T* Tony Stone Images/John & Eliza Forder *CL* David W. Jones *CR* National Trust/Robert Thrift *BL* National Trust *BR* Collections/Ashley Cooper **65** Reproduced by kind permission of the Museum of Lakeland Life and Industry, Abbot Hall, Kendal, Cumbria **66-7** Val Corbett **68** E. A. Bowness **69** Derry Brabbs **70** *L* By permission of the President and Council of the Royal Society *R* Science Photo Library **71** Val Corbett **72** *L* Eye Ubiquitous/B. Pickering *R* Science Photo Library/University of Dundee **73** The National Trust Photo Library/William R. Davis **74** *TL* Carlisle Library *R* The Wordsworth Trust, Dove Cottage *BL* Cumbria Record Office and Local Studies Library, Whitehaven **74-5** Christie's Images **75** Val Corbett **76** Aerofilms **77** David Ward **79** Val Corbett **80** Courtesy of the Board of Trustees of the

V&A **81** Mary Evans Picture Library **82** *L* The Royal Collection © Her Majesty The Queen *R* Rex Features **83** The Wordsworth Trust, Dove Cottage **84** Bill Birkett **85** Val Corbett **86** *TL* © Cumberland Pencil Co. *TR* Geoscience Features *CL* © Cumberland Pencil Co. *CR* Illustration from *The Snowman* by Raymond Briggs (Hamish Hamilton 1978) © Raymond Briggs 1978 Reprinted by permissions of Penguin Books Ltd *BL* © Cumberland Pencil Co. *BR* © Cumberland Pencil Co. **87** David Ward **88** The National Trust Photo Library/Joe Cornish **89** Keswick Museum and Art Gallery **90** Mary Evans Picture Library **91** Val Corbett **92-3** The National Trust Photo Library/Val Corbett **94** *T* Bill Birkett *B* Chris Bonington Picture Library/Alan Hinkes **95** Chris Bonington Picture Library/Chris Bonington **96** Lord Inglewood **97** Cumbria Picture Library/Julie Fryer **98** *T* Carlisle United *L* Carlisle Library *R* Photograph by Jonathan Becker courtesy of *Cumbrian Gazette* **99** English Heritage **100** *T* IPC International Syndication/Trevor Meeks © *Horse & Hound B* Bruce Coleman Ltd/Colin Varndell **101** PA News/Michael Stephens **102** Science Photo Library/David Taylor **103** N. Howard Esq/Greystoke Castle **104** *L* Val Corbett *R* The National Trust Photo Library/Joe Cornish **105** Courtesy *The Cumberland News* **106-7** Val Corbett **107** Action Plus/Peter Tarry **109** Andy Williams **110** Collections/Ashley Cooper **111** Val Corbett **112** Collections/Ashley Cooper **113** Val Corbett **114** Derry Brabbs **115** Reader's Digest **116** *L* © Ordnance Survey *R* © Ordnance Survey/John Paddy Browne **117** © 1992 Michael Joseph Ltd **118** Val Corbett **119** Val Corbett **120** *L* By courtesy of the National Portrait Gallery, London *R* Photograph by D. L. Booth **121** The National Trust Photo Library/Alasdair Ogilvie **122** Val Corbett **123** Images Colour Library **124** Abbot Hall Art Gallery and Museum **126** The Wordsworth Trust, Dove Cottage **127** *T* The Royal Collection © Her Majesty The Queen *B* Val Corbett **128** Mary Evans Picture Library **129** Bridgeman Art Library, London/Dove Cottage Trust, Grasmere **130** *T* Cumbria Picture Library/Eric Whitehead *B* Collections/Brian Shuel **130-31** Woodmansterne **131** *T* Collections/Brian Shuel *B* Val Corbett **132** Val Corbett **133** The Wordsworth Trust, Dove Cottage **135** Val Corbett **136** David W. Jones **137** Val Corbett **138** Courtesy *The Cumberland News* **139** *T* Cumbria Record Office, Carlisle *B* Collections/Brian Shuel **140** Val Corbett **141** Miller Howe Hotel, Windermere **143** Permission of the Trustees of the British Museum **144** *L* David Ward *R* Mary Evans Picture Library **145** Science Photo Library/M-SAT LTD **146** *TL* Images Colour Library *TR* BBC Natural History Unit/Mike Wilkes *CL* Oxford Scientific Films/Peter Gathercole *CR* Institute of Freshwater Ecology/David Tipling **148-9** Images Colour Library **150-51** David Tarn **152** Val Corbett **153** *TL* Collections/Ashley Cooper *TR* Val Corbett *CL* Val Corbett *CR* Robert Harding Picture Library/Roy Rainford *B* Val Corbett **154** *L* Ivan J. Belcher Colour Picture Library/David J. Belcher *R* David Tarn **155** *T* C & J Clark Archive *B* George Romney Ltd **156** Cumbria Picture Library **157** *T* The National Trust Photo Library/Stephen Robson *BL* Aerofilms *BR* Frank H. Westwood/© 1950 United Features Syndicate **158** *T* David W. Jones *B* The National Trust Photo Library/Rob Talbot **159** *T* Roy P. Chatfield *B* Ashley Cooper **160** *T* Colorific!/Patrick Ward *B* David Ward **161** *L* Val Corbett *R* Environmental Images/Paul Glendell **162** *T* Robert Harding Picture Library/Roy Rainford *C* Woodfall Wild Images/Tapani Räsänen *BL* NHPA/Laurie Campbell *BR* Woodfall Wild Images/Peter Wilson **163** Images Colour Library **164** *T* BBC Picture Archives *B* Rex Features/Julian Makey **165** *T* Hulton Getty *C* By courtesy of the National Portrait Gallery, London *B* Reader's Digest **166** *L* By courtesy of the National Portrait Gallery, London *R* The Wordsworth Trust, Dove Cottage **167** *L* The Wordsworth Trust, Dove Cottage *R* Network/Homer Sykes **168** *T* Sharrow Bay Country House Hotel *B* Youth Hostels Association of England and Wales **169** Colorific!/Patrick Ward

SEPARATIONS Studio One Origination Limited, London
PAPER Périgord-Condat, France
PRINTING AND BINDING Printer Industria Gráfica SA, Barcelona, Spain